*For each and every Feng Shui enthusiast
who strives to make a difference*

Four Pillars
of
Destiny

A Guide to Relationships

Jerry King

iUniverse, Inc.
Bloomington

Four Pillars of Destiny
A Guide to Relationships

iUniverse books may be ordered through booksellers or by contacting:

iUniverse
1663 Liberty Drive
Bloomington, IN 47403
www.iuniverse.com
1-800-Authors (1-800-288-4677)

ISBN: 978-1-4620-0684-7 (pbk)
ISBN: 978-1-4620-0686-1 (clth)
ISBN: 978-1-4620-0685-4 (ebk)

Printed in the United States of America

iUniverse rev. date: 04/20/11

Table of Contents

PART THREE

Special stars

Putting it All Together

~

APPENDIX

Author's Preface

1.

For countless generations in China, the Chinese have been drawn to the Four Pillars system for its accurate method of divination. For many, this system is commonly known as the "Eight Characters", or in Chinese: "八字". This system has allowed practitioners the ability to analyze many aspects of one's life and how to go about capitalizing one's cosmic flow when good luck comes about. The destiny blueprint each of us receive at birth can be used to reveal options and paths that we can act upon during good and bad times in life. With this blueprint, we can evaluate where our limits lie, and what we are truly capable of achieving. The Four Pillars of Destiny allows us to understand why we connect with certain people. The types of partnerships that we have with others, be it in business or in personal relationships, can also be explained through this ancient method. This powerful blueprint—formally identified as the Four Pillars "birth chart"—is composed of simple, fundamental building blocks: the year, month, day and hour.

Why do we want to study and understand our Four Pillars of Destiny chart?

There are ten reasons that I'd like to list out, but this list is by no means exhaustive. They include:

1. Knowing one's **cosmic life force**
2. **Career** directions
3. Knowing one's **potential**
4. Avoiding **pitfalls** and enhancing **luck**
5. Capitalizing on **good cosmic energy**
6. Enhance one's **lifestyle** through the use of good cosmic flow
7. Enhance **relationships** with others
8. Establishing **business** and making proper **investments**
9. Avoid **failures**
10. Assist others in their **life** whether it is their health, relationship, career, or finances.

However, it is impossible to explore all of these topics within one book due to the amount of information that can be extracted from a birth chart.

2.

Interpretations of a Four Pillars chart require testing and the knowledge of key events in one's life to ensure accuracy. For borderline cases (meaning birth charts composed of two or more different elemental flows), it is necessary that a practitioner question their clients about major events during certain luck cycles or years to determine the cosmic flow. Since a Four Pillars chart is never stagnant and is subjected to the changes of the luck cycle and annual energy, an experienced practitioner can narrow down on a few key elements and questions for a precise consultation. At times, even experienced practitioners need to ask questions to ensure the accuracy of their readings. Those questions pertain to life events and negative or positive changes. Determining cosmic flow is the most challenging part of a Four Pillars analysis, and this is what makes the whole practice exciting and mind-stimulating.

Aside from the historical data of a person, there are other key factors that play an important role in shaping one's destiny. Even if some people share the same birth date, they may lead different lives. It is essential to look at every aspect that may influence the cosmic energy of one's life. DNA, siblings and family background, profession, hobby, education, environment, nutrition, mentality, and life choices all play a role in a destiny analysis.

Lily Chung, one of my teachers, has provided many key insights into analyzing relationships through cosmic flow and there will be references to some of the examples that she has written in her Chinese book on relationships.

There have not been any major texts published in English regarding the subject of relationships and the Four Pillars system — and this has motivated me in providing a compilation in English for practitioners with a limited knowledge of the Chinese language. Traditional methods of the Four Pillars of Destiny, cosmic identity, personal experience and real life examples are the key drivers for this book. The names employed for the case studies in this book have been changed to protect the confidentiality of my clients.

When looking at the Four Pillars, borderline elemental flows require testing and questioning. Playing the "weak" and "strong" game on a chart can cause more mishaps and misfortunes. We have to understand that cosmic flow is the key driver in the Four Pillars. It is about identifying the leading forces and energy in a chart, and how the luck cycles and annual cycles affect oneself. When I mention cosmic flow, I am referring to the utilization of the key elements in one's life chart. The five elements are water, wood, fire, earth, and metal. Due to cosmic flow, some birth charts may only stand to benefit from

I have came across many practitioners who use the "weak" or "strong" approach in their analysis, where they would use a balancing act of the elements. Some may use calculators or computer programs which would rank a chart by a scale of one to ten. How much truth is there to the utilization of computer programs to determine destiny and energetic flow? We are dealing with real life human beings where cosmic flow is impacted by different cycles, different birth places, and different family background. Can a computer tell us what our family background is? Can it tell us what our professions are and what we have studied in school?

one element while other birth charts can utilize more than one. birth charts can utilize more than one element.

With this book, I hope to equip practitioners with the knowledge of how cosmic reality and cosmic flow affect one's relationship. The identification of cosmic flow can help all of us "go with the flow" and live in harmony. Principles of Yin and Yang and the Five Element Theory are crucial to our understanding of flow. The birth charts of the examples provided in this book uses the Lunar Calendar. Years of effort in research and testing by Lily Chung accompanied by my own personal experience and research concluded that the Lunar Calendar provides an accurate interpretation of birth charts. Birth dates lying on the borderline of a changing cosmic flow, identified by the climate divider, between the lunar and solar months require more testing. Therefore, it is important for practitioners of the Four Destiny to have an open mind when interpreting a birth chart. Questioning the person is the best way to determine flow.

When referring to relationships, utilizing the Four Pillars can also enable one to seek a suitable business partner. Therefore, if some of you intend to use this book to evaluate business partners, co-workers and colleagues, it can also be possible. To ensure harmony, those who share commonalities in cosmic flow within the workspace tend to benefit more. The possibilities and analysis of a Four Pillars system is practically unlimited. I decided to write a book on the Four Pillars with a narrow focus because of the overwhelming number of encounters I have had with clients and customers involved in relationship struggles. I hope my research can contribute to the field of study in the Four Pillars system—it is impossible for anyone to claim ownership of such a complex system. The Four Pillars has been tested throughout time by many people in different generations. This system of testing and verification on mankind has been practiced by local fortune tellers, scholars and leading officials who worked for past emperors in China. Unfortunately, many of the analysis and manuscripts from the past have been eroded away and some Feng Shui masters have choosen to keep the secrets of the Four Pillars to themselves.

3.

Since some of the principles and guidelines mentioned in this book are taken from ancient scripts, the translations are not made exactly word-for-word, but the interpretations and meanings are very close to the originals. Some of the interpretations, methods, and analysis presented within this book are taken from books by Chinese writers and classical texts. Classical texts and writers like Feng Shui master Lily Chung have contributed extensively to the practice of the Four Pillars of Destiny, and some excerpts from their findings will be presented in this book. I will also present many of my own findings by using real examples. I hope that those who read this book will be able to understand cosmic flow and know how to utilize it in their relationship life. For those who are only interested in the cosmic flow aspect of a Four Pillars chart, this book also provides a fundamental basis of how flow is determined, and the types of characteristics that a person may possess.

Part One

Opening Doors

1.
Introduction

There has been a growing trend in the recent years regarding the behaviour of men in relationships. It is no longer a shock for me to hear that the "mission impossible of this century" is now meeting a mature man. It could be easily concluded that this is a mere coincidence—that I confront people with a certain type of mentality when they seek my service. It is true that most people have had their fair share of hiccups in their relationship life. Living together with someone you love may be more challenging than what it used to be. What once was a harmonious and exciting marriage may crumble without any warning. Those who are dating may find their partner a nuisance and wonder why they had ever decided to jump into a relationship from the very beginning. For some, relationship may just be child's play—a game of tag, or hide and seek. The more one treasures and pampers the other in a relationship, the more the other would take things for granted.

In order to make a greater sense of what is causing these problematic patterns in our society, the current ruling period from a Feng Shui point of view, accompanied by astrological birth data of individuals, can provide us with key insights.

We are currently in period 8, symbolized by the Gen (艮) Gua in the 8 trigrams; this period began in 2004. This ruling period plays a very influential role in how people behave. We are all cosmically driven by the ruling period aside from our astrological traits. Cosmic energy and astrology is analysed logically through an intricate system of calculations and evaluations utilizing the five element theory. Contrary to popular convictions, there are no specific beliefs or religions involved in such an analysis. Some may consider the practice of Feng Shui a superstition, and myself was no exception. I, too, was once guilty of this stereotype when I was a child, but after further research and intensive studies over the past decade, I have realized the validity of Feng Shui and the Four Pillars of Destiny.

The Gen trigram, has two Yin lines on the bottom represented by the two

"Gen Gua"

This is one of eight trigrams of the 'Ba Gua'. In Chinese, Gen is written as '艮'. The trigram is often used in Feng Shui practices representing the Northeast sector. Each of the eight sectors possesses a specific type of energy. For the Northeast sector, the energy is earth. This trigram is also associated with the current period which is period 8. This period began in 2004 and lasts until the end of 2023. The attributes of this trigram includes the youngest son, mountain, stomach, spleen and pancreas.

broken lines while a solid Yang line is on the top. Gen Gua is one of the 8 trigrams representing young men and boys. The ruling energy in this period impacts the human psyche, especially young men and boys. It is a global phenomenon. Period 7, a period that represented the mouth, saw the rise of singers such as Michael Jackson, Madonna, and so forth, while period 8 presented us with a new theme.

Cosmically speaking, the ruling period has created a population of people who are immature and irresponsible. Such immaturity has been found on Wall Street and throughout America in the recent years. The financial stress created through irresponsible lending and subprime mortgages are prime examples of the instability of people's behaviour in period 8. From a relationship standpoint, this immaturity has translated into many divorces, affairs, and marital problems. Unfortunately, the ruling period of the Gen trigram does not end until year 2024.

Even though many people have behaved recklessly like rebellious teenagers, there are many successful stories that have come about. The partnership and relationship of the Google duo is a perfect example of two young men coming together with a business that revolutionized the way we do things on the internet. The birth systems of Sergey Brin and Larry Page, founders of Google will be evaluated later in this book. Other young and successful business entrepreneurs have brought about the likes of YouTube, Twitter and Facebook. How often in the past did the world turn their heads to great stories of young boys like Michael Zuckerberg of Facebook? In 2004, the gaming industry saw a rise of a young man by the name of Daigo Umehara, who became a superstar in the arcade world. Would money and fame be crowned to a "professional gamer" twenty years ago? Even online dating companies are being rewarded on this band wagon as many of the love-promising websites are founded by young men. It is a period where young men are becoming more and more successful. These young men are capitalizing on the speed of information and technology. Since the ruling period is period 8, it is much easier for young men to achieve fame. The ruling period is defined by the nature of the cosmos and represented by the Gen trigram. Justin Bieber and Jayden Smith are examples of how boys are capturing the attention of thousands and melting the hearts of millions.

This youthful enthusiasm has also brought about traumatizing relationships for many, as the younger generation no longer cherish the "stable and steady" values of the past. Couples now have less patience to maintain a marriage or work out issues before filing for a divorce. Again, it can be simply concluded that this is a trend only for certain cultures, especially in North America. In the past, in Asia, the Middle East and other traditional societies, couples would not think about the concept of divorce. Relationship issues are a global phenomenon and divorces are now common, even in traditional societies. About a half a century ago, that generation had experienced a period of war and governmental instability. Communism had made life difficult for some countries in Eastern Europe and Asia. During the postwar period, energy was spent on making money through difficult times. In contrast, money and material goods are much more readily available in this generation. Infrastructure, hot water, electricity and transportation are services we take for granted. It is fair to say that people have been spoiled by economic and industrial growth in multiple ways. Some of these privileges have affected relationship lives indirectly as you will see from the evaluation of birth charts.

Throughout my practice, I have observed a trend amongst women in many parts of the world, from traditional cultures such as the Chinese, Koreans, Japanese, Arabs, to less conservative societies like North and South America. More than 70 percent of all the women that I have met and consulted were concerned about 'relationships'. Again, this can be a result of my profession as a Feng Shui specialist. For those who are single, they are finding it more and

"FOUR PILLARS CHART"

This is often referred to as birth charts, birth system, or cosmic system. These terms are used interchangeably. A Four Pillars chart is composed of the birth year, month, day and hour. It is like a blueprint of our own energetic makeup determining many aspects of our lives. The calculations are made through Chinese astrological calculations. The explanations of life through the use of the chart are logical."

more difficult to meet the perfect man or someone who is reliable. These concerns are not limited to women — even men are interested in their own relationship life. My research and studies are drawn from a cosmic and astrological point of view with many individuals' birth charts. Examples from all walks of life, from famous celebrity couples to the working class, will be examined in the first section. Stories and real life encounters are presented in the latter chapters of this book.

Relationships have always been an integral part of many people's lives; in terms of relationships, I would also include associates, family, friends, and the people around us, not just our relationship with our spouse or partner. As a society change, so do people's mentality, especially in modernized and prosperous countries. The desire for wealth and career growth becomes secondary once one has met his or her basic needs in life. There are those who feel the need of having someone special, some who are afraid of being alone, and some who wish to share their happiness and joy with a partner. As a Four Pillars practitioner and researcher, I have noticed a continual shift and change in societal needs in the past few decades; this is probably because of the aforementioned change from period 7 to period 8, which began in 2004. Today, health and relationship becomes a high priority in many people's lives. My next book will touch upon how cosmic flow and the Four Pillars of Destiny bring about wealth, scholars and innovative minds, but for this book, I will primarily focus on relationships.

Cosmic flow is of utmost importance when looking at a couple's relationship within the Four Pillars. To quickly sum up, cosmic flow is the leading energy or element within one's birth system; this energy, when favourable to the birth system, allows one to benefit from good luck and fortunes. Of course, going against the flow will lead to misfortunes. Identifying the most favourable cosmic energy is the key to unlocking the code in a Four Pillars birth chart.

The case studies will reflect upon cosmic reality and how we can use one's birth chart to determine what is good or bad for them. Empirical analysis combined with the rules and guidelines left to us by Chinese sages and ancient scripts on Bazi (八字) is the best way to analyze the truth behind cosmic reality. The Four Pillars of Destiny, or Bazi, is not a system founded by one single person. It is a system tested throughout time from observation and analysis. This trial and error process has existed ever since it was practiced by the masses in China for centuries. Today, the Four Pillars system is used all over the world by Feng Shui practitioners. It is a collaborative field shared by trained practitioners with a common interest.

The analysis of the Four Pillars chart of both parties in a relationship would give us a complete picture of what can transpire or what has transpired within a relationship. There are, of course, instances when only one chart can be obtained for analysis when one party does not know the birth chart of their spouse. Many answers and logical explanations can still be provided from one birth chart. This book will proceed to cover the analysis of males and females separately, illustrating guidelines and rules in terms of evaluating one's partner. Afterwards, both males and females will be explored in greater depth with the use of combinations, flows and illustrations of examples.

Necessity is another key component to the Four Pillars and relationships. If both parties involved in a relationship require a specific element, they would be drawn towards each other and may thrive together by utilizing the same energy. Relationships can also come to an abrupt end at times due to the change in the luck cycle. If one of the couples encounters an element that he or she needs in the luck or annual cycle, this person may have a change in attitude and can separate from the relationship. Evaluating both parties can provide aclearer picture as to whether the relationship would be harmonious or unstable.

"LUCK CYCLE"

It does not mean good luck, nor does it mean bad luck! A luck cycle is an interval or period calculated to measure your interaction with that specific period of time in your life. All luck cycles are identified in ten year periods where the upper row of the luck pillar represents 5 years while the lower row represents another 5 years. Although 5 years is often used by practitioners, there should be an overlap of energy as one move from one luck cycle to another."

2.
Reality or Superstition?

As I previously mentioned, many still believe that Feng Shui and Four Pillars are superstitious gimmicks. It is difficult to believe in these concepts because we cannot see the energy in action. The energy around us is not physically visible in which we can immediately identify a "water" or "fire" flow. Many of the calculations are based from thousands of years of collaborative research and studies. The information of a birth chart is taken from a Chinese Thousand Years Calendar It requires years of study, practice and experience in order to be proficient in reading one's destiny and life. There are patterns involved in our lives because living beings are composed of energy. Some of the super-stition may have stem from inexperienced practitioners who lack the proper knowledge to present accurate information in this field. The erroneousness in readings can be disastrous and unjust to the study of Feng Shui as a whole.

In Chinese Astrology, there are two schools of studies, Purple Star As-trology (or Zi Wei Dou Shu), or Four Pillars (Bazi). Many of the concepts come from the I Ching, principles of Yin and Yang, and the five element theo-ry. These concepts are all logically composed, and they can be combined with the utilization of Chinese Astrology to interpret and analyze one's fortunes.

In Hong Kong, at Temple Street, there are practitioners that focus on using proper methods, while some are out to fool others without intending on giving readings with substance. Those who are less fortunate and encoun-ter 'fraud' practitioners may stereotype that Chinese Astrology is a supersti-tion. Some may continue to seek the truth, hoping to find an explanation of what has transpired and how they can rectify their life issues. The explanations that I provide in this book has been derived from clearly stated steps based on logic. I personally believe that our life events can be explained through a logical evaluation of our birth chart. If the events cannot be explained from a logical perspective, the birth date may be incorrect. I have encountered people who have given me the wrong birth date, which can bring about an incorrect interpretation. By questioning about one's past through an analysis using the five element theory can allow us to predict the future.

Although the future can be predicted, we are often provided with options in terms of how to behave. If you were presented with 10 years of bad luck, it is not the end of the world. The bad luck can be dealt with through good karma and hard work. I find it more important to identify bad luck and present people with options in terms of how to approach it. Staying low and avoiding conflict is always the best solution. Solutions can come via the use of Feng Shui remedies. I have seen cases where some of my customers came to me and explained to me that they were told to give money to a certain institution or practitioner on a monthly basis in order to remove themselves of bad luck. Remedies often come from the mind. Knowing what to do and how to behave according to the natural laws of the I Ching is the best solution. There are practitioners who would take advantage of one's misfortunes and continually mislead others to benefit themselves financially. These unethical practitioners have led many to approach Feng Shui with hesitant doubt. Whether a destiny or life reader uses Chinese Astrology or other methods, the interpretations should be very similar. The approach within Chinese Astrology is logical and based upon the five element theory.

If a birth chart does not like water, it does not mean that a person should not drink water, if this is the case, approximately 1/5 of the world's population would suffer from drinking water. The effects of water could come from coastal regions. Some may not like the feeling of living by the waters, others may fear swimming or riding in a boat. The water energy can also come from a specific year or seasonal weather affecting our mood.

3.
Five Element Theory

The five elements are wood, fire, earth, metal and water. Each of these elements can be related to one of the five Confucian virtues. Everyone has an element, be it Yin or Yang, associated to oneself in the Four Pillars chart. It is referred to one's self element found in the day stem. The day stem can be found by using a Chinese Thousand Years calendar by looking at the day you were born. The elements possess certain identifiable traits on its own but Four Pillars practitioners must understand that these traits are very dynamic due to the complexities of a birth system. For example, identifying or describing a wood person solely on the element itself without understanding the entire make up of the birth chart is erroneous. The same can be said with labelling an animal to a specific birth year and concluding that they would possess the characteristics of an animal. The nature of each element should be first understood to complete an evaluation. The season that the element was born in and its interactions with other elements within a Four Pillars chart makes a huge impact in chart classifications.

Each of the five elements has a Yin and Yang designation, and these designations can be labelled as one of the ten gods in relation to the self. Knowing the ten gods (十神) is imperative when using this book as many references will be made to them. Do not be alarmed if you do not have a deep understanding of the ten gods, an explanation of the ten gods will be provided later on.

The ten gods include the following: Direct Resources (正印), Indirect Resources (偏印), Friend (比肩), Direct Wealth (正財), Indirect Wealth (偏財), Rob Wealth (劫財), Officer (正官), Seven Killings (七煞), Eating God (食神) and Hurting Officer (傷官). Each of the ten gods plays certain roles within a relationship and a family. The ten gods are not considered to be "specific stars" since they are only named in relation to the self, rendering easy identification for practitioners to seek out key features and characteristics of a person. For those who are not familiar with the five element theory, understanding the ten gods will be a challenge. The foundation of the ten gods is derived from the five element theory. The appendix in this book provides a table illustrating the ten gods in relation to the self. For those who are familiar with the five element theory and the basics of the Four Pillars system, you can move on to Chapter 2.

The descriptions presented here on each element are only a general overview.

Wood is associated with kindness, in Chinese it is "仁", pronounced as 'ren'. Ren is the virtue of benevolence, charity and humanity. Just imagine a tree or a plant that is growing. Flowers and potted plants are fragile, yet they are kind and gentle. In Feng Shui

"Ten Gods"

They are not gods or deities. It is a direct translation of how the Chinese interpreted each element within a Four Pillars chart in relation to the self element. There are ten different types of elemental interaction with the self, hence the term Ten Gods. The Ten gods is often used for practitioners to label the symbols in the chart making it easier to extract information."

and Four Pillars, there is a Yin and Yang aspect to every element. For wood, Yang would represent a big oak tree or a forest. An overly strong tree makes the tree stubborn; trying to chop and hack a big tree requires tremendous energy. Potted plants on the other hand require less effort and the plotted plants can often be referred to as and hack a big tree requires tremendous energy. Potted plants on the other hand require less effort and the plotted plants can often be referred to as Yin Wood.

Fire represents propriety, good manners, politeness, ceremony and worship and this virtue is called "禮", in Chinese, pronounced as 'li'. Yang fire can be equated to a bright sun or fire with great radiance. Fire that is overly strong may want to overshadow everything else around it while fire that is weak may be hidden from attention even though it wants to shine. Yin Fire, when it is pure and beautiful, is like a candle providing warm and comfort on the dinner table. On the other hand, Yin Fire burning in coal or bad lumber may ignite unwanted fumes.

Earth, like a mountain is steady, stable and trustworthy. It is referred to the Confucian virtue of "信", or xin. This is the virtue of faithfulness and integrity. Yang Earth is like a big dam, concrete barrier or mountain which can conquer nature when it is strong and solid. Alternatively, being overly strong may make it difficult to penetrate; as a result, influencing or changing the minds of these individuals may become difficult. Yin Earth, when moist and fertile can absorb a tremendous amount of information. The moist earth can also bury secrets. Moist earth being wet and soggy may pollute water leading to evil thoughts and intentions.

Metal can be referred to as being upright, virtuous and honest. It symbolizes "義", pronounced as yi. Yang Metal is like a broadsword wielded by a brave soldier standing strong along the forts providing defense for the emperors of ancient China. Loyalty, bravery, and honesty are characteristics of the metal. Yin Metal in its purest form can be sharp and attractive like gold and jewelry. Metal that is polluted or corrodes like rusted pipes may be deemed useless.

Water with its versatility and dynamic nature is the virtue of zhi, or "智". It simply means knowledge and wisdom. Yang Water can flow like a gentle river or crash like a waterfall. Water in its most violent form can wreak havoc to nature and bring about chaos. Water, when gentle, can present a calm feeling. Mist and rain can sooth nature with its Yin form.

The five elements can all be interpreted with positive and negative features, whether they are in the form of Yin or Yang. Remember

> **In Chinese metaphysics, each of the elements represents a specific organ and specific careers or industries. Metal is often associated to music. The sound of music comes from metal. Metal also represents the vocal cords and the lungs, hence, its relations with singing."**

that there is no single element superior to another element. Being born of a Yang element by no means concludes that it is better than a Yin element, and vice versa. The intricate interaction amongst the elements delivers different dynamics according to each element's distinctive characteristics. A Four Pillars birth chart exhibits many of these different dynamics.

Understanding how they interact with each other is a fundamental basics in understanding the Four Pillars system.

Within the Five Element Theory, there is a production cycle, a reduction cycle and a destruction (or controlling) cycle. The cycle of the elements serves as the foundation of the Four Pillars of destiny and must be understood clearly in order to do a preliminary analysis on relationships. Knowing the Five Element Theory is not enough to determine the outcome or compatibility of a relationship either. There are many cosmic combinations influencing elemental flows that need to be understood in order to do a thorough analysis on the relationships and compatibility of partners. The image below illustrates the growth cycle of the five element theory.

Production Cycle

The best way to remember the five element theory is to use imagery. To begin with, you can picture the wood as fuel for the fire. Turning from fire to earth, visualizing a volcano is one of the best ways to remember that fire generates earth. As the fire and lava erupt from a volcano, it creates and generates earth. Earth, on the other hand, produces metal. Precious metals such as gold, silver and copper are unearthed from the ground, and as a result, earth produces metals. From metal to water, water-soluble organics are dissolved metal salts of a combinations of many different compounds. This is how metal is seen as producing water. Last but not least, water is used to grow plants and trees. So there you have it, each element produces another element in a cycle.

Reduction Cycle

As one element produces another element, one element is reduced. For example, trees reduce water, utilizing its nutrients. On the other hand, fire reduces wood when the fire wants to continue to burn. Earth reduces fire and serves as a great way to fight forest fires. One of the ways to reduce the energy of fighting forest fires is to use earth. Bulldozers and mining trucks made of metal are used to reduce earth. Finally, water corrodes metal by rusting it away. As one element gives birth to another element, another element is subjected to a reduction or a weakening process.

Destruction/Control Cycle

The destruction cycle is where one element seeks to control another element. The simplest example comes from water controlling fire. When there is fire in the kitchen, you would most likely douse it off with water. Moving onto wood, the best way to control the growth of the tree is to use metal as metal chops wood. On the other hand, fire melts metal, therefore, fire controls metal. For earth, wood would be the controlling element as the roots of a vibrant and growing tree can penetrate the ground. Earth's strength comes from its ability to curb and control water and it can be symbolized by a dam. The controlling cycle is illustrated below.

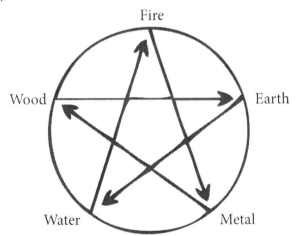

From the Four Pillars chart of a male, the element that he controls is considered the 'wealth' element. The 'wealth' element also represents the spouse. To keep it simple, if the male is a wood self, meaning being born on a wood day, the element that he controls would be earth, hence, earth would be his wealth and spouse. This is only one way of looking at the spouse as there are many other factors that are used to determine the spouse. On the other hand, for females, the element that controls the female is sometimes referred to as the 'Officer' and it can represent her spouse also. For example, if the female is a wood self, the element that controls her would be the metal.

4.
The Four Pillars

The Four Pillars chart is composed of eight characters. The name "Four Pillars" comes from the fact that the birth chart is divided into four sections, the Year, Month, Day and Hour. In each pillar, there are two characters. One of the character represents the heavenly stem while the other represents the earthly branch. For some people, they do not have their birth hour but the cosmic flow of the chart can still be determined with the year, month and day. In some cases, it could be harder to determine if the chart is considered a borderline without a defining flow. Generally speaking, in the practice of the Four Pillars, the effects of the birth hour are much more pronounced later in life. Nevertheless, the birth hour plays an important part of the overall makeup of a Four Pillars chart. Some of the examples used in this book may not contain the birth hour but the cosmic flow is clearly discernible.

The heavenly stems have ten symbols while there are twelve earthly branches. The eight characters in a Four Pillars chart are derived from the symbols of the stems and branches. Every symbol in the Four Pillars chart plays an important role in relation to the self. Knowing that you are a specific element does not mean that you must strengthen it with resources, nor does it mean that one element is more superior than another. Below is a list of symbols that can be found in a Four Pillars chart. Note that the symbols are placed in sequence starting from wood and the season of Spring to water in the Winter.

Heavenly Stem	Symbol
Yang Wood	甲
Yin Wood	乙
Yang Fire	丙
Yin Fire	丁
Yang Earth	戊
Yin Earth	己
Yang Metal	庚
Yin Metal	辛
Yang Water	壬
Yin Water	癸

Earthly Branches	Symbol	Polarity	Hidden Elements
Tiger	寅	Yang	甲丙戊
Rabbit	卯	Yin	乙
Dragon	辰	Yang	戊乙癸
Snake	巳	Yin	丙戊庚
Horse	午	Yang	丁己
Goat	未	Yin	己丁乙
Monkey	申	Yang	庚戊壬
Rooster	酉	Yin	辛
Dog	戌	Yang	戊辛丁
Pig	亥	Yin	壬甲
Rat	子	Yang	癸
Ox	丑	Yin	己辛癸

Each of the earthly branches holds one or more hidden elements, which can alter the structure of a birth chart. The hidden elements must be memorized as these elements play a very critical role in identifying the flow and characteristics of the birth system. Every Lunar year begins with the Tiger (寅) as the first month of the year and ends with the Ox (丑) as the twelfth month. Just like the heavenly stems, each of the earthly branches also has a Yin or Yang designation to it.

One of the simplest approaches to analyzing the strength of the self element is to identify its behaviour and interaction within the birth month. This is always the first step in analyzing a birth chart. Unfortunately, it is more complicated than just analyzing the self element's interaction with the birth month and counting symbols to evaluate the strength of the self. There are many combinations involved which can change the balance of power within a birth system. Being a strong self or a weak self does not necessarily mean much without analyzing the big picture. Even after a birth system has been classified, the luck cycle must also be evaluated to ensure that it is in favour of the flow. If it isn't, misfortunes are bound to occur.

Structure of the Four Pillars Birth Chart

The structure of the Four Pillars birth chart is very simple to put together. The Appendix explains how to plot a Four Pillars birth chart. The upper row of the Four Pillars birth chart is called the heavenly stems while the bottom row is called the earthly branches. This is why the Four Pillars is also commonly known as Bazi (八字), for the eight characters in the birth chart.

Each pillar is composed of two characters: the heavenly characters and the earthly characters. The Four Pillars includes one's birth Year, Month, Day and Hour. Some may wonder if it is possible to obtain a reading without the hour. The answer is yes. As the first three pillars, Year, Month and Day, governs the majority of one's earlier part of life, this information is often suffice to determine the classification and characteristics of the birth chart.

Hour	Day	Month	Year	
	Self Element			Heavenly Stems
				Earthly Branches

The table above illustrates how to find one's self element. The self element is located in the day pillar of the heavenly stems. Remember that only one of the ten stems can be in the day stem. The twelve branches can only be in the bottom row. Each of the earthly branches is either Yin or Yang and it has to be paired up with a stem of the same polarity. Therefore, a Yang Metal (庚) cannot be paired up with a Snake (巳) since the Snake (巳) is Yin. When plotting the Four Pillars chart using the Ten Thousand Years Lunar Calendar, each of the pillars come in a pair so it is difficult to make this mistake. has to be paired up with a stem of the same polarity. Therefore, a Yang Metal (庚) cannot be paired up with a Snake (巳) since the Snake (巳) is Yin. When plotting the Four Pillars chart using the Ten Thousand Years Lunar Calendar, each of the pillars come in a pair so it is difficult to make this mistake.

"SELF ELEMENT"

This is the element that is used as a reference point for the entire structure of the birth chart. The self element is often referred to as the day master, day stem, or the self. The self element can be classified with many terms: weak self, strong self, surrender, dominant self, transformed self and so forth.

5.
Seasons, Climate, and Location

Since there are four seasons in a year, each of the season possesses certain traits allowing some elements to be prosperous while other elements to be in a trapped or dead state. Being in a dead state is not so bad. In many cases, it can be rewarding as witnessed with some of the richest people in the world. Examples of these types of people will be presented in this book and in my future publications. There are three animal symbols representing each of the four seasons but always remember the complexion and strength of the animals can be altered through clashes and combinations. This will be covered when we talk about cosmic flow and combinations. Before we take a brief look at the seasons, it is important to note that the last month of each of the season has plenty of earth energy that can sway the classification of the birth system.

For example, the last month of spring is the month of the Dragon (辰). The Dragon (辰) possesses hidden earth and other elements that we will cover later on. The four earth animals are the Dragon (辰), Goat (未), Dog (戌), and Ox (丑). Although they belong in one of the seasons, the hidden elements within these animals can be easily dragged out as seen with some of the examples in this book.

Spring

In the Spring, the Tiger (寅), Rabbit (卯) and Dragon (辰) represents prosperous wood energy. From a five element theory perspective, when wood is strong, obviously, the earth energy is considered dormant since wood controls earth. Fire, on the other hand, is considered to be growing during this period as the climate becomes warmer while there is an ample supply of wood to support the growth of fire. Spring water is in its reduction phase as the wood is draining the energy of the water. Metal, just like earth, lacks the energy during this period to become strong and it will have to yield to the prosperity of wood.

Summer

The summer is represented by the Snake (巳), Horse (午) and Goat (未). In the summer, fire dominates the season and as it produces earth, earth during the season also becomes prominent. Earth is particularly hard and hot during the last month of the summer in the month of the Goat (未). As the fire burns away the wood, wood now belongs to the reduction phase where it begins to weaken.

Water and metal in the summer lacks vital energy to fight the heat. Try to picture water in the dry hot desert; the water supply is limited and is almost nonexistent. For metal, imagine metal being thrown into the hot furnace: it would bend and melt as the flaring heat reduces its power to fight the fire.

Autumn

Autumn brings about a rich supply of metal energy led by these three animals, Monkey (申), Rooster (酉) and Dog (戌). With metal at its most prosperous state, wood is too weak in this season to withstand it. From a nature perspective, the leaves of trees start falling, giving us a hint of the weakening and disappearance of the wood energy. Since metal feeds water in the five element cycle, water is considered as growing. As metal becomes prosperous, the energy of earth begins to dwindle. Although earth's energy is being reduced by the metal, the month of the Dog (戌) must be taken into account. A person born in the month of the Dog (戌) with earth as their self element may experience more strength than the other autumn months. For fire, the damp weather in the autumn prevents it from growing. As a result, its limited capacity can do very little damage to metal.

Winter

The last three months, represented by the Pig (亥), Rat (子) and Ox (丑) brings about a cold and wet weather chill upon the other elements. During the winter, the energy of water is vigorous and thriving while metal is being corroded. Rust comes to mind when water and metal is mixed, but even rusty metal pipes can still be functional in the winter. Fire on the other hand lacks strength to provide light during the winter unless it is heavily supported by wood. It is during this time of the year that wood begins to grow again while earth, being wet and moist, is being penetrated by the roots of trees.

Each element responds differently to different months even within a season. These elements and the types of energy that a birth system interact with affects how we react to one another, whether it is in a marriage, or simply within the workplace. As a luck cycle changes, and annual energy is altered, so does the way we react and respond.

Climate and Birth Location

Birth location makes a difference in a Four Pillars chart reading. Imagine a person being born in the summer months which include the Snake (巳), Horse (午) and Goat (未) months. Summer to those who are in the Northern Hemisphere would be winter in the Southern Hemisphere. Although in a country like Australia where winter would be during June, we do not reverse the order of the months. A birth chart in Australia requiring additional water would receive more water energy than those in Canada. Elemental imbalances can be offset by where a person was born in. Elemental imbalances can also be enhanced depending on where the person was born. There are practitioners who reverse the month pillar because of the difference in Southern and Northern Hemisphere. This method does not work. Think about it from a logical perspective: if a person enjoys a water flow from the winter months, would not switching from hemisphere to hemisphere between seasons allow that person to enjoy a full year of good luck? This would not be plausible.

At the time we were born, we would receive a specific type of energy which can be calculated and evaluated from the Four Pillars chart. Being born near the ocean does not mean anything to your birth chart unless the birth chart has been classified properly. A chart following the flow of water would have its flow enhanced from the moment the baby was born by the waters. On the other hand, a birth chart enjoying the flow of fire would benefit from being born in warmer climate. From research and studies, birth location places an influence on our birth charts. The birth chart of Nicole Kidman is an example of how the birth location enhanced her fire flow.

6.
Cosmic Forces

It is important as a practitioner to accept cosmic reality whether it is good or bad news in relationships. Divorces, marital affairs, accidents, deaths and loss of wealth are all part of cosmic reality that has to be accepted. Some of the best ways to avoid mishaps is to select a partner that conforms to one's cosmic flow and cosmic connection, but this can prove to be a difficult task for many. By understanding how the cosmic flow and connections work, practitioners of the Four Pillars can provide answers to their clients about how they can live in harmony and better prepare themselves for upcoming issues. One of the greatest ways to avoid problems or endure hardships is to study the I

Ching. The I Ching also teaches us how to manage a relationship and family as specified by hexagrams numbered 31, 32, and 37. I highly recommend having a look at the natural laws and wisdom of the I Ching because each hexagram presents a different moral and theme.

Before looking at a Four Pillars chart and determining whether one's spouse or partner is favourable or not, it is essential that the flow and useful elements are identified for the chart. Without such knowledge, it is difficult to understand what kind of role the spouse palace plays in the Four Pillars chart. The spouse palace is identified as the symbol that sits underneath one's self element. In addition to flow, the cosmic combination between a married couple or people who are in relationships make a difference in achieving a harmonious relationship. No relationship is perfect since it is very difficult for couples to have perfect combinations and flows that connect them for an indefinite period of time. Although it may be difficult to have perfect combinations, by doing the right things at the right time and going with the flow of our energy, mishaps can be averted. By accepting and understanding our cosmic birth system, we would be able to know why one would behave the way they do, and the types of challenges that we are presented with in life.

Luck cycles and cosmic combinations often change and can cause separations and marital problems. This is the cosmic truth and by understanding cosmic truth, Four Pillars practitioners can provide remedies and different forms of counselling to better prepare couples for the inevitable. It is also possible in some cases to use Feng Shui as a form of remedy. When there is cosmic bonding through combinations and flow between the couple, the necessity of

Feng Shui and Four Pillars counselling in the aspects of relationships can be reduced and practitioners can focus their attention on other parts of people's lives which include career, health, and wealth creation.

Cosmic Flow and Combinations

1.
Combinations

In the Four Pillars system, there are ten heavenly stems and twelve earthly branches. Within the stems and branches, they form various combinations, clashes and punishments—all of which must be incorporated into a holistic view of a relationship analysis. These different combinations have specific patterns which were analyzed and practiced for thousands of years in China. The patterns correlate with the five element theory and the principles of Yin and Yang. It would be great if everyone can connect or meet with people who have the perfect cosmic combination with themselves. Unfortunately, such cosmic unity is constantly affected by annual and periodic changes in the energetic flow.

Combinations can simply mean cooperation. For the business world, it can be used in reference to partnerships and joint ventures. For personal relationships, an ideal combination can bring about a harmonious and long lasting romance. In sports, good combinations can bring about strong team spirit and competitive success. Politicians can benefit from having good combinations and cosmic flow with their closest supporters. So what are these combinations? There is the combination of the heavenly stems. In the branches, the combinations include Six Harmony, Directional, and Trio. The list of combinations will be referred to throughout this book, and for those in the learning of how combinations function, this chapter will provide a good starting point.

Heavenly Stem Combinations

Yang Wood 甲	+	Yin Earth 己	=	Earth 土
Yin Wood 乙	+	Yang Metal 庚	=	Metal 金
Yang Fire 丙	+	Yin Metal 辛	=	Water 水
Yin Fire 丁	+	Yang Water 壬	=	Wood 木
Yang Earth 戊	+	Yin Water 癸	=	Fire 火

When looking at the birth charts of a couple, utilizing the stem combinations presented above can provide practitioners with details in terms of whether there are cosmic connections or bonding between them. The focus of the stem combinations should be on the day stem. For example, the two charts presented next demonstrates an example of when both the male and female have a cosmic combination in the stems.

Male			
Hour	Day	Month	Year
X	甲 Yang Wood	X	X
X	X	X	X

Female			
Hour	Day	Month	Year
X	己 Yin Earth	X	X
X	X	X	X

The charts of the male and female exemplify a powerful bonding between them — as represented by the Yang Wood (甲) of the male's day stem and the Yin Earth (己) of the female's day stem. The combination results from one of many methods utilized by practitioners to determine the presence or the absence of cosmic harmony between couples. Harmonic cosmic bonding produces a greater chance of a lasting relationship. The pairing in this example can be identified by using the stem pairing chart. The harmonious bonding can be seen from the Yin and Yang relationship between the male and female.

The Yang Wood (甲), being a Yang element is controlling the Yin Earth (己) element. In the Four Pillars practice, the controlling element of the Female Self Element is considered the spouse or the partner. However, for those who are currently in a relationship, do not be alarmed if you and your partner lack possession of the bonding shown in the above example. There are many other combinations to consider in a relationship. This stem pairing is by no means ideal or perfect in all walks of our life.

Six Harmony Combinations

The next bonding to look at is the day branch which involves the twelve cosmic animals. The table below illustrates the connections between the animals and the possibilities of transforming into a specific element.

Rat 子	+	Ox 丑	=	Earth 土
Tiger 寅	+	Pig 亥	=	Wood 木
Rabbit 卯	+	Dog 戌	=	Fire 火
Dragon 辰	+	Rooster 酉	=	Metal 金
Snake 巳	+	Monkey 申	=	Water 水
Goat 未	+	Horse 午	=	Sun/Moon-Fire

The bonding is sometimes referred to as the "Six Harmony Combinations". Having the combination of the entire day pillar cosmically bonded with the partner definitely provides a greater chance of harmony in a relationship. In order to have two charts with the day pillars bonded, both the self element and the day branch must be connected via the combinations listed above. The day pillar bonding provides an energetic attraction between the couple, making it difficult for them to separate unless cosmic or external factors should be present and a clash occurs. Below is the combination of the animals illustrated in a circular pattern.

Depending on the position and the season, these combinations have a possibility of transforming into a different element once combined. (As mentioned earlier, within a Four Pillars chart, these combinations have a possibility of transforming into a different element once they are combined, depending on their positioning and the season.) If a person, born in the month of the Rooster (酉) with a Dragon (辰) right beside in either the day or year branch, the chances of a transformation is much higher and it can affect the makeup of the birth system. These branch pairings can be utilized to prevent a clash from happening. If a clash is experienced in that system for a specific luck cycle or year, he or she can utilize the branch pairing to team with the animal in question to avoid misfortune.

The Chinese often utilize symbols and images of certain animals to represent specific years. For example, if you were born in the year of the Dragon (辰), the Dog (戌) would clash with the Dragon. To avoid or counter any misfortunes that may arise from the clash in this example, one may use images of the Rooster (酉) in bracelets or paintings for that entire year. Think of it this way: the Dog (戌) would not try to battle with the Dragon (辰) since the latter now has a "friend" to play with.

From a relationship standpoint, being with a person who possesses an animal that combines with the day branch in your chart can reduce the impact of a clash and can also ensure greater harmony as a couple. In the Rooster (酉) month of a Rabbit (卯) year, this person can wrestle off a clash by being with someone with a Dragon (辰) in their birth system. Better yet, if the Dragon (辰) is found next to the Rooster (酉), the amount of harm the Rabbit (卯) can bring about would be limited. The same can be said if a Dog (戌) appears to eliminate the Dragon (辰). Having a partner or a spouse within the birth chart can help ward off unwanted enemies.

Male			
Hour	Day	Month	Year
X	甲 Yang Wood	X	X
X	子 Rat	X	X

Female			
Hour	Day	Month	Year
X	己 Yin Earth	X	X
X	丑 Ox	X	X

Above is an example of the cosmic combination between the day pillar branches of the male and female. As illustrated by the highlight column, the earthly branch presents an additional combination to solidify the bond. The Rat (子) and the Ox (丑) combines into earth as seen in the "Six Harmony Combination" and those combinations can also be utilized in determining a couple's bonding. By bonding, it means that the connections involved with the animals found in the birth chart. Bonding is logically determined through patterns and interactions from the various animal combinations used in the practice of Four Pillars.

To further examine the evidence of a solid bonding, one could also scrutinize the year pillar to locate existing combinations. The chart below illustrates a combination that is considered strong, and such strength can result in long lasting relationships. In addition to the combinations, the male possesses Yang elements that are considered properly positioned with the Yin elements that the female possesses. The Yin and Yang relationship enforces the cosmic connections between the two genders. This scenario presents a perfect situation where all the elements are in cohesion with each other—unfortunately, perfect combinations do not occur very often. We don't live in a perfect world after all.

Male			
Hour	Day	Month	Year
X	甲 Yang Wood	X	丙
X	子 Rat	X	辰

Female			
Hour	Day	Month	Year
X	己 Yin Earth	X	辛
X	丑 Ox	X	酉

In the various cosmic combinations presented, a solid chance of harmony in relationships can be found, but these charts are, by no means, the only guideline that one should follow when evaluating a couple's relationship. What if there are no combinations between the couple that you are providing a Four Pillars consultation for? Keep in mind that there other determining factors exist in keeping couples together or causing them to separate at certain times. Bonding amongst couples also depends quite heavily on the cosmic flow of the Four Pillars chart.

Directional and Three Harmony Combinations

There are two other types of combinations that can have an impact on the leading flow of one's birth composite and it will be explained in further detail in the next section. It is imperative that these combinations be remembered when trying to understand the birth chart. They include: the Directional Combination and the Three Harmonious Combination.

Spring 春	Tiger 寅	Rabbit 卯	Dragon 辰
Summer 夏	Snake 巳	Horse 午	Goat 未
Autumn 秋	Monkey 申	Rooster 酉	Dog 戌
Winter 冬	Pig 亥	Rat 子	Ox 丑

The Directional Combination

Each of the Directional Combinations is made up of three animal symbols representing a season. The directional pattern is easily discernible once the symbols are drawn according to order starting from the first month of the year until the last month of the year. Below is a graphical illustration of the order of the directional combination. The lunar year begins with the Tiger (寅) and ends with the Ox (丑). Imagine the cycle from a seasonal point of view.

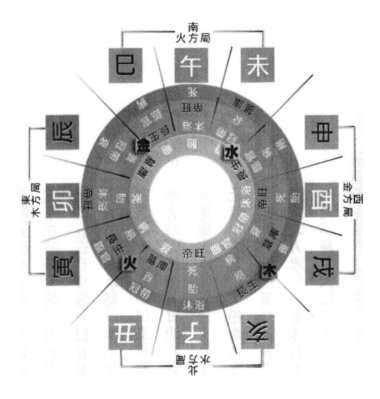

Each of the directional combinations is led by the cardinal symbols. For the Spring, the Rabbit (卯) leads the team of wood. In the Summer, the Horse (午) leads the fire. During the Autumn, the Rooster (酉) would lead the metal while the Rat (子) leads the water in the Winter. The unique characteristic of the directional combination is that all three of them must be seen in the birth chart in order to be classified as having a directional combination. Having two out of the three symbols in a chart cannot be considered a directional combination. If a person encounters the third animal symbol in the year or luck cycle, it is possible that the entire combination is completed, barring any other combinations or clashes found in the chart. Normally, directional combinations are considered unstable and can be broken up by other combinations.

Another key cosmic combination to look for in a Four Pillars chart is the Three Harmonious Combination shown in the chart below.

Water Structure 水局	Monkey 申	Rat 子	Dragon 辰
Wood Structure 木局	Pig 亥	Rabbit 卯	Goat 未
Fire Structure 火局	Tiger 寅	Horse 午	Dog 戌
Metal Structure 金局	Snake 巳	Rooster 酉	Ox 丑

Three Harmony "三合局"

In the Three Harmonious combination, the leader of each group is also the main cardinal direction just like the Directional Combination. The difference with the Three Harmonious combination is that even if the main cardinal symbol does not exist in the chart, the specific elemental structure can still be formed. Whether the element transforms or not depends on the season that the person was born in and the flow of the birth chart. For example, the water structure is made up of the Rat (子), Monkey (申) and the Dragon (辰). If a Four Pillars chart only has the Monkey (申) and the Dragon (辰), the water structure is still formed although it may not be as strong and pure with the absence of the Rat (子); nevertheless, water is still present in the birth system. If the person encounters a Rat (子) luck cycle or the year of the Rat (子), the structure is complete and the team of water would be unified. This unified structure, when found in a chart born in the correct season, has the greatest chance of providing a leading flow. The pattern of the Three Harmonious combination is presented below.

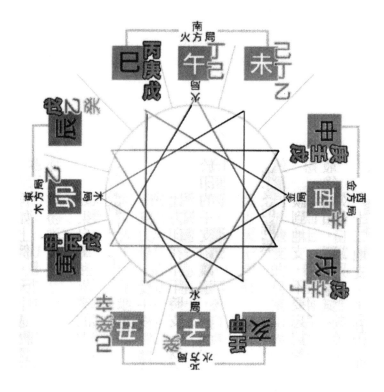

Notice the triangles linking the three animal symbols together, the pattern of combination is developed from the triangles. The strength of the combination is dependent upon which animals are present in the Four Pillars chart and which season the person was born in. Take another example, if the combination of the Pig (亥) and Goat (未) is found in the chart while the person is born in the month of the Rooster (酉), the team of wood is considered very weak due to the fact that this person is born in a period where metal is the leading energy in Autumn. In addition, the energy of wood in Autumn is considered trapped. This type of chart may want to follow a wood flow, but fails to do so because of the stronger metal flow in Autumn. Timing is very critical to the formation of an elemental structure. Poor timing can lead to disharmony.

The Three Harmonious combination is considered a tighter nit group compared to the Directional Combination. A Four Pillars chart containing two of the three animals in the structure is known as stronger and harder to have one of the animals clashed away. Take this analogy: if two people teams up together to form a partnership in a wrestling match, an intruding enemy would think twice before fighting the two of them. From a relationship standpoint, those who have bonds in the year or day branch of the Three Harmonious combination tend to have good connections with each other. For example, Latin American singer Juanes has a Monkey (申) sitting in the day branch while his wife, actress and model, Karen Martinez, has a Rat (子) sitting in the day branch. The combination is highlighted next.

Juanes (August 9, 1972)			
Hour	Day	Month	Year
X	壬 Yang Water	戊 Yang Earth	壬 Yang Water
X	申 Monkey	申 Monkey	子 Rat

Karen Martinez (August 1, 1979)			
Hour	Day	Month	Year
X	庚 Yang Metal	辛 Yin Metal	己 Yin Earth
X	子 Rat	未 Goat	未 Goat

This combination provides a good chance for a harmonious relationship. In addition to the bonding of their day branch, Karen possesses metal in her chart, aiding the metal and water flow of her spouse. Combinations and flow come hand in hand. Having combinations that are not supportive of the leading flow can lead to misfortunes. As explained earlier, having a wood combination in a chart while being born in the incorrect timing can lead to struggles in life. Hence, birth systems with the correct combinations and the right timing are considred to be in cosmic harmony. Keep in mind that both types of birth systems do not guarantee success or failure; it also depends on the timing of the luck cycle and the annual cycle. If the cycles are in favor of the chart, flowing with useful elements, fame and success can be achieved with ease. However, if the luck cycle is going against the flow, poor timing can lead to disharmony and misfortunes.

2.
Clash and the Effects in a Relationship

In Four Pillars, each of the earthly branches has a clashing partner. Whether a clash is good or bad depends on the overall makeup of the Four Pillars chart. Often, when a person encounters a clash with the annual branch animal or the luck cycle, a period of change is expected. If the clash is found within the birth chart, instability within relationships is highly possible, especially if the clash occurs with the day branch. However, changes and instability does not always denote something negative, as clashes can sometimes be good for a chart if it clashes away an unfavorable branch or element in a birth chart. Below is the pattern that forms a clash.

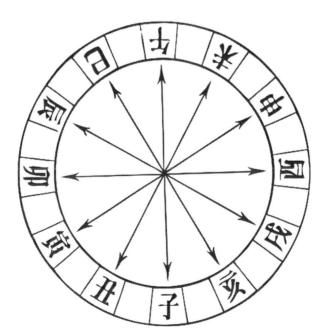

As seen in the pattern, each animal symbol clashes with the animal located directly opposite from it. If a clash occurs between the month and the year branch in a person's birth chart, most often his or her relationship with their parents is poor. Perhaps the person lived away from their parents at a very early age, or perhaps constant arguments arise between the person and the parents. Of course, it is not always the case that the latter occurs. In some cases, the person may be working away from their parents but still maintains a very close relationship with them. Both Nelly Furtado (December 2, 1978) and Katie Holmes (December 18, 1978) have clashing month and year branch but their relationships with their parents have been seemingly peaceful (they haven't had a volatile relationship with their parents).

Nelly Furtado			
Hour	Day	Month	Year
X	戊 Yang Earth	甲 Yang Wood	戊 Yang Earth
X	戌 Dog	子 Rat	午 Horse

Katie Holmes			
Hour	Day	Month	Year
X	甲 Yang Wood	甲 Yang Wood	戊 Yang Earth
X	寅 Tiger	子 Rat	午 Horse

Nelly Furtado first sang at the age of four performing a duet with her mother at church. She acknowledged her family as the source of her strong work ethic. Nelly and her family immigrated from Portugal to Canada and never experienced any major issues with her family. In 1996, she moved to Toronto and lived with her sister. This is a case where having clashing month and year branches does not automatically result in issues with the parents. For Nelly Furtado, it only meant moving away from her parents at a very young age. The same can be said about Katie Holmes as she also moved away from her parents at an early age because of her career aspirations.

Clashes between the day branch and the hour or the month branches have different cosmic reactions compared to the two examples above. Whenever the day branch possesses a clash with the month or hour branch, relationships with the spouse or partner would become unstable, although there are exceptions. If the day branch is combined with another animal next to it, the volatility of the relationships can be reduced or nullified.

All clashes and combinations discussed in this chapter must be well-learned in order to be utilized effectively in classifying birth charts. The key is to practice as much as possible — which will aid the memorization process. With the combinations and charts studied, patterns can be quickly spotted and interpreted. The next section here will explain the functions of the combinations, and by remembering these combinations, understanding the examples within this book will prove to be an easier task.

3.
Stem Transformations: Examples

Before moving forward with the interpretations of cosmic flow, the fundamentals of the combinations and transformations must be understood. Just because symbols combine with each other, this does not guarantee that an elemental structure is created, nor does it mean that an element has been completely transformed. Some of the combinations may result in transforming into the element designated by the patterns, while other combinations may fail to transform altogether. Combinations can be favourable and unfavourable depending on the cosmic flow of the birth system. Be cautious when examining stem transformations as there are unlimited variations of combinations in transformations, borderline transformations, or disabled transformations (inability to transform).

Let's begin by looking at the heavenly stems. Yang Wood (甲) has a combination with Yin Earth (己) which can transform the Yang Wood (甲) into earth. Whether it is transformed into earth depends on many factors. The most important criterion to evaluate is the month of birth. Here is a simple example:

Hour	Day	Month	Year
X	甲 Yang Wood	己 Yin Earth	X
X	X	酉 Rooster	X

The Yang Wood (甲) in the day stem has a natural combination with the Yin Earth (己) in the month stem. The birth month is in autumn, the month of the Rooster (酉), hence the transformation does NOT occur. Although the transformation does not occur, nothing can be concluded from this chart until the cosmic flow is identified. Sometimes, it is better not to transform than to transform.

For the Yang Wood (甲) to transform into earth, the combination has to occur at the proper timing. The next example illustrates the transformation.

Hour	Day	Month	Year
X	甲 Yang Wood	己 Yin Earth	X
X	X	丑 Ox	X

Being born in the month of the Ox (丑) allows earth to transform with much more ease as Ox (丑) represents wet earth. If a transformation occurs at a time when the resource of the transformation is found in the luck cycle, this person will be in an auspicious period. Since this is an earth transformation, fire being its resource would be favourable. Additional earth would also reinforce the transformation.

If this person is born in the month of the Snake (巳), a borderline transformation may occur. Although the Snake (巳) is not one of the earth animals, its fire and the season of the summer makes the Yang Wood (甲) transform.

To make this example even more complicated, let's say the person is born in the day of the Monkey (甲) and the month of the Snake (巳).

Hour	Day	Month	Year
X	甲 Yang Wood	己 Yin Earth	X
X	申 Monkey	巳 Snake	X

There are two events happening with this example. The Yang Wood (甲) and Yin Earth (己) are combining to form earth, but if you refer to the 'Six Harmonious' combinations, the Monkey (申) and the Snake (巳) also wants to combine and form water. Both combinations in the stems and the branches would find it difficult to combine. The transformation at best would be unstable.

There are birth charts where the combinations are separated by a pillar. The transformations in the stems are then less likely to occur, as shown in the example below.

Hour	Day	Month	Year
X	丙 Yang Fire	X	辛 Yin Metal
X	X	子 Rat	X

The Yang Fire (丙) here wants to combine with the Yin Metal (辛) to transform into water. This chart is definitely in the correct season. The issue here is that the two stems cannot combine and transform because they are separated by the month stem.

Sometimes, birth systems with stem combinations can still transform into the specified element even if they are not born in the correct season. There may be symbols in the branches where they would combine with each other and form an elemental structure. As the structure is formed, it would create a cosmic shift, allowing the stems to transform. The stem combination between the Yang Fire (丙) and the Yin Metal (辛) presented below illustrates a transformation of water that can be deceiving because the birth month is the Snake (巳), the first month of summer.

Hour	Day	Month	Year
X	丙 Yang Fire	辛 Yin Metal	X
X	辰 Dragon	巳 Snake	子 Rat

For the Three Harmony combinations, remember that the Rat (子), Dragon (辰) and Monkey (申) can form a water structure. As long as two of the three are found in the chart, they can still form a structure despite the separation of the two symbols. The Yang Fire (丙) and Yin Metal (辛) in this birth system transforms into water due to the half alliance between the Rat (子) and the Dragon (辰). It would most certainly benefit from the Rooster (酉) since the Rooster (酉) and the Snake (巳) form half a metal structure, which would in turn, feed the water and solidify the transformation.

Taking things further, transformations of the stems can also occur in the month and year stem. If the month stem is a Yang Water (壬) and the year stem is a Yin Fire (丁), they would be attracted to combine and form wood. Being born in the month of the Tiger (寅) would allow the transformation to happen.

Hour	Day	Month	Year
X	辛 Yin Metal	壬 Yang Water	丁 Yin Fire
X	X	寅 Tiger	X

The Yin Metal (辛) self in this example now possesses wealth elements next to it. If more wood and water are encountered in the luck cycle, the transformation would be solidified and enhanced. A scenario where the elements will fight to combine may occur. For example, if the birth system presented above encounters a Yang Water (壬) or a Yin Fire (丁) in the annual or luck cycles, the elements will fight to combine. Fighting to combine may result in third party disputes and the level of dispute varies depending on the elements involved. Yet sometimes, fighting to combine may enhance the transformation. Fighting to combine and transforming within a birth system can also result in a dysfunctional life. It depends on the elements that are involved.

In my practice, I have encountered sports athletes that thrive in systems that fight to combine. They enjoy competition so it is not always unfortunate when there is competitive urge for elements to combine within a birth chart.

Hour	Day	Month	Year
X	丁 Yin Fire	壬 Yang Water	丁 Yin Fire
X	X	寅 Tiger	X

The Yin Fire (丁) self is fighting the Yin Fire (丁) in the year stem to combine with the Yang Water (壬). If this is a birth system of a female, it is very likely that she will often be involved in third party relationships. She would want to compete with the other Yin Fire (丁) for a man, but after the fight is over, she may lose her interests and move on to another man. This is one probable scenario. The degree of fighting and competing depends on the strength of the self and the strength of the transformation. A female with multiple controlling elements combining with the self is often led to many unwanted romances. She will tend to have more than one man in her life, and this can be a result of greed, or sometimes, a lack of self-security.

Hour	Day	Month	Year
丙 Yang Fire	辛 Yin Metal	丙 Yang Fire	丙 Yang Fire
X	X	子 Rat	X

The Yin Metal (辛) self in the previous chart is being combined by at least two Yang Fires (丙) in the birth system. The third Yang Fire (丙) in the year stem would want to leapfrog over the other Yang Fire (丙) and combine with the self. A person like this would most likely live an unhappy marriage life; it is best for her to avoid getting married. The multiple combinations would also create an uncomfortable situation for her spouse.

"FIGHT TO COMBINE"

This does not mean that there are people fighting with you when a 'Fight to Combine' occurs. Combinations are involved where two or more elements may want to combine with a specific element in the birth chart. In Chinese, it is called '爭合'. The positioning of the symbols and the structure of the birth chart would be able to tell us what will transpire. The natural course of Four Pillars is to avoid a 'Fight to Combine'.

4.
Branch Transformations and Clashes

Within the branches, there are three main types of combinations which include Six Harmony, Three Harmony, and Directional/Seasonal combinations. Each of the types of combinations possesses different qualities and attributes and must be prioritized properly. The Three Harmony combination is the most powerful type of combination in the Four Pillars system. The Directional/ Seasonal combination ranks second amongst combination strength due to the fact that all three symbols representing a season must be present. For the Six Harmony combination, the symbols need to be right next each to each other, just like the heavenly stem combinations. If the Six Harmony combinations are separated by a pillar, they cannot combine. The transformation of the Six Harmony combinations does not occur as easily as the Three Harmony combinations. Being born in the correct season is crucial to its transformation. The example below illustrates a transformation of the Rooster (酉) and the Dragon (辰) into the controlling element of the self, metal.

Hour	Day	Month	Year
辛 Yin Metal	甲 Yang Wood	X	X
X	X	酉 Rooster	辰 Dragon

On the other hand, what if the Dragon (辰) is in the month branch and the Rooster (酉) is in the year branch? Usually, the transformation into metal would not occur since the birth month is in the spring. Yet, there are exceptions to this rule. If metal is found in the month or year stem, the transformation to metal can still occur in the branches.

Hour	Day	Month	Year
辛 Yin Metal	甲 Yang Wood	X	X
X	X	辰 Dragon	酉 Rooster

Birth systems having the Six Harmony combination separated by a pillar cannot combine, let alone transform. For example, an Ox (丑) and Rat (子) may want to combine and transform into earth, but it is not possible if the elements are separated, as illustrated by the chart below.

Hour	Day	Month	Year
X	丙 Yang Fire	己 Yin Earth	戊 Yang Earth
子 Rat	申 Monkey	丑 Ox	X

In this example, the Ox (丑) cannot combine with the Rat (子) because of their separation. Instead, the Monkey (申) and the Rat (子) combines and forms a water structure instead due to their proximity. However, some Chinese texts may state that the Ox (丑) combines with the Rat (子), in addition to the water structure that is formed between the Rat (子) and the Monkey (申). This is not possible from a logical standpoint. The Three Harmony combination supersedes the Six Harmony combination. Assuming that the Rat (子) and the

Monkey (申) exchanges position, with the Rat (子) ending up in the day branch beside the Ox (丑), the Ox (丑) may fight to combine. Essentially, the Rat (子) and the Monkey (申) are natural partners and are naturally attracted to each other. The Ox (丑) and Rat (子) would fail to combine and form earth. When multiple combinations are found within branches, it is highly likely that the person is approachable and has a lot of friends. But prior to making such an assumption, it is important to first sort out favourable elements to the birth chart. If the branch combinations are favourable to the entire birth chart, chances remain that this person is enjoyable to work with.

Just like the stem combinations, there are also possibilities of having a fight to combine in the branches. The two Monkeys (申) in this example illustrate a fight to combine with the day branch, the Snake (巳). This type of combination, where two Monkeys (申) compete for the day branch, often creates misfortunes in marriages.

Hour	Day	Month	Year
X	癸 Yin Water	X	X
申 Monkey	巳 Snake	申 Monkey	X

The partner of the spouse in this birth chart may be having affairs or another relationship. There is potential for the spouse to have another family already. Or perhaps the spouse has been divorced, but still needs to tend to children from a previous relationship. Another common situation for a person with a chart like this is that their spouse is often never content with be-ing in only one relationship. This may sound terrible for those who place a lot of emphasis on their relationships. However, clients who possess this type of birth chart are often willing to accept this news and understand that they have to live with such circumstances. Therefore, the delivery of the message through a reading is very important, and must be treated appropriately and cautiously. Four Pillars practitioners should try to avoid injecting their own emotion onto other people's lives. It is essential to diagnose without bias. A Four Pillar con-sultation examines the life of another human being — and problems will arise if sessions are dealt unprofessionally by taking personal beliefs and imposing them onto your clients.

Hour	Day	Month	Year
X	癸 Yin Water	X	X
X	巳 Snake	申 Monkey	巳 Snake

Let's say the fight to combine has now shifted to the month and the day branch. This may explain a conflict within the previous generation. The conflict can involve marital problems or a dispute of family wealth. If the person was born in the hour of the Monkey (申), the additional Monkey (申) may nullify the conflict. Cosmically, each of them have their own partners and will not choose to fight with one another.

Hour	Day	Month	Year
X	癸 Yin Water	X	X
申 Monkey	巳 Snake	申 Monkey	巳 Snake

This example can be considered unstable. Furthermore, the instability can be brought about by the changes in luck and annual cycles. Imagine this: what would happen during the year of the Snake (巳)? A new person will emerge, wanting and trying to pull away one of the partners. Some practioners place a greater emphasis on the month and year pillars for the earlier part of life, while heavily weighting on the day and hour pillars for the latter part. There is some truth to this method, but we must be inclined to look at the overall structure of the birth chart first. We cannot nullify the year pillar when a person enters the age of 60. With this example, you can look at the age of this person and determine whether the Snake (巳) targets the Monkey (申) in the month or hour branch. If this person was in his teenage years, most likely the Snake (巳) would affect his or her parents more because of the heavier weight placed upon the month branch.

The Six Harmony combinations usually have a much more difficult time in transforming as it requires the birth month to be in the right season. These combinations also need to be beside each other. The Three Harmony combinations are different as they can still form an elemental structure even though they are separated (the degree of separation depends). Transformations would still occur but the elemental structure would be considered weak.

Hour	Day	Month	Year
X	X	X	X
酉 Rooster	子 Rat	辰 Dragon	丑 Ox

The branches in this example present two combinations occurring. In the inner branches, between the month and the day, the Rat (子) and the Dragon (辰) combine to form half a water structure. On the outer branches, the Ox (丑) and the Rooster (酉) can combine to form half a metal structure. Since metal produces water, it can be deduced that there is a slight interbreeding of elements within this example. The metal structure formed on the exterior is considered weaker, but they still combine. When a clash is encountered from the luck or annual cycles, the impact of the clash would depend on the animal symbol that is under attack. If this chart enters a Horse (午) or a Dog (戌) cycle, the clash is minimized due to the combination of the Rat (子) and the Dragon (辰) standing side by side. The potential for negative impacts diminishes. On the other hand, if it is a Goat (未) or a Rabbit (卯) year, the exterior combinations are not so fortunate. The distance between the Rooster (酉) and Ox (丑) would be too far for them to come together to defend against negative impacts of the clash. Keep in mind that the strength of a clash also depends on the cosmic flow of a birth system. The scenarios provided here are all theoretical.

For Directional Combinations, all three animal symbols must exist in a birth system. Having just the two animals out of the three will not be enough to form a Directional Combination. It is not possible for the birth chart below to form half a Winter Direction.

Hour	Day	Month	Year
X	己 Yin Earth	X	X
酉 Rooster	亥 Pig	子 Rat	寅 Tiger

Although the birth month is a Rat (子), it is missing the Ox (丑) to form a complete Directional combination which would unite together with the Pig (亥). By encountering an Ox (丑) year or luck cycle, the Directional combination would be temporarily formed. If an Ox (丑) is present in the birth system, the Directional combination is complete and a winter water structure is formed.

Hour	Day	Month	Year
X	己 Yin Earth	X	X
戌 Dog	亥 Pig	子 Rat	丑 Ox

Note that the Directional Combination does not require the animals to be next to each other. The only requirement is that all three symbols have to exist within the branches. The problem with a Directional Combination, however, is that it can be broken up by a clash in the luck cycle, or eliminated by another combination. With the example above, even though the complete direction of the Pig (亥), Rat (子) and Ox (丑) is present, this team of water can be broken up if it encounters a Horse (午). The Horse (午) may choose to fight with the Rat (子), or it may choose to combine with the Dog (戌) in the hour branch. A Rabbit (卯) year can also pull apart the team as it may want to combine with the Pig (亥) to form a half wood team. A birth system like this may find it difficult to lead with a water flow as it is constantly restrained by other elements in play. Thus, frequent frustrations may arise. As you can see, there are endless possible scenarios in terms of combinations and clashes.

"BRANCH VS. STEMS"

Branches vs Stems – Always remember that the Stems are only in the upper row of the Four Pillars chart while the Branches are in the lower row of the Four Pillars chart. Stems are seen and visible to people while the Branches are hidden. The exterior characteristics of a person can be seen through the analysis of the Stems.

5.
Cosmic Flow Theory

Determining cosmic flow and cosmic necessity in a relationship is probably the most difficult task when dealing with the Four Pillars. By cosmic necessity, it can be specific elements that a person requires in his or her chart that can make them happy and successful. For example, a person may need a specific element and the partner could possess the necessary resources to complement one's chart. Some relationships can be one-sided where one needs the partner more. Of course, the best situation to have is that both sides have elements that they need so that they can complement each other.

When the flow of the luck cycle changes, meaning a seasonal or an elemental shift in the luck cycle, some may feel even more attracted to one another while some couples could lose their feelings, resulting in difficulties and struggles in their relationship. In order to determine the flow of a birth composite, the month where one is born is crucial. Each season is dominated by a leading element, an element that is considered to be in full bloom. In spring, wood is in full bloom, while in the summer, fire blazes in brightness. In autumn, metal becomes the leading element, a time when the heat cools and metal solidifies. During winter, water corrodes the metal and the cold, wet season dominates. Picturing the four seasons in the mind allows practitioners to understand how the eight characters in a chart come together.

With the knowledge of the earthly branch combinations, practitioners can make precise judgement on what the leading flow of a chart would be. It is not always the case that cosmic flow can be defined clearly in a chart. Many practitioners fall into the trap of counting symbols and dismissing the combinations in the birth chart. This is a common pitfall and habit that can result in the incorrect reading of flow. In order to minimize the amount of errors made in a consultation, questioning and verification of past historical or key events can help avoid mistakes.

As a chart moves into a different cycle with a favourable element in play, questions should be asked to determine whether it is in fact a favourable element, or sometimes referred to as the "useful god". The questions should pertain to one's health and wealth. Obviously, a great year would be a year of good health and financial success. On the other hand, if one move into a bad cycle or run into an element with an opposing flow, it can have a detrimental effect on the person. In this case, the opposite would occur as health and wealth properties suffer during bad periods. Remember, no definite blueprints or rules on determining the useful god exists in the practice of Four Pillars. Since the nature of cosmos is constantly changing, some birth systems are easier to understand while others require tedious effort to decipher. The constant change of energy and where we were born creates different the lives and luck cycles we have.

After the main flow has been determined, other factors become secondary such as the use of special stars, punishments, harms, and penalties. Those secondary factors are calculated based upon patterns. Since we are primarily concerned with the flow of the elements in this chapter, we will explore some of the secondary factors in later chapters. There is a general tendency for practitioners to evaluate special stars, such as peach blossom, romance, scholar, guides and noblemen stars, before looking at the flow and patterns of a Four Pillars chart. Without a clear identification of the flow, there is not much use in plotting the special stars. For example, how would one determine the impact of a special star if they do not know a scholar or nobleman star may be unfavourable to the flow of the elements in a birth chart? The positive features of the specific star can be more harmful to the entire Four Pillars chart than one may think. This sort of analysis can be compared to the Feng Shui analysis of a house. In Feng Shui, there is a method where practitioners would use Flying Stars to determine the good and bad energies of a house. What if the house has a terrible exterior or the house is facing bad energy in its front yard? We must always turn to the big picture first. There are other methods in Four Pillars where people would count symbols and label each symbol individually with one of the Ten Gods. Again, without defining the flow of the birth system, identifying individual symbols in a birth chart will result in an erroneous reading.

Clashes on the other hand are important parts of a Four Pillars reading. Clashes can be determined as to whether it is a good clash or a bad clash, likewise with combinations. A self element being born in the wrong season has a great chance of surrendering to a leading flow. For example, a Yin Water (癸) self born in the month of the Rabbit (卯) in the spring has a high possibility of surrendering to the wood flow. This is assuming that there are wood combinations in a chart while there is an absence of resources and the self element. Borderline cases are much more difficult to determine by just looking at a chart. It requires questioning about a person's history and past events.

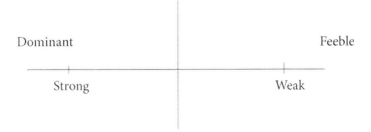

When analyzing the strength of a birth chart, using the above line graph allows us to classify where the chart would stand. There are two ends of the spectrum when we classify charts. Charts can be classified as feeble, or surrendering to a leading flow. On one end, dominant charts can be found where the self element is usually born in the proper season at the right timing, solidifying the self. In addition, combinations supporting the self would ensure that the charts remain dominant. Four Pillars charts can be classified as any being located somewhere along the lines between feeble and dominant. It would be much easier to classify a birth system by picturing where one would be on the line. The different types of classifications and how it can influence a relationship will be explored as we take a look at the various types of flows in this chapter. The best way to evaluate and analyze a Four Pillars chart is to keep the line graph in mind. Determine where one would stand, then identify the leading flow. If there isn't a leading flow, there is a high possibility that these people would stand between the weak and the strong. During a chart analysis, it is good to get into a habit of picturing where the chart would stand according to the line graph.

On the other hand, those who are born feeble would be able to enjoy the benefits of the cosmos. Imagine helpless babies: being the opposite of a dominant self will attract and receive all the attention, love and care. By possessing a feeble chart, a person can enjoy great fortunes and success with lots of assistance. They would benefit most if the luck cycle is in their favour. By being in their favour, it means that the elements within the luck cycle should enhance the leading flow. Let's say water is the leading flow, obviously, this person would enjoy great luck and fortune with water and metal in the luck cycle.

Earth and fire would impede the flow as earth controls water and fire creates conflicts with water. Contrary to feeble systems, those who belong on the dominant self classification needs to work hard like a responsible adult forced to job hunt in order to feed an entire household. Dominant selves can be just as successful if the luck cycles are in their favour. Those in between the weak and strong may have a more difficult time but it also depends on the luck cycles. Remember that 'luck cycles' do not mean 'good' or 'bad' luck, it is a term that defines the interval that we are in. This interval is represented by a symbol. The nature of the luck is then determined by whether the element of the symbol is favourable or not to the entire birth chart.

"DOMINANT SELF"

This is a term given to birth charts where it is classified as having a dominant element throughout the chart. The chart can be composed of the same element as the self with elements supporting the growth of the self element. A person with a dominant self chart will enjoy good fortunes as long as the luck and annual cycles continue to support its dominance.

The luck cycle has a major influence on whether the feeble or the dominant selves can enjoy the benefits that they were given with at birth. A feeble self empowered by resources would no longer be like a baby. In extreme cases, they can behave like rebellious teenagers. On the other hand, a dominant self encountering a controlling element may enter a period of difficulties as the controlling element would seek to break apart the newly formed connections between elements within the birth system. The breakup can lead to struggles in life. Once again, by "going with the flow", people would stand a greater opportunity in achieving their goals and objectives.

"FEEBLE OR SURRENDER"

Although being feeble or surrendering has somewhat of a negative connotation, in Four Pillars practice, by being feeble or surrendering to a leading elemental flow, success, wealth and fame are easily accomplished as long as the birth chart remains feeble and goes with the leading elemental flow. It is when a feeble birth chart suddenly becomes strong that mishaps will occur. Four Pillars is not about balance, it is about going in harmony with the leading flow.

The following section about the cosmic flow of each element serves as a guideline, but it is by no means absolute. As mentioned earlier, aside from understanding main principles of the flow, testing and verification plays a vital part in a consultation. The relationship between the seasons and the elements is one of the keys to determining the strengths of the cosmic flow and whether the flow is pure or disruptive.

Wood Flow

In spring, wood is leading the seasonal flow, therefore, in a Four Pillars chart, if a person was born in the month of the Tiger (寅), Rabbit (卯) or Dragon (辰), that person should pay attention to the wood flow's relationship with the self element. It is also important to note that each of the three animals have combinations with other animals that can transform into a different element. Naturally, it is easier to say that Rabbit (卯) leads the team of wood and represents the Eastern cardinal direction. If a chart possesses one or both of the Goat (未) and the Pig (亥), the wood flow would be solidified by a half or a trio wood combination. Such combinations are considered to be more stable than a directional combination composed of the Tiger (寅), Rabbit (卯) and Dragon (辰).

An earth self surrenders in the spring as wood penetrates earth during this period. The surrenders is based on the assumption that there is a lack of fire and other earth elements in the birth system. Earth lacks energy in this season to withstand the strength of the wood. If a birth composite lacks a wood "alliance" in the branches and the self is supported throughout the chart by resource elements, it would be difficult for the self element to surrender to the wood.

Below is an example of a birth composite with a wood flow even though this was born in the month of the Pig (亥) during the winter.

Hour	Day	Month	Year
X	己 Yin Earth	丁 Yin Fire	乙 Yin Wood
X	未 Goat	亥 Pig	卯 Rabbit

60	50	40	30	20	10	0
庚 Yang Metal	辛 Yin Metal	壬 Yang Water	癸 Yin Water	甲 Yang Wood	乙 Yin Wood	丙 Yang Fire
辰 Dragon	巳 Snake	午 Horse	未 Goat	申 Monkey	酉 Rooster	戌 Dog

This is the birth composite of Ralphael Enthoven, born on November 9, 1975 where the leading flow is obviously wood. The Yin Earth (己) self lacks energy even though it is sitting on top of a Goat (未). In this case, the Goat (未) combines with the Pig (亥) and the Rabbit (卯) to form a complete wood trio. The Yin Fire (丁) in the month is too weak to burn up the wood and it is not strong enough to strengthen the earth. From a relationship standpoint, Ralphael would enjoy being with a person who would have a water and wood flow. By tracing back to recent history, it is evident that he benefits from wood and water, as he obtained a qualification in philosophy during his Yang Wood (甲) cycle. During the Yin Water (癸) cycle between the ages of 30 and 34, he became an everyday icon in a program (The new paths of knowledge) for France Culture in 2008-2009. This example goes to show that he benefits from a water and wood flow.

From a relationship standpoint, Carla Bruni, French singer, songwriter, and former model, fell in love with Raphael and had a son with him in 2001. So what brought the both of them together and took them apart? By analyzing the cosmic flow of their charts, Carla Bruni also enjoys a water and wood flow. She was born on December 23, 1967, at the hour of the Rooster (酉) and below is her chart:

Hour	Day	Month	Year
丁 Yin Fire	辛 Yin Metal	壬 Yang Water	丁 Yin Fire
酉 Rooster	酉 Rooster	子 Rat	未 Goat

75	65	55	35	45	25	15	5
庚 Yang Metal	己 Yin Earth	戊 Yang Earth	丁 Yin Fire	丙 Yang Fire	乙 Yin Wood	甲 Yang Wood	癸 Yin Water
戌 Dog	酉 Rooster	申 Monkey	未 Goat	午 Horse	巳 Snake	辰 Dragon	丑 Ox

Water and wood played a critical role in Carla Bruni's birth system, and the flows attracted Raphael to her. Looking at the birth system of Carla, she was born in the month of the Rat (子) where her metal is receding in strength while wood is beginning to grow. In addition, she was born in Turin, where metal does not have enough strength to fight with the harsh winter conditions. It is clear that Carla needs to follow the flow of the water. In order to truly surrender to the flow of wood and water, the Rooster in her day branch must be taken away from her system. In terms of timing, Carla was in the Rabbit (卯) cycle at the time when she was with Raphael, and that was when the Rabbit (卯) clashed away the Rooster (酉) while it combined with the Goat (未) in the year branch to form half a wood alliance. The strength of the wood can be attributed to the stem combinations. The Yang Water (壬) in the month stem combines with the Yin Fire (丁) and wants to transform into wood. This process is possible if the timing is correct. Since Carla's birth system had an abundance amount of wood and water, the attraction and timing was perfect. In Raphael's birth system, he was in the Monkey (申) cycle when Carla's Rat (子) month attracted the Monkey (申) to form more water. The unfortunate part is that their relationship could not last long because of the Rooster (酉) sitting in her day branch, inducing the pure metal of the Rooster to chop away at Raphael's wood flow. Once her cosmic cycle departed from the Rabbit (卯), the power of the metal Rooster (酉) pushed the both of them apart. Carla mentioned to the media that she felt that there was not enough commitment made in their relationship. From a Four Pillars point of view, the Rooster (酉) in Carla's birth chart presents her with problems in relationships. The Rooster (酉), a cardinal metal animal, is seen as a rival to her own self element which is the Yin Metal (辛).

Both Carla and Ralphael enjoy and prosper from the wood flow, as illustrated in this example. In order to decode the underlying theme of their chart, it is important to know all the cosmic combinations and understand the strengths and weaknesses of each element within a particular season. For Raphael, his Yin Earth (己) self element lacks energy to withstand the wood in the branches while Carla's Yin Metal (辛) self is in a reduction phase during the winter month of the Rat (子). Carla's month and year stem also had the capabilities of transforming into wood if the timing is right.

Fire Flow

Summer is the season when fire is the most prosperous. The three months of the summer are the Snake (巳), Horse (午), and Goat (未). The Horse (午) represents the South cardinal direction. Chinese books often use directions to explain the change in the luck cycle. For example, they may mention that the luck cycle is changing towards a southerly flow, meaning the three animals in the Summer. The Horse is the leader of fire and it can combine with the Dog (戌) and the Tiger (寅) to form a fire trio. A fire self born in the fire season has the possibility of becoming a fire dominant self, but there must be a team of fire to support the dominant self. In other words, without a team, the fire could be too hot and it may require a water flow to reduce the heat.

Knowing when the fire flow is leading requires a vast amount of experience, especially when the self is earth or wood. When questioning about the fire periods, where a person may pass through the Yang Fire (丙), Yin Fire (丁)

and Horse (午) cycles are crucial. Also, the month that the person is born in is just as important. Imagine a person born in the month of the Dog (戌) with the complete fire trio: it is not always the case that fire will be the leading flow. If the birth composite possesses a certain amount of water and metal, it can change the classification of the chart as a strong self that requires water to cool the system. Once a chart is classified as a strong self, weakening the chart by using the controlling or output elements will prove to be beneficial. The weakening process can come about through a luck cycle or through the use of Feng Shui and specific colors. If a strong fire self encounters additional resources in the luck cycles, health problems related to the heart may occur.

Canadian actress and model, Pamela Anderson, provides an example of a Four Pillars chart cosmically driven and led by the fire flow. She is a Yang Fire (丙) self born in the heat of the summer on July 1, 1967.

Hour	Day	Month	Year
庚 Yang Metal	丙 Yang Fire	丙 Yang Fire	丁 Yin Fire
寅 Tiger	寅 Tiger	午 Horse	未 Goat

The fire is led by the Horse (午) which teams with the Tiger (寅) to form a half fire alliance. On the other hand, the Horse (午) wants to combine with the Goat (未) to form fire but the strength of the Tiger (寅) and Horse (午) is more pronounced. When analyzing combinations, remember that the Three Harmony (trio) combination takes precedence over other combinations. In Pamela Anderson's case, the Tiger (寅) and the Horse (午) are closer to each other than the Horse (午) and the Goat (未). The Horse (午) would be the first to attract the Tiger (寅) as the two form half of a Three Harmony combination. Although the Tiger (寅) naturally partners with the Horse (午), the Goat (未) is constantly fighting to combine with the Horse (午). The fight to combine is one of the causes for her multiple marriages.

Tommy Lee			
Hour	Day	Month	Year
X	甲 Yang Wood	庚 Yang Metal	壬 Yang Water
X	戌 **Dog**	戌 Dog	寅 Tiger

Kid Rock			
Hour	Day	Month	Year
X	壬 Yang Water	己 Yin Earth	己 Yin Earth
X	寅 **Tiger**	丑 Ox	丑 Ox

Rick Salomon			
Hour	Day	Month	Year
X	癸 Yin Water	癸 Yin Water	丁 Yin Fire
X	巳 Snake	丑 Ox	未 Goat

Pamela's attraction to fire is evident in her relationships with her former spouses Tommy Lee (October 3, 1962), Kid Rock (January 17, 1971), and Rick Salomon (January 24, 1968). Each of them possess key symbols that are fire related in the birth chart. The previous page presents their birth charts with the cosmic fire energy highlighted.

Unfortunately, her three spouses do not have enough wood and fire in their chart to give her the cosmic connection that she truly needs. The fight to combine within her birth composite accompanied by partners who do not have a pure fire flow resulted in multiple marriages. Out of the three men identified here, Tommy Lee would be the most suitable partner for Pamela Anderson due to the existence of the Dog (戌) in his day branch. The Dog (戌) would complete the team of fire Dog (戌), Tiger (寅) and Horse (午) that Pamela Anderson would enjoy. Since Pamela already possesses the Tiger (寅) and the Horse (午), she would naturally be more in tuned to Tommy Lee's birth system.

Hollywood actor and producer Tom Cruise, born on July 3, 1962 at the hour of the Horse (午), represents another clear example of a birth composite in need to follow the flow of fire. "Lights, camera and action!"—a representation of fire—has placed Tom Cruise into Hollywood's Walk of Fame. The abundance of fire in his birthchart has provided him with great success in the movie industry. He can also benefit from wood elements, as wood fuels fire with supple flames.

Hour	Day	Month	Year
丙 Yang Fire	壬 Yang Water	丁 Yin Fire	壬 Yang Water
午 Horse	寅 Tiger	未 Goat	寅 Tiger

41	31	21	11	1
壬 Yang Water	辛 Yin Metal	庚 Yang Metal	己 Yin Earth	戊 Yang Earth
子 Rat	亥 Pig	戌 Dog	酉 Rooster	申 Monkey

Tom Cruise is a Yang Water (壬) self sitting on top of a Tiger (寅). The fire in the month burns on a sturdy foundation as the Yin Fire (丁) is supported by the fire and wood Goat (未) underneath it. In addition, the Horse (午) in his hour branch teams up with the Tiger (寅) to form half a fire alliance. Much of Tom Cruise's success came early in his acting career in the Dog (戌) cycle which was roughly between 1988 and 1993. From his birth chart, the Dog (戌) cycle is found between the ages of 26 to 30 in his luck cycle. The Dog (戌), Horse (寅) and Tiger (寅) in his chart combined to unleash the fire. It was during that period where he became famous in Hollywood for his movies. It is evident that many of his blockbuster hits were released in fire-related years. Below is a list of big box office hits featuring Tom Cruise.

- **1986,** THE YEAR OF THE YANG FIRE TIGER (丙寅) SAW THE RELEASE OF TOP GUN.

- **1996,** THE YEAR OF THE YANG FIRE RAT (丙子), the first Mission Impossible was released and box office gross was more than $400 million.

- **2002,** THE YEAR OF THE YANG WATER HORSE (壬午) SAW THE RELEASE OF Minority Report, another big box office hit grossing more than $300 MILLION. THE HORSE (午), BEING A CARDINAL SYMBOL OF THE SOUTH PLAYED A MAJOR ROLE IN HELPING TOM CRUISE STAR IN ANOTHER BIG MOVIE RELEASE.

- **2006,** THE YEAR OF THE YANG FIRE DOG (丙戌), MISSION IMPOSSIBLE III was released and box office gross was nearly $400 million.

Similar to the example of Pamela Anderson, evaluating the birth chart of Tom Cruise's ex-spouse Nicole Kidman (June 20, 1967) and his current spouse Katie Holmes (December 18, 1978) confirms his need for fire and wood.

Katie Holmes			
Hour	Day	Month	Year
乙 Yin Wood	甲 Yang Wood	甲 Yang Wood	戊 Yang Earth
亥 Pig	寅 Tiger	子 Rat	午 Horse

Nicole Kidman			
Hour	Day	Month	Year
甲 Yang Wood	乙 Yin Wood	丙 Yang Fire	丁 Yin Fire
申 Monkey	卯 Rabbit	午 Horse	未 Goat

From looking at both birth composites, Katie Holmes and Nicole Kidman possess a great deal of wood and fire in them. Kidman's birth chart is more obvious as she is born in the month of the Horse (午) and both her month and year stem has fire. Yin Wood (乙), being her day stem, lacks strength and she has to surrender to the fire. With Katie Holmes, she also has a Horse (午) in her chart and is surrounded by wood.

Since the primary concern of this chapter is on cosmic flow, there will be more references made to Tom Cruise's relationship life later in this book. Let us now focus on Nicole Kidman's birth chart.

She was born on June 20th, 1967 at approximately 3:15pm. As mentioned earlier, the effects of the birth hour tend to come later in life. The fortunate part of Nicole's Four Pillars chart is that the cosmic flow can be clearly defined by the amount of fire that she possesses. In addition, she was born in the heat of the summer in Honolulu, Hawaii. The location of birth provided additional fire to her cosmic system. The primary focus a birth system like Nicole's should be whether she surrenders to the fire or not. Below is her luck cycle.

44	34	24	14	4
辛 Yin Metal	庚 Yang Metal	己 Yin Earth	戊 Yang Earth	丁 Yin Fire
亥 Pig	戌 Dog	酉 Rooster	申 Monkey	未 Goat

Key Events of Nicole Kidman

One of the easiest ways to evaluate the flow of a birth chart is by evaluating the key events of a person's life. For Nicole Kidman, fire is the main element in question. Since her birth chart indeed surrenders to fire, one way of determining the main element is to turn to what has transpired in the Horse (午) years, since the Horse (午) is a cardinal symbol of Southern fire. Both

1990 and 2002 were years of the Horse. In 1990, it was Nicole's first American debut in the movie Days of Thunder and it was one of the highest grossing films of the year. Fast forward to 2002, she received an Academy Nomination for her role in Moulin Rouge and was given the leading role in the movie, "The Others". To cap off 2002, she won an Academy Award for Best Actress in the movie, "The Hours".

The Dog (戌) is also good for Nicole Kidman because of the half fire trio which would form with her birth system. To reiterate, the fire trio is composed of the Horse (午), Tiger (寅), and the Dog (戌). Nicole Kidman was made a 'Companion of the Order of Australia' in 2006 and was also the highest-paid actress in the movie industry. One final confirmation should be made: an examination of the Rabbit (卯) found in the day branch. If her chart is a true surrender to fire, then having the Rabbit (卯) out of the picture would grant her greater results. When she was near the end of the Rooster (酉) cycle, the Rooster (酉) clashed and eliminated the strength of the Rabbit, leading to an Academy Award in 2002 as the Best Actress. On the line graph, Nicole Kidman's birth system teeters between 'Feeble' and 'Weak'. It is much better for her to remain in the 'Feeble' classification, this means that as long as her luck cycles keeps the wood in check, she can continue to benefit from the cosmic flow.

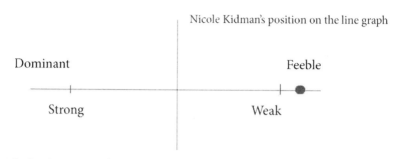

Nicole Kidman's position on the line graph

Dominant   Feeble

Strong   Weak

The birth system of Nicole Kidman illustrates a few key points in cosmic flow. Being in the right industry or career is an important factor for achieving success. For Nicole, just like her ex-husband Tom Cruise, it was being in the spotlight of Hollywood. Having movies released in a year of favourable cosmic flow gave her an opportunity to win an Academy Award. Nicole's Four Pillars chart also demonstrates that by having "unwanted" elements and symbols eliminated or weakened, one can gain favourable results. Once again, a clash does not always result in an unfortunate event or period.

Earth Flow

There are four key branches that would lead an earth flow and they are the Dragon (辰), Goat (未), Dog (戌) and Ox (丑). Whether they lead earth in a birth chart is highly dependent upon which month the person was born in and whether there is an abundance of earth within the chart. Out of all five elements, earth requires extra attention due to the fact that earth can be found in all four seasons. In the spring, earth is found in the Dragon (辰). Hidden within the Dragon (辰) are three elements, Yang Earth, Yin Wood and Yin Water. The element that plays a more prominent role in the Dragon (辰) depends on the presence of other combinations and what is found in the heavenly stem. If earth and fire is present above the Dragon (辰) in the heavenly stems of a chart, the earth would be firmly rooted by the Dragon (辰). On the other hand, if there are combinations that involve the Rat (子) and Monkey (申), water would take a stronger stance in the chart. Having more wood in the chart would most likely reinforce the presence of the wood from the Dragon (辰).

Moving onto the summer, the month of the Goat (未) is the third month of summer and it possesses Yin Earth, which is dry and hot. In addition, hidden in the Goat (未) is Yin Fire and Yin wood. Similar to the Dragon (辰), the combinations and the elements that are found in the stems can shift the strength of the elements in the Goat (未). For example, if the Rabbit (卯) and/ or Pig (亥) were found in the chart, the chart would lean towards a wood flow. If the wood flow is not in the correct season, classification becomes difficult. Wood flows are much stronger if the person was born in the winter or spring.

Once combinations are understood in the Four Pillars practice, similar patterns can be found for the Dog (戌), which represents the last month of the autumn. The same can be said for the Ox (丑), representing the last month of winter. The Dog (戌) possesses Yang Earth, Yin Fire and Yin Metal while the Ox (丑) possesses Yin Earth, Yin Metal and Yin Water. Another major difference to note between the two animals is that the Dog (戌) has hidden fire elements, creating hard earth, whereas wet earth can be classified for the Ox (丑).

The hard earth and fire can be brought about easily from the Dog (戌) if it encounters a Horse (午) in the chart, the luck cycle or annually.

Theoretically, an earth person being born in the summer months has a greater possibility of becoming earth dominant. Fire solidifies the earth energy found throughout the hot summer months. The "textbook approach" to verifying the interaction between the two elements is to single out the fire combinations and earth elements for traces of water, wood or metal. Ideally, it would be good to go with the flow on a Dominant Earth chart by using fire and earth. Real estate tycoon, Donald Trump, is certainly a prime example of a person in need of fire and earth. He was born on June 14th, 1946, where the combination of fire and earth are leading the flow as illustrated in his birth

Hour	Day	Month	Year
己 Yin Earth	己 Yin Earth	甲 Yang Wood	丙 Yang Fire
巳 Snake	未 Goat	午 Horse	戌 Dog

67	57	47	37	27	17	7
辛 Yin Metal	庚 Yang Metal	己 Yin Earth	戊 Yang Earth	丁 Yin Fire	丙 Yang Fire	乙 Yin Wood
丑 Ox	子 Rat	亥 Pig	戌 Dog	酉 Rooster	申 Monkey	未 Goat

composite.

By determining the importance of fire and the leading cosmic flow of his chart, both the day stem and the month branch are key components to look at. Trump is a Yin Earth (己) born in the month of the Horse (午). Due to the number of combinations occurring within his birth chart, his birth system must be analyzed carefully. The most obvious combination that Trump has is the complete Southern directional combination in his branches, composed of the Snake (巳), Horse (午), and Goat (未). Although the Southern combination is complete, the Horse (午) is naturally drawn to team up with the Dog (戌) in the year branch and greedily forms a half-fire alliance. The possibility of the Horse (午) joining with two different types of combinations creates chaos and instability in his birth chart. This sense of instability can be translated into his relationship life. In addition, the Horse (午) also has a "six harmonious" combination with the Goat (未) in the day branch. Going to the stems, the Yang Wood (甲) in the month stem combines with the Yin Earth (己) day master to transform into earth. The transformation in this case occurs since it is in season and is supported by the fire and earth underneath him.

Classification of Donald Trump

Looking at the big picture and all the combinations, it is obvious that the flow is fire and earth. This type of chart is typically labelled as a "Dominant Self" (專旺格). The dominant earth flow is strongly supported by the fire in his branches. The above graphical illustration of Donald Trump places him beyond a strong self. Utilizing water in this instance would not be a good idea as it will destabilize the structure and cause the two Yin Earths (己) in the stems to fight for wealth. By evaluating his luck cycle, Trump had been through quite an abundant amount of fire and earth cycles especially during the period between the 1970s and 1980s. This was the time where he was in the Yang Earth Dog (戊戌) luck pillar. Since it has been mentioned that he would enjoy a fire and earth flow, the luck cycles at the time benefited him. Much of his financial success was found in that period. From a relationship standpoint, Trump

Hour	Day	Month	Year
戊 Yang Earth	辛 Yin Metal	丙 Yang Fire	己 Yin Earth
子 Rat	巳 Snake	寅 Tiger	丑 Ox

65	55	45	35	25	15	5
癸 Yin Water	壬 Yang Water	辛 Yin Metal	庚 Yang Metal	己 Yin Earth	戊 Yang Earth	丁 Yin Fire
酉 Rooster	申 Monkey	未 Goat	午 Horse	巳 Snake	辰 Dragon	卯 Rabbit

would enjoy a partner who has earth and fire in the birth composite.

Ivana Trump, born on February 20, 1949 married Donald Trump in 1977. Her birth composite is presented on the previous page. The luck cycle is highlighted, Yin Earth (己), is the period when they were married.

Looking at Ivana Trump's chart, she possesses an abundant amount of fire and earth. The entire year pillar presents wet earth with the Yin Earth Ox (己丑). The Yang Fire (丙) in the month pillar is strongly 'rooted' by the Tiger (寅). It is not too difficult to see that Donald Trump is attracted to Ivana cosmically through the supply of fire and earth that Ivana's birth composite has. In order for Ivana to secure a fire and earth flow, she would need the Dog (戌) and the Horse (午)—two distinct elements found in Donald's Four

Pillars chart. Throughout their marriage, Ivana has helped Donald in his business and family life; this is a result of the need of fire and earth of Donald's chart.

Following cosmic flow and finding a partner that fit the cosmic needs of one's birthchart can ensure a harmonious relationship. Unfortunately, when there is a change in luck cycle or energetic flow, difficulties in a marriage can occur. In 1991, the year

of the Yin Metal Goat (辛未), Ivana Trump decided to file for divorce alledged-ly due to the circulation of rumors regarding Donald's affairs with another woman. The Yin Metal (辛) is her self element and as she encounters another Yin Metal (辛) either in the year or the luck cycle, the cosmic energy of the metal would create competition for her. Both Yin Metals (辛) seek to combine with the Yang Fire (丙) in her month stem. The Yang Fire (丙) can be inter-preted to represent problems related to divorce and affair, and in her case—ru-mors about another woman having an affair with Donald Trump. Soon after their divorce, Ivana married Riccardo Mazzucchelli but the marriage did not last. Ivana filed a breach of contract suit against Mazzucchelli for violating the confidentiality clause in their prenuptial agreement. The lawsuit was settled out of court. All of this had transpired between 1995 and 1997, coincidentally, Ivana was in the Yin Metal (辛) cycle which lasted between her age of 45 to 50.

Dominant Earth

People with dominant earth charts that are characterized as borderline may display personalities of dominance, although dominant earth individuals tend to have a stronger sense of discomfort and insecurity. The earth within the chart can work for them or against them so that they are constantly on the lookout and on the defensive. True dominant selves are more assertive, intel-ligent and have an aura of supremacy. Donald Trump can be classified as a true dominant self as his chart does not possess any element that would go against the earth flow, aside from the hidden elements. Below is an example of a 'fake dominant self' chart.

Hour	Day	Month	Year
癸 Yin Water	戊 Yang Earth	辛 Yin Metal	己 Yin Earth
丑 Ox	戌 Dog	未 Goat	未 Goat

A few points can be used to demonstrate why this chart is not considered a true dominant self. Firstly, the Yin Metal (辛) found in the month weakens the foundation of the earth. Secondly, there is Yin Water (癸) located in the hour stem, dragging up some of the water hidden in the Ox (丑); the transformation to fire between the Yin Water (癸) and Yang Earth (戊) becomes unstable. At times, this chart can be completely dominant, especially if it encounters Yang Fire (丙). The Yang Fire (丙) would combine and take away the qualities of the Yin Metal (辛), rather than transforming it into water since this person is born in the summer. The instability of the earth dominance can be found in the Goat (未). Whenever this person encounters the Rabbit (卯) in the luck cycle or during the year of the Rabbit, it can transform one of the two Goats (未) into wood and upset the system. This example will be explored later in depth within the theories of the ten gods.

Surrendering to Earth

There are often misconceptions about the term "surrender". There are 'borderline' surrenders, 'fake' surrenders, and 'true' surrender. In traditional Chinese texts, a self that is too weak and born out of season have a greater chance of following a leading flow; this is the definition of surrender in Four

Pillars terminology. People with a Four Pillars chart that surrenders to a clearly defined flow or pattern has a greater chance of becoming successful in their chosen profession or in investments, as witnessed from some of the examples used in this book. Nicole Kidman is one prime example. Those teetering on the edge of the borderline also have a chance at gaining fame and it ultimately rests upon the luck cycle to push the birth system into a complete surrender as seen with the Four Pillars chart of Carla Bruni-Sarkozy. Whether a chart is a 'fake', 'borderline', or 'true' surrender, they all stand a chance in becoming rich and famous as long as the luck cycle is in their favour.

The leading flow of metal, water, fire and wood are easier to discern and verify in comparison to the flow of earth. The problem in earth lies with the four earthly animals, Dragon (辰), Goat (未), Dog (戌) and Ox (丑). All four of these animals have hidden elements that can immediately shift the makeup of the chart, depending on their combinations. Both the Dragon (辰) and the Ox (丑) have wet earth—meaning water and metal can be extracted from the two. Similarly, the Goat (未) and Dog (戌) possess earth that has been hardened with fire. Practicioners need to understand hidden elements for an accurate reading.

For elements to surrender to the leading flow of earth, it is much more desirable when the person is born in the summer. A water self being born in the summer most likely would surrender to a fire or an earth flow. It is dependent upon whether there are more earth or fire elements in the chart. If there is a fire combination in the stems when the metal resource for the water is limited or nonexistent, it is most likely that the self will surrender to the fire.

A wood self being born in the summer has a greater opportunity to surrender to the fire rather than to the earth. Wood being born in the month of the Dog (戌) would also be more likely to surrender as it lacks the energy to withstand the autumn metallic energy. Keep in mind that there should be a lot of earth found in the chart in order for the wood to surrender to the earth. If both water and wood are found in the birth chart, it may become a weak self rather than a surrender. A fire self can surrender to earth much easier if the person is born in the month of the Ox (丑). Since fire is weak during the winter months, it is difficult for the fire to fight the wet earth.

Let's bring up an example of a birth system whereby earth is prevalent throughout the Four Pillars chart. For this illustration, we turn to Julia Roberts. Julia Roberts was born on October 28, 1967 in the hour of the Rat (子). As mentioned in the last paragraph, wood lacks energy to withstand the metal energy of the autumn. Since Julia was born in the month of the Dog (戌), the conditions for a Yin Wood (乙) self to survive and fight the atrocious weather would present a difficult proposition. Below is the birth system of Julia Roberts.

Hour	Day	Month	Year
丙 Yang Fire	乙 Yin Wood	庚 Yang Metal	丁 Yin Fire
子 Rat	丑 Ox	戌 Dog	未 Goat

44	34	24	14	4
乙 Yin Wood	甲 Yang Wood	癸 Yin Water	壬 Yang Water	辛 Yin Metal
卯 Rabbit	寅 Tiger	丑 Ox	子 Rat	亥 Pig

The earth found in the cosmic system of Julia Roberts is plentiful. It also represents her wealth element. This sort of a birth structure is often misinterpreted as a weak self with a lot of wealth. By looking at the overall makeup of her birth system, the Yin Wood (乙) in the day stem is all alone by itself where there is no support whatsoever. She is better off obeying the flow of earth since it is dominating her birth system. How do we know that the earth is dominating her chart? The earth is found in three of her branches, represented by the Dog (戌), Ox (丑) and the Goat (未). Those who have been practicing Four Pillars for awhile would notice the 'Bullying Punishment' of the three aforementioned animals. This "punishment" can be defined as a situation where people would get into some terrible predicaments due to their own carelessness. When a practicioner approaches a client's Four Pillar cosmic flow, determining flow should be prioritized over punishments and special stars.

Adding an interesting twist to her birth system is the existence of the Rat (子) in the hour branch. The Rat (子) is often associated with water, but in Julia's system, the Rat (子) combines with the Ox (丑) and partially transforms into earth. Why the partial transformation? During Pig (亥) months or years, the Pig (亥) may want to break apart the transformation; likewise, the same could be said about the Monkey (申) and the Dragon (辰). Therefore, the combination of the Rat (子) and the Ox (丑) in Julia's chart is fragile and unsteady. Nevertheless, the Rat (子), during the majority of her life, transforms into earth in her cosmic system.

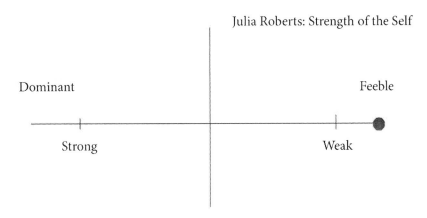

The line graph above illustrates where the cosmic system of Julia Roberts stand. In order to benefit, her luck and annual cycles have to abide by the elements fire and earth. Let's briefly discuss her history of major awards.

Julia Roberts' fame came as she was in the Ox (丑) cycle. In her case, the Ox (丑) did not clash with the Goat (未), but teamed with the Rat (子) first to form more earth. The additional Ox (丑), which appeared when she entered in her luck cycle, combined with her hour branch and it brought about periods of major success. The new combination created even more earth. Let's quickly do the math here to confirm whether the earth in the Ox (丑) is good for her. She was born in 1967 and the power and strength of the Ox (丑) came to the fore-front in between her ages of 28 and 33. That meant one of her best cycles were between the years of 1995 and 2000. This was at the time when she was given the main roles in My Best Friend's Wedding, Runaway Bride, Notting Hill, and Erin Brockovich. Although she was nominated for an Academy Award for Best Actress for the movie, Pretty Women (1990), her time did not come as she was still in the Yin Water (癸) cycle. 1990 was the year of the Horse (午), and these movies and nomination foreshadowed what would be an amazing career in Hollywood for Julia.

• **1990** – YEAR OF THE YANG METAL HORSE (庚午) PRETTY WOMEN, NOMINATED FOR AN ACADEMY AWARD FOR BEST ACTRESS

• **1997** – YEAR OF THE YIN FIRE OX (丁丑) MY BEST FRIEND'S WEDDING, GOLDEN GLOBE AWARD FOR BEST ACTRESS.

• **1999** – YEAR OF THE YIN EARTH RABBIT (己卯) RUNAWAY BRIDE AND NOTTING HILL, MTV MOVIE AWARD FOR BEST FEMALE PERFORMANCE, GOLDEN GLOBE AWARD FOR BEST ACTRESS.

• **2000** – YEAR OF THE YANG METAL DRAGON (庚辰) ERIN BROCKOVICH, ACADEMY AWARD FOR BEST ACTRESS

Ever since the Ox (丑) cycle, she has yet to receive any major awards or nominations for any of her roles. This is attributed to the rivalry in the Yang

Wood (甲) cycle where it is competing with the self for fame and fortune. We will touch upon rivalries in greater depth later in this book. Birth systems that surrender to a leading flow dislike the same element or a resource element that strengthens the self. Referring back to the line graph, it is imaginable that she is no longer in a feeble position, therefore, the benefits of the cosmos is no longer rewarding for her. From a Four Pillars perspective, the best position for the leading flow is to remain feeble. Once the self becomes stronger, the benefits that one had been experiencing would dissipate. From a relationship standpoint, her former spouse, Lyle Lovett (Born on November 1, 1957), has an abundant amount of fire and earth that brought them together—but only for a short period of time. Below is his birth chart.

Hour	Day	Month	Year
X	丁 Yin Fire	庚 Yang Metal	丁 Yin Fire
X	丑 Ox	戌 Dog	酉 Rooster

The instability of the earth was one of the main reasons that didn't allow their relationship to last long. The earth in his chart was constantly weakened by the Yang Metal (庚) in the month stem and the Rooster (酉) in the year branch. Another reason from a cosmic standpoint is the fact that the year of the Pig (亥) in 1995 disrupted the leading earth flow in the system of Julia Roberts. The Pig (亥) forced the Ox (丑) and the Rat (子) to form a directional combination while she was in the Yin Water (癸) period. This brought about a conflict against her leading flow when the water was fighting the earth.

Julia Roberts has a birth system that is easily identifiable as to where her leading flow would stand and what she benefits from. The birth month provides a very good indication to practitioners as to where she may stand on the line graph. Earth is by far the most deceptive element in the Four Pillars system due to its appearance all year round and its abilities to transform into another element completely when the timing is right.

Verifying Earth

The combination of experience and verification is crucial when testing earth. Each of the four earthly branches can combine and transform into a different element. Therefore, an evaluation on the luck and yearly cycles can provide a clearer picture on the impact of the branches and its relationship to the earth element. The impact of the branches can be caused by clashes and combinations. Both the Dog (戌) and the Dragon (辰), and the Ox (丑) and the Goat (未) create friction with one another. These earthly animals and their clashes can induce disharmony and interrupt the flow of earth. An obvious earthly flow can instantly change through combinations into a new flow. A chart possessing all four earth symbols in the branches does not guarantee a true earth flow. The stems and season of birth must also be evaluated. In many instances, fire can be used as a litmus test to verify earth. If good events happened during the fire cycles, it can possibly determine that earth is a favourable element to the chart — assuming that the self element is not fire.

Metal Flow

The autumn months represents a period where metal energy is predominant during this period. The leader of this group is the Rooster (酉). The three animal symbols for this season are the Monkey (申), the Rooster (酉), and the Dog (戌). Just like the other seasons, two of the three animals, the Monkey (申) and the Dog (戌) can be easily transformed into a different element depending on their positioning and combinations. The Rooster (酉), when partnered up with the Snake (巳) and/or the Ox (丑) can have a possibility of providing a metal leading flow within a birth system. It also depends on the self element of a birth chart. If the self element is a Yin Wood (乙), the wood will lack the energy to go against the flow of metal, especially if it is surrounded by metal in the branches and stems. The same can be said for earth and fire. On the other hand, those who possess the self element of metal or water may lean towards a dominant system as the metal combinations in the branches can strengthen the self, or in the case of water, the metal can serve as a resource to the self.

Since some of the previous examples have been clearly defined with a unanimous flow, the next will illustrate how a borderline chart can benefit from going with a leading flow. Below is the birth chart of Daniel Westling, Duke of Västergötland, born on September 15, 1973.

Hour	Day	Month	Year
X	甲 Yang Wood	辛 Yin Metal	癸 Yin Water
X	寅 Tiger	酉 Rooster	丑 Ox

62	52	42	32	22	12	2
甲 Yang Wood	乙 Yin Wood	丙 Yang Fire	丁 Yin Fire	戊 Yang Earth	己 Yin Earth	庚 Yang Metal
寅 Tiger	卯 Rabbit	辰 Dragon	巳 Snake	午 Horse	未 Goat	申 Monkey

He is born in the month of the Rooster (酉) with an Ox (丑) next to the month branch, combining to form half a metal alliance. In addition, there is Yin Metal (辛) found in the month stem on top of the Rooster (酉). The metal seems to be leading the charge in his birth system. On the other hand, the Yang Wood (甲) in the day stem is considered to be "rooted" in the Tiger (寅) while there is Yin Water (癸) serving as resources to the self. The question is, can his birth chart surrender to the metal flow or is this considered a weak self?

In a birth system, it is always favourable to have a distinct leading flow. Upsetting the leader produces negative discrepancies, and in Westling's case, the Rooster (酉) is the leader in his chart. Having conflicting flows can be disastrous, because the birth chart would not know which elemental flow to favour. Conflicting flows often lead to struggles in life. For example, a birth chart with branches composed of both fire and metal without a distinctive, defined flow would result in a conflict between the two elements. Fortunately for Daniel Westling, his chart has ample opportunities within the luck cycles to remain loyal to the flow. Ever since he was born, his luck cycles were going with the flow of earth and metal. In his late 30s, he moved on to the Snake (巳), and although the Snake (巳) represents fire and the Summer, it combined with the Rooster (酉) and the Ox (丑) to form a complete metal trio. It is also within the Snake (巳) period that Daniel Westling became the husband of the Crown Princess of Sweden. At the time, Daniel was a personal trainer and served as the CEO of Balance Training, which had three gyms in Stockholm. The gym had metal equipment which was also in his favor.

Coincidentally, during the period when Daniel and the Crown Princess of Sweden, Victoria, met, the princess was in the middle of her metal cycles. Below is the birth system of Victoria (July 14, 1977).

Hour	Day	Month	Year
X	壬 Yang Water	丙 Yang Fire	丁 Yin Fire
X	申 Monkey	午 Horse	巳 Snake

38	28	18	8
庚 Yang Metal	己 Yin Earth	戊 Yang Earth	丁 Yin Fire
戌 Dog	酉 Rooster	申 Monkey	未 Goat

The Crown Princess was in the Rooster (酉) cycle at the time of her marriage and it combined with the Snake (巳) in her year branch, forming more metal energy which proved beneficial to Daniel's Four Pillars chart. The case of Daniel Westling illustrates how a birth system can enjoy harmony and ensure happiness as long as the system is loyal to the flow.

Many actresses, super models, and singers tend to have a flow of metal and water. Metal is representative of the lungs and the vocal cords. Those requiring the use of metal succeed easier in music. The sound of music in general comes from metal. It is very often that metal and water work hand in hand and the next few examples will illustrate their collaboration.

Water Flow

Water comes to the forefront during the winter season and it is led by the eleventh lunar month of the Rat (子). The three wet months of the winter are found in these three symbols, the Pig (亥), the Rat (子) and the Ox (丑). To reiterate, being born in these months does not guarantee that water leads the flow of the chart. Each of these animals can be eliminated or combined and transformed into another element, reducing the strength of the element in a chart, changing the dynamics of a birth system. The graphical illustration of the Three Harmonious combinations presents the water trio of the Rat (子), Dragon (辰) and the Monkey (申). Having two of the three branches in a Four Pillars chart while being born in the winter months would provide a greater opportunity for water to lead the birth chart. A fire self would lack the energy to fight that water in the winter, assuming that there isn't enough wood and fire to support the self. On the other hand, a fire self born in the summer can also surrender to the flow of water.

Sandra Bullock's birth system illustrates a borderline chart. Although she was born in the incorrect season for a water flow to occur, her birth system still enjoys a water make-up. Sandra Bullock was born on July 26, 1964.

Hour	Day	Month	Year
庚 Yang Metal	丙 Yang Fire	辛 Yin Metal	甲 Yang Wood
寅 Tiger	子 Rat	未 Goat	辰 Dragon

36	26	16	6
丁 Yin Fire	戊 Yang Earth	己 Yin Earth	庚 Yang Metal
卯 Rabbit	辰 Dragon	巳 Snake	午 Horse

Sandra is a Yang Fire (丙) self born near the end of summer in the month of the Goat (未). The chart is flanked on both sides by water, represented by the Rat (子) and the Dragon (辰) as they seek to combine to form a half water structure. Another notable feature is the stem pairing between the Yang Fire (丙) and the Yin Metal (辛), which unite to transform into water. The transformation is considered shaky or unstable due to the Goat (未) separating the water structure. Nevertheless, the transformation does transpire, especially if there is an appearance of more water and metal. Although there is Yang Wood (甲) found in the year stem, the wood is too far and weak to aid the self and strengthen it. Animals such as the Monkey (申), Rooster (酉), Ox (丑), Rat (子) and the Dragon (辰) can all come to the aid and ensure that water is the leading flow in her chart. To test this hypothesis, we can look at her key events.

- **1993** – YIN WATER ROOSTER YEAR (癸酉), first major appearance IN THE MOVIE DEMOLITION MAN.

- **1996** – YANG WATER RAT YEAR (丙子), DRAGON (辰) CYCLE, NAMED ONE OF THE MOST BEAUTIFUL WOMAN IN PEOPLE'S.

- **2000** – YANG METAL DRAGON YEAR (庚辰), STARRED IN MISS CONGENIALITY, NOMINATED FOR BEST ACTRESS IN THE GOLDEN GLOBE AWARD.

- **2004** – YANG WOOD MONEY YEAR (甲申), STARRED IN CRASH, A MOVIE THAT WON THE BEST PICTURE IN THE ACADEMY AWARDS IN 2006.

- **2005** – YIN WOOD ROOSTER YEAR (乙酉), STARRED IN MISS CONGENIALITY 2.

In 2009, the year of the Ox (丑), Sandra Bullock topped movie charts as she won an Academy Award for Best Actress for her role in the movie, The Blind Side. This is a perfect example of what a positive clash can do to her chart as the Ox (丑) removed the Goat (未), allowing the Rat (子) and Dragon (辰) to lead the water structure and ensure a solidified transformation of water in her birth system. From the listings of her positive key events in life, it is determined that metal and water are favorable to her birth system. To make an additional verification to her chart, an evaluation of her spouse, Jesse James, would be appropriate. Jesse James was born on April 19, 1969 and below is his Four Pillars chart.

Hour	Day	Month	Year
X	甲 Yang Wood	戊 Yang Earth	己 Yin Earth
X	子 Rat	辰 Dragon	酉 Rooster

35	25	15	5
甲 Yang Wood	乙 Yin Wood	丙 Yang Fire	丁 Yin Fire
子 Rat	丑 Ox	寅 Tiger	卯 Rabbit

Coincidentally, Jesse James possesses some of Sandra's most favourable cosmic animals. Both birth systems have a half water structure where the Rat (子) and the Dragon (辰) is present in the chart. There is also a Rooster (酉) in the Four Pillars chart of Jesse James where it can breed the water in both of their cosmic system.

Combined Flow

There are many birth systems that can utilize multiple elements to strengthen or enhance the flow. In order to pinpoint these systems, more than one element must be tested on the birth chart. Testing a birth system means to evaluate the history of a person and pinpoint all the key events — both positive and negative. This next example illustrates how the utilization of two elements can ensure a prolonged period of fame and success.

Hour	Day	Month	Year
X	壬 Yang Water	戊 Yang Earth	壬 Yang Water
X	申 Monkey	申 Monkey	子 Rat

50	40	30	20	10
癸 Yin Water	壬 Yang Water	辛 Yin Metal	庚 Yang Metal	己 Yin Earth
丑 Ox	子 Rat	亥 Pig	戌 Dog	酉 Rooster

Juan Esteban Aristizábal Vásquez, known as Juanes, was born on August 9, 1972, the year of the Water Rat, in Medellin, Colombia. Juanes is a Yang Water (壬) self. From initial examination, his water may be seen as strong. However, this is not a strong water chart where it should be weakened with wood or earth and an overall picture must be painted in order to understand the entire structure. This birth system is a Yang Water (壬) born in the month of the Monkey (申) where water is being bred by the metal in two of the Monkeys (申) lying in the branches. The water in this birth system is further strengthened by the year pillar where the Yang Water Rat (壬子) is found. The water is flowing smoothly with some hard earth in the month stem partially impeding the flow. In order to completely rid itself of all the earth in the system, metal can be used as a filtration system to purify the water. Additional water would be just as good as it can flush away the excess earth.

This chart is clearly a "Dominant Self" where water rules. In Chinese, it is called "專旺格". 滴天髓, one of the leading Four Pillars writers from China centuries ago wrote "一清到底有精神." Having a pure flow makes one strong, brilliant and energetic. The "Dominant Self" of Juanes' chart can also be illustrated by the combination between the two Monkeys (申) and the Rat (子). The Rat (子) itself is a pure water animal, with the Rat (子) and the Monkey (申), they form a water alliance that supports the self. As mentioned, the flaw in his system is the Yang Earth (戊) where it impedes the flow of water from time to time. The best way to get rid of the Yang Earth is to use metal. Fortunately in his luck cycle, Juanes has a long metal luck cycle that began with the Rooster at the age of 15 and it lasts until his mid-30s, then the water cycle commences and ends at about his mid 50s.

Classification of Juanes

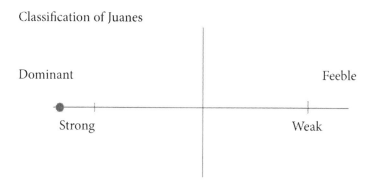

The line graph above demonstrates where Juanes' birth system stands. In order for him to capitalize on his system, the best elements to use in his chart are definitely water and metal. Dominant selves rely upon resources and the self element to remain dominant. Similar to the cosmic system of Donald Trump, they want to stay dominant rather than to impede the flow. Since the Yang Earth in the month branch impedes the flow of water, using metal would be more beneficial as it reduces the earth and feeds the water self. So how can we prove that metal and water are his best elements? Using historical data by analyzing his career and life would be the best way to prove this analysis. Metal symbolizes the voice and music, and it played an important role to his rise to success.

Life and Career of Juanes

Since it has been mentioned that metal is his best element, obviously, pure metal came into his chart at the age of 16. So what happened at the age of 16 for Juanes? He started a metal rock band in 1988 and released an album in the same year. His band included the likes of Alejandro Sanz and Ricky Martin. He eventually disbanded the group and pursued his own career as a solo artist in 1998. Coincidentally enough, between 1998 to 2002, he was in the Dog (戌) cycle, which has a lot of Yang Earth and Fire in it. As a result, he was quiet during that period within his career. It was obvious that earth blocked the tide of his success.

At the age of 30, year 2002, Juanes' luck cycle moved back into a metal flow when the Yin Metal (辛) came to the forefront. His first solo album, Un dia normal (A Normal Day), was released in 2002 and it coincided with the metal flow of his luck cycle. The album was certified gold in Colombia upon its first day of sales and it remained in the top ten of Billboard's Top Latin Albums chart for 92 weeks. Within the next five years, Juanes established himself as one of the leading singers in Latin America.

Fast forward to 2005, the Year of the Rooster (酉), it is a year of pure metal. At the 2005 Latin Grammy Awards, he took home three awards for the Best Rock Song "Nada Valgo Sin Tu Amor", Best Rock Solo Album for Mi Sangre, and Best Music Video for "Volverte A Ver". In that same year, he was invited to Germany at an international gala celebrating the 2006 FIFA World Cup Final Draw event and performed one of his most popular songs, "La Camisa Negra". Also in 2005, he was named by Time Magazine as one of the world's 100 most influential people.

In 2006, the year of the Yang Fire Dog (丙戌), he began a year-long sabbatical to spend time with his wife and two daughters. Again, the year of the Dog (戌) is characterized as hard Yang Earth with fire, as a result, his singing career took a one year break.

In 2007, the year of the Pig (亥), and 2008, the year of the Rat (子), Juanes came back to the forefront as he released a new album titled "La Vida... Es Un Ratico". On December 11, 2007, the month of the Yang Water Rat, he appeared at a Nobel Peace Prize Concert in Oslo, Norway and it was broadcast live to over 100 countries around the world. On November 13, 2008, the year of the Rat (子) in the Yin Water Pig (癸亥) month, he swept the Latin Grammys winning all five nominations. The cosmic system of Juanes illustrates what can happen when water is pure and supported by metal. A birth system staying loyal to the flow ensures an easier path to success and fame.

We can also evaluate the birth system of his wife, Karen Martinez, to confirm Juanes' attraction to water and metal.

Hour	Day	Month	Year
X	庚 Yang Metal	辛 Yin Metal	己 Yin Earth
X	子 Rat	未 Goat	未 Goat

As mentioned previously, the Rat (子) found in the day branch of Karen Martinez has a natural attraction with the Monkey (申) that Juanes possesses in his day branch. This attraction is strengthened by the amount of metal that Karen has in her birth system, which includes both the Yin and Yang Metals found respectively in the day and month stems. In summary, to be in harmony with the cosmic flow, it is essential for a person to utilize elements beneficial to their birth chart. Juanes plays guitar, an instrument made of metallic strings, and sings, a vocal talent that uses metal; the utilization of metal has provided him with great success in the music world.

Necessity Based Flow in a Relationship

Some birth systems may have deceiving cosmic flow while others may not even have a flow until the energy is untapped by the luck or annual cycles.

The latter can still thrive if a person's marriage partner possessed the right factors required for them to become successful. Liliane Bettencourt (Born on October 21, 1922), principle shareholder of L'Oreal, exemplifies such an example. By looking at her birth system, it would look somewhat like a weak self requiring resources and the same self element to aid the self. Her Yang Water (壬) lacks any roots from the branches to support her.

Hour	Day	Month	Year
X	壬 Yang Water	庚 Yang Metal	壬 Yang Water
X	戌 Dog	戌 Dog	戌 Dog

74	64	54	44	34	24	14	4
壬 Yang Water	癸 Yin Water	甲 Yang Wood	乙 Yin Wood	丙 Yang Fire	丁 Yin Fire	戊 Yang Earth	己 Yin Earth
寅 Tiger	卯 Rabbit	辰 Dragon	巳 Snake	午 Horse	未 Goat	申 Monkey	酉 Rooster

It can be argued that the Yang Metal (庚) in the month utilizes the earth found in the Dog (戌) to enhance the water, but it is highly unlikely that the earth can support the metal. The Dog (戌) possesses earth that is too dry and hard; metal requires wet earth such as the Dragon (辰) and the Ox (丑) to support. Liliane's birth system is very deceiving. The three Dogs (戌) in her branches actually have an incredible amount of buried wealth. The hidden elements are vital components in Four Pillars analysis and the hidden Yin Fire (丁), Liliane's direct wealth element, is found within each of the branches. In order to unearth its full potential, she needs the Horse (午) or Tiger (寅) which would put her truly in surrender mode towards the fire flow.

Her husband, André Bettencourt (April 21, 1919) has exactly what she needed and more. Not only did he possess the Rabbit (卯) in his system, but also, André had a sufficient amount of earth in his system to block the tide of water in Liliane's system.

Hour	Day	Month	Year
X	癸 Yin Water	戊 Yang Earth	己 Yin Earth
X	卯 Rabbit	辰 Dragon	未 Goat

Liliane's luck was in full swing as she approached her fire cycles in her mid 20s. André and Liliane were married in 1950. She had a combination of fire luck in addition to the aid of her husband's cosmic system. This luck brought about a tremendous amount of wealth and fame. Liliane, being born at the right time in the right family with a great cosmic system accompanied by a supporting spouse, was able to achieve financial success with great ease. Being married to a spouse who has the specific elements to support oneself is very important to one's success. However, having the perfect marriage may not be enough—the energy within each of our bodies need to be physically close to the person we are attracted to in order to make a difference. For those who are fortunate and in a good cycle, like Liliane, it was much easier for her to attract the energy of her husband. People who are in bad cycles may attract energy that is not favourable. The interaction of positive energy amongst couples usually translates into happiness, financial, and career success.

Borderline Systems

Some birth systems are very straightforward where the leading flow is easily determined by the birth month and the combinations solidifying the flow. In some cases, it is not that simple as the birth month may want to team up with two different elements. Difficult cases are those who possess rivalries in their charts, placing their Four Pillars classification on the edge of feeble and weak self. These cosmic systems require tedious effort and verification to ensure that the favourable and unfavourable elements are properly determined. For example, Princess Diana, born on July 1, 1961, Dog (戌) Hour possesses a system that can be classified as a borderline helpless self. This borderline classification can be explained by the wood rivalry in the stem of the birth month. The Yang Wood (甲) found in the month wants to support

the Yin Wood (乙) self, preventing it from becoming completely helpless to the fire.

Hour	Day	Month	Year
丙 Yang Fire	乙 Yin Wood	甲 Yang Wood	辛 Yin Metal
戌 Dog	未 Goat	午 Horse	丑 Ox

32	22	12	2
戊 Yang Earth	丁 Yin Fire	丙 Yang Fire	乙 Yin Wood
戌 Dog	酉 Rooster	申 Monkey	未 Goat

Lily Chung has provided a more detailed analysis of Princess Diana in her book, Truth of Ups and Downs (p.73-74). She determined and verified that Diana's birth chart requires following the flow of fire and how she had benefited from the fire. Since this is a book on relationships, the main focus of her birth system here is on how Princess Diana, who was a commoner, was able to marry a Prince. One of the main reasons behind this is that her chart, when it surrenders, can be classified as 'Surrendering to Offspring.' In Chinese, it is called "從兒格". Even though it is not a pure surrender to the offspring, she still benefits from such a classification. When a birth system surrenders to the output or offspring element, in Diana's case, wood surrendering to fire, these people are usually lucky as they are often rewarded with good and easier careers. During good cycles, if they decide to work, they can easily obtain a job without putting much effort into looking. They are usually friendly, approachable, and know how to speak and behave in the public. The flip side of such a classification is that when they are in bad cycles, they can easily upset their bosses. For Diana, her relationship with Queen Elizabeth was not a very harmonious one. Other issues that may occur in bad cycles would include health complications, or to some extreme levels, they can become depressed and suicidal.

Borderline systems can easily upset the leading flow; Therefore, these people rarely lead normal lives. They constantly have one foot in the door but the other foot out. When the flow is in one's favour, everything in their life become rosy and comfortable. If these birth systems encounter resources or the self element, they can easily rebel. Lily Chung also made a case of this citing Adolf Hitler and Christopher Reeves as example of a borderline birth system in her book (P. 75-78). Another example of a borderline system would be the birth chart of Tenzin Gyatso, also know as the 14th Dalai Lama. Dalai Lama was born on July 6, 1935. Below is his Four Pillars chart.

Hour	Day	Month	Year
X	癸 Yin Water	癸 Yin Water	乙 Yin Wood
X	未 Goat	未 Goat	亥 Pig

79	69	59	49	39	29	19	9
乙 Yin Wood	丙 Yang Fire	丁 Yin Fire	戊 Yang Earth	己 Yin Earth	庚 Yang Metal	辛 Yin Metal	壬 Yang Water
亥 Pig	子 Rat	丑 Ox	寅 Tiger	卯 Rabbit	辰 Drag- on	巳 Snake	午 Horse

Again, just like Princess Diana, Dalai Lama can be classified as a borderline surrender to the output element, which is wood in his case. He is a Yin Water (癸) self born in the summer month of the Goat (未), where it is dry and hot in the mountains of Tibet. The other Yin Water (癸) found in the month stem tries to empower the self but it is sitting on top of hot earth, preventing it from pushing Dalai Lama's birth system into a weak self. To push the self further towards a feeble self, the Pig (亥) in the year branch unites with the Goat (未) to form half a wood team. The wood is solidified and strengthened by the Yin Wood (乙) in the year stem. With the half wood team formed between the Pig (亥) and the Goat (未), the strength of the water in the Pig (亥) is weakened. Dalai Lama's fame and fortunes can be traced back to the Rabbit (卯) and Yang Earth (戊) cycle, which placed him into a complete helpless feeble self. It was during this period where he had made numerous trips around the world to promote peace and stability. In 1989, his hard work and dedication was finally paid off with a well-honoured Nobel Peace Prize.

The birth system of Dalai Lama was far from perfect as the water in the month stem constantly gave him many rivals to tangle with—none bigger than the Chinese government. The water in his birth system had always been a thorn to his life and it became apparent in 2008, the year of the Rat (子) during the Rat (子) cycle. In October of 2008, he was suffering from abdominal pain and was hospitalized in India where he had a surgery to remove a gallstone. Earlier that year, his supporters were blamed by the premier of China for the growing arrest and violence in Tibet.

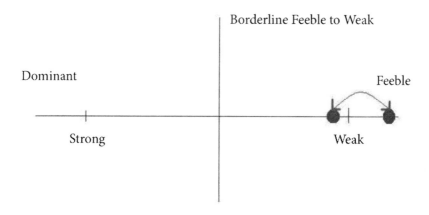

Dalai Lama, Princess Diana, and Adolf Hitler all possessed birth composites that are classified as borderline systems. These borderline systems allowed them to gain fame and power when they were in their good cycles. As long as the self element remained feeble to the leading flow, their birth systems were in harmony with the cosmos. When they encountered elements that empowered the self, they were no longer loyal to the flow and they were presented with many problems. The graph above explains how these borderline systems oscillate between the classifications of weak and feeble.

> ## "BORDERLINE CHART"
>
> Charts classified as being in between weak and fee-
> ble, and strong and dominant, belong in the border-
> line classification. The luck and annual cycles can enhance or
> reduce the strength of the flow. If borderline charts are moved
> into a weak state, the flow of the birth chart can be interrupted."

Awaiting Flow

There are many birth systems that may not have a team of combinations within the branches, rendering its flow more difficult to be determined.
Most borderline systems have teams, as witnessed with Princess Diana and
Dalai Lama, where a specific flow can still be unearthed from the branches.
What if there is an overwhelming amount of a specific element, and yet no
combinations of the branches are present? The Four Pillars chart of Jude Law
is a perfect example of such a case. Jude Law was born on December 29, 1972
at 6:00am and below is his birth chart.

Hour	Day	Month	Year
丁 Yin Fire	甲 Yang Wood	壬 Yang Water	壬 Yang Water
卯 Rabbit	午 Horse	子 Rat	子 Rat

42	32	22	12	2
丁 Yin Fire	丙 Yang Fire	乙 Yin Wood	甲 Yang Wood	癸 Yin Water
巳 Snake	辰 Dragon	卯 Rabbit	寅 Tiger	丑 Ox

Jude Law is a Yang Wood (甲) self born in the month of the Rat (子) where the month and year pillars possess an overwhelming amount of water. The Yang Wood (甲) in this scenario lacks the power to control the torrent pace of the water. This scenario reflects the flaws of a big tree but rootless tree along the gushing streams of a cold icy river. There are multiple ways to approach an analysis of Law's birth system. With the cold weather, Jude Law's system would actually benefit from some heat and lighting, which can be found in the hour stem as represented by the Yin Fire (丁). Although it seems like the wood can surrender to the gush of water, the Rat (子) lacks a water team to completely put his chart into an absolute feeble stage. In addition, the Horse (午) found in the day branch is constantly waging war on the Rat (子) in the monthly branch, bringing about uncertainty and discomfort. If Law's chart surrendered to water, the Dragon (辰) and the Monkey (申) should clearly provide good fortunes and remove the discomfort in the system.

Tracing back to the most recent Dragon (辰) year, in 2000, Jude Law was given a lead role in Enemy at the Gates and also starred A.I. (Artificial Intelligence). These roles did not catapult him to the top of the Hollywood scene due to the fact that he was still in the Rabbit (卯) cycle when the wood found in the Rabbit (卯) was competing with the self. The movie Cold Mountain was Jude Law's big breakthrough as he entered the Yang Fire Dragon (丙辰) period of his luck cycle. The movie was nominated for multiple awards in 2003 including an Academy Award Nomination for Best Actor. In 2004, the year of the Monkey (申), Jude Law was given more roles as he starred in I ♥ Hucka-bees, Closer, Sky Captain and the World of Tomorrow, Alfie, The Aviator, and Lemony Snicket's A series of Unfortunate Events. The Dragon (辰), Monkey (申) and Rat (子) completed the water structure in his birth chart. During this

Dragon (辰) cycle, he also starred in Sherlock Holmes, playing the role of Dr. John Watson, as well as returning onto the London stage to portray the title role in Shakespeare's Hamlet.

Jude Law's fame coincided with the appearance of the Dragon (辰) in his luck cycle and his re-nowned celebrity status proved the advantage of having team branches. Even though the birth system of Jude Law does not possess a team of ani-mals with a specific flow, he can still capitalize on a temporarily-formed team when a missing member ap-pears in the luck or annual cycle.

6.
Questioning Flow

How do we question flow? It is quite often that the four cardinal symbols play a vital role in a chart or in a luck cycle in relation to the self element. The four cardinal symbols of the Rat (子), Rabbit (卯), Horse (午) and Rooster (酉) can shift the balance of power in a cosmic system. They can also empower the leading flow, bringing about great fortunes. Those who lack experience in the practice of the Four Pillars can always use one or more of those symbols to identify flow. Questioning and verifying what had transpired during one of the four years when the cardinal symbol appeared can help practitioners extract a great deal of information. If someone dislikes metal, ask what happened during the Rooster (酉) year or cycle. For example, assuming that a practitioner has determined that the client likes water and enjoys swimming, it can then be evaluated what did transpire in the year of the Rat (子). Was it a financially successful year? How did you do in a Rat (子) year while you were in school? The information found in your list of historical events can be used to determine flow. Those historical events may have certain patterns involved. You can also explore your health records to see which months of the year you would experience the flu or certain illnesses. It is most certain that everyone has caught a cold within their lifetime. Knowing when it happened can help you reduce the possibilities of another cold or illness when that time of the year comes along in the future.

The easiest ways for people to benefit from their flow is to choose the industry that belongs to the leading element in their birth system. Studying a topic related to a specific element allows one to succeed with greater ease. For example, if metal is the most favourable element, careers in music, automobiles, and the use of metallic tools would bring about greater success. The same goes with relationships. A person in need of metal should choose a partner who has a metal flow to ensure happiness and harmony. In the past, some societies, like ancient China, denied people of the freedom to choose marital partners through the enforcement of arranged marriages. Today, many people have greater choice and freedom. It is quite normal for those in a bad cycle to choose the wrong marriage partner, resulting in affairs, divorces and other marital issues. In order to prevent mishaps, experienced Four Pillars practitioners can help clients avoid negative consequences.

I find that relationship can be a very sensitive issue in a Four Pillars consultation. Nobody wants to hear bad news, especially when a couple is engaged and has planned to spend the rest of their lives together. Many people may be emotionally attached to their spouse or partner; Therefore, providing them with the truth can be a difficult proposition. At times, clients are worried about their relationship life while they are dating. Of course, there are numerous ways for practitioners to deliver bad news. Regardless, I believe it is necessary to remind lovers to enjoy each and every moment in the dating process. On the other hand, those who are in a troubled relationship may require help. The assistance can come in the form of counselling after an evaluation of the Four Pillars chart of the couple. By understanding the characteristics of the parties involved, consultants can use specific gestures and words to deal with them. There are no written rules or guidelines in terms of how to approach people with bad news. Do we even need to give them the bad news? As a Four Pillars practioner, it is not my role to doom a relationship, nor should I dazzle my audience with a positive spin on the situation. Some clients may not be willing to accept answers to a question they did not ask. Knowledge of flow, accompanied by the knowledge of the Ten Gods, allows practitioners to determine how people would accept bad news. The next chapter will go on to explain how the Ten Gods influence flow, and their significance in analyzing relationships.

"TESTING FLOW"

The best way to test the favourable and unfavourable elements is to evaluate the history of positive and negative events. Once the history of events has been documented, the information can be mapped to specific years and cycles. There is often a noticeable pattern that can be found through the history of events.

Part Two

Ten Gods And Relationships

1.
The Importance of the Male and Breadwinner

When looking at a spouse or a marital partner, most of the attention is focused upon the day pillar's branch and the wealth of the chart from a male's standpoint. The reason why wealth is traditionally seen in the Four Pillars as a male's spouse is because it is traditionally considered his "possession"; the wealth element can be used to determine the characteristics and attributes of the spouse in the Four Pillars. The relationship between the self stem and the day branch is another way of determining the characteristics of the spouse or marital partner and whether the spouse is helpful to the man of the household. The day branch is often referred to as the "House of Spouse" or "Spouse Palace". Prior to evaluating the spouse, it is always important to understand the flow of one's chart, then decide whether the spouse palace has a symbol that is beneficial to the flow. Without the ability of determining the flow, it would be difficult to understand the relationship between the spouse and the self. There are many rules and guidelines offered by Chinese classics that I have seen regarding marital partners. One of my objectives is to translate as much information from these classics and present them to you in an understandable and meaningful way.

Most people would like to have a helpful and supportive partner in their lives. When the spouse palace has a specific branch interrupting or clashing against the flow, it may be better to advise the person not to get involved in a relationship. They would become a happier person if they did not get involved in a relationship. If they choose to get involved in a relationship, sleeping in separate rooms and working abroad are possible solutions. I have seen cases where the luck cycles have brought a couple together but once the luck cycle passes, there is a mutual understanding between the couple that they will need to see each other less. This is the cosmic reality of life and as long as we accept cosmic reality and go with the flow, happiness and harmony can be achieved. There are exceptions where the cosmic flow and the makeup of the birth system can override the role of the spouse palace. This will be explained shortly in this chapter.

I find that many practitioners in Hong Kong look at a man's chart over the woman due to the fact that men are often seen as the breadwinner of the household. However, if we want a bigger picture of how the wife influences the entire family and her spouse, it is important to look at both charts. If the woman of the household is the main breadwinner, a practioner's own creative judgement in their understanding of the main principles of the Four Pillars of Destiny can also provide an accurate analysis in terms of her relationship life. We can also evaluate a spouse or partner of a woman from the chart. The controlling element is often looked upon as the indicator for the spouse of a female's chart. Similar to a male's birth chart, the day branch for a female's chart is also designated as the "House of Spouse" or the "Spouse Palace."

The information presented here are some of the key guidelines for those practicing Four Pillars when their clients inquire about their spouse or marital partners. These guidelines or rules are by no means absolute, but they are accurate when used accordingly to analyze a relationship. After understanding some of the guidelines and rules of a chart, we can evaluate the bonding of a relationship. The evaluation of the spouse palace, wealth element(s) of a male's birth chart, and controlling element(s) of a female's chart, and the combinations involved, all bring together a clear picture of a couple's relationship. Within a relationship, there are those whose partner can benefit the breadwinner tremendously by providing sound advice, yet on the other hand, there are those who would give their partner problems and troubles in life. Many would seek advice regarding their relationship looking for good news rather than accepting reality. By utilizing the knowledge of Yin and Yang and the Five Element Theory, practitioners of the Four Pillars can look into the cosmic makeup of a couple's relationship. This cosmic makeup would tell us whether the relationship would be beneficial or not and what the long term outlook is for such a relationship.

Changes in the luck cycle and the flow can bring people together, but also push people apart from one another. By better understanding ourselves, we would know when tough times may come in a relationship and strategize in terms of how we can reduce the misfortunes within a relationship. Just because bad cycles can come about, it does not mean that you are doomed in your relationship life. There are ways to avoid relationship issues. It may be better to live apart for awhile. When there is a clash encountered in the spouse palace, it does not mean that a divorce is supposed to happen. The couple may be separated due to work for a prolonged period of time. Perhaps a child may be accepted into a good school overseas and requires the supervision of a parent while the spouse is working at his or her home country. Separation by choice is better than waiting for the flow to create issues. Some relationship issues are manageable due to minor differences in characteristics. Others may consist of major concerns, such as one partner being cheated on. Once the trust is broken, I find it very difficult for the couple to retain their relationship. The scenarios in evaluating relationships are boundless.

2.
Spouse Palace

Let us begin by looking at the Spouse Palace. The Spouse Palace in a Four Pillars chart is located in the Day Pillar directly below the Self Stem. It can also be referred to as the Day Branch. The relationship between the self element and the spouse palace is one of the ways to evaluate the strength of the partner. The palace provides details in terms of what type of spouse a person is likely attracted to. The spouse palace can also present information about whether the person would marry more than once. For this example, we can go back to the birth composite of Tom Cruise.

Hour	Day	Month	Year
丙 Yang Fire	壬 Yang Water	丁 Yin Fire	壬 Yang Water
午 Horse	寅 Tiger	未 Goat	寅 Tiger

The spouse palace here is duplicated in the Year branch represented by the Tiger (寅). It is quite common for those who have a spouse palace symbol duplicated elsewhere in the chart to marry more than once. Since the spouse palace is duplicated in the Year branch, there is a very high likelihood of him getting married early in life which he did. Tom Cruise had married Mimi Rogers in 1987 at the age of about 24. His other spouses include Nicole Kidman and Katie Holmes. The duplication of the spouse palace in the luck cycle can also lead to marriage, or for those who are married, they may remarry again during that period.

After defining the flow of a birth system and locating the nature of the spouse palace, the element hidden within the spouse palace can give a minor indication in terms of what type of a spouse one may be attracted to. Many practitioners refer to the Ten Gods approach for its accuracy in determining the type of partner and also the characteristics of the self.

"SPOUSE PALACE"

Often referred to as the 'House of Spouse', is located in the day branch directly underneath the day stem. The spouse palace is not the only place in a Four Pillars chart used to describe a person's partner or relationship. Flow and the use of the Ten Gods are also integral parts of spouse analysis.

These Ten Gods are not special symbols or actual gods that belong in a religion—it is only a term used to refer to an element in relations to the self. They include the Eating God, Hurting Officer, Direct Wealth, Indirect Wealth, Friend, Rob Wealth, Officer, Seven Killings (Indirect Officer), Direct Resources and Indirect Resources. Lots of information can be extracted from the use of the Ten Gods when analyzing a Four Pillars chart. Each of them is paired in polar opposites and will be explained in the following sections. Below are some of the characteristics of the Ten Gods. My second book on the Four Pillars of Destiny will go into further detail about the Ten Gods.

Eating God (食神)/Hurting Officer (傷官) and the Self

Intentions: Curb the controlling elements, support the wealth elements, reduce the strength of the Rivalries and the self.

Both the Eating God and the Hurting Officers are output elements of the self. The output element refers to the element that the self produces. The difference between the Eating God and the Hurting Officer is that the Eating God represents the output element of the same polarity whereas the Hurting Officer is of opposite polarity. Simply put, the Eating God of the Yang Wood (甲) self is the Yang Fire (丙), whereas the Hurting Officer of the Yang Wood (甲) self is the Yin Fire (丁). The output element represents performance, expression, and intelligence. People with output elements found in the stem are often talented, logical, responsible and artistic. The strength and nature of their intelligence comes from whether it is useful to a birth system or not. Remember that the output element is also the element that reduces the self. Weak birth systems possessing too many output elements may not have the strength to perform or express all that they have acquired through learning. Having one of the output distinctions over another does not mean that one of them is better than the other. It depends on the cosmic flow and the overall makeup of the birth composite. Some charts prefer the Eating God over the Hurting Officer. Each of them serves a different purpose. Combinations can take away its effectiveness, yet it can also enhance its positive qualities, depending on the needs of the birth chart.

The location of the output element and its relationship to other elements with the birth system are important factors in evaluating relationships. For example, if the spouse palace's relationship to the self is the Eating God with limited indirect resource, the spouse would typically be physically overweight but she can provide assistance and advice to the person in charge of the household. Below is a chart where the Self sits on top of the Eating God, the Self being a Yang Earth (戊) while the Monkey possesses a Yang Metal (庚) within it.

Example: Eating God			
Hour	Day	Month	Year
X	戊 Yang Earth	X	X
X	申 Monkey	X	X

Please note that as long as the resources to the self are limited or not present, the partner or spouse would not be negatively affected. So for the case above, if there is an overwhelming amount of 'Fire' located in the chart, the Yang Metal (庚) that is sitting underneath the Monkey (申) could be harmed. Translating this into real life, the spouse may feel stressed and tired in this relationship. Picture this: the metal is being 'controlled' by the fire, and as a result, the partner would feel controlled by the breadwinner in this relationship.

For men who have the Hurting Officer in the spouse palace, if the Hurting Officer is beneficial to the flow of the chart, it is quite often that his spouse or partner would be very attractive and helpful to the self. A strong self having an eating god or hurting officer underneath the chart would tend to result in a good spouse or partner, but if there are sibling rivalries in the chart, the result would be the opposite. Most often, when a chart has a sibling rivalry, meaning the same element as the self in the stem, these people are dissatisfied or unhappy in their personal relationship life. Prince Charles is a good example of what happens with a sibling rivalry and the eating god sitting in the spouse palace. He was born on Nov. 14, 1948, a Yin Water (癸) self whereby the other Yin Water (癸) in the month is rooted by the Pig (亥).

Hour	Day	Month	Year
X	癸 Yin Water	癸 Yin Water	戊 Yang Earth
X	卯 Rabbit	亥 Pig	子 Rat

By just looking at the chart itself, the chart wants to follow the output/offspring flow, which is wood from the Rabbit (卯) and Pig (亥) combination. The Yin Water (癸) in the month pillar is partially controlled by the Yang Earth (戊) in the year pillar, and as a result, his chart can surrender to the offspring flow at certain times if Wood becomes prominent. The unfortunate part is that whenever water becomes heavy, the flow is instantly interrupted. Consequently, happiness tends to be short lived within such a chart. Some people might say that he's the "Prince", but a Prince with no power or authority, subjected to the control of the Queen, has a bitter pill to swallow. The cosmic flow of his birth chart is in line with his life situation. This is not based on chance, this is cosmic reality.

Hour	Day	Month	Year
丁 Yin Fire	乙 Yin Wood	丙 Yang Fire	壬 Yang Water
亥 Pig	亥 Pig	午 Horse	戌 Dog

66	56	46	36	26	16	6
癸 Yin Water	壬 Yang Water	辛 Yin Metal	庚 Yang Metal	己 Yin Earth	戊 Yang Earth	丁 Yin Fire
丑 Ox	子 Rat	亥 Pig	戌 Dog	酉 Rooster	申 Monkey	未 Goat

Prince William of Wales serves as a better example of a birth system that surrenders to the output element. He was born on June 21, 1982 at 9:03pm and his Four Pillars chart is on the previous page.

Prince William is a Yin Wood (乙) self born in the heat of the summer in the month of the Horse (午). His self element is flanked on both sides by fire serving as his output elements. The unfortunate part of his birth chart is that there are two Pigs (亥) in his branches found in the day and hour. Those two symbols are trying to empower the self, preventing the Yin Wood (乙) from completely surrendering to the fire. Luckily for Prince William, the power of the fire is solidified by the half fire alliance of the Horse (午) and the Dog (戌). Finding a suitable marriage partner for Prince William could be a daunting task as the Pig (亥) is residing in the spouse palace and it serves as an "unwanted" symbol in his birth system. To make matters worse, the Pig (亥) is duplicated in the hour branch, which may lead to remarriage later in life. For Prince William, having a spouse who has an abundant amount of fire in the birth system can become beneficial to him and prevents marriage tensions from a cosmic stand-point. Since Prince William surrenders to the output element, fame and fortune comes easily as long as his birth system remains loyal to the cosmic flow of fire. There is also no doubt that he is very intelligent and boisterous.

The birth system of Prince William possesses both the Eating God and the Hurting Officer in the stems. This is a case where having two of the same elements of opposite polarity would not create any conflict in his system since he is surrendering to fire. As a result, having either Yin or Yang Fire in his Four

Pillars chart is beneficial to the flow. Obviously, water would cause problems and damage the cosmic flow of fire since water controls fire. The Yang Water (壬) found in the stem appear to cause problems to his birth system, but since it is sitting on top of hot molten fire and earth found in the Dog (戌), the damage the water can do to the flow is limited. The wealth element for Prince William, earth, can be used to curtail water. The next section will explain what wealth means to a birth system.

Direct Wealth (正財) and Indirect Wealth (偏財) and the Self

Intentions: Ruin/harm resources, support and feed the controlling element, weaken the output element, induce a fight amongst rivalries or allow the rivalries to come together and take the wealth (depends on the chart classification).

The wealth is the element that the self controls. Since wood controls earth, earth is the wealth of the self. Fire controls metal, therefore, metal is the wealth of the self, and so forth. Direct wealth is the element of opposite polarity that the self controls while the indirect wealth is the element of the same polarity that the self controls. For example, the direct wealth of a Yang Wood (甲) self would be the Yin Earth (己), while the indirect wealth of a Yang Wood (甲) is the Yang Earth (戊).

If the Spouse palace possesses the wealth element in relation to the self, the partner or spouse would be very beneficial to the head of the household;

but like any other of the Ten Gods, this is assuming that the wealth element is supportive to the flow of the entire chart. A Four Pillars chart classified as a weak self would not have a favourable spouse if the wealth element resides in the spouse palace. Wealth stars are exposed in the heavenly stems of the chart, unless the chart surrenders to the wealth flow. Having wealth in the stems can also result in the loss of wealth, the difficulty in maintaining wealth, and a possibility of losing your partner to another person. The probability of such misfortunes is much higher especially if the wealth encounters a "Rob Wealth" or a "Friend cycle". Rob Wealth and Friend are the same element as the self. The best scenario is to have the wealth element located in the day pillar branch, hidden and useful to the flow. Not only would the spouse be helpful to the self, but also the wealth element is well protected.

Example: Wealth			
Hour	Day	Month	Year
X	戊 Yang Earth	X	X
X	子 Rat	X	X

The chart above illustrates the wealth element of the Yang Earth (戊), the Rat (子), being protected underneath the self in the day pillar. If more Earth elements were encountered in the stems or in the luck cycle, there could be possibilities of a loss of wealth or another person taking away the spouse or partner Since the wealth element is buried in the stems, the loss of wealth is much less likely to occur;. it is said to be 'protected'. The breakup would also depend on the bonding of the couple, and this will be discussed later. The more wealth stars there are located in a Four Pillars chart, the easier it is for the person to lose his wife and wealth. Birth charts with a weak self and a strong wealth element are more susceptible to relationship issues. The spouse or partner of such a chart would tend to be weak with the possibilities of health issues. In addition, the spouse or partner would not be able to support the breadwinner mentally by providing him with sound advice.

When the wealth is weak with hurting officers or eating god present in the chart, and if resources are also present, there is a likelihood that a tragic accident or death will befall the spouse. However, a chart with a weak wealth does not always signify that negative events will occur. As long as the resource elements are not seen, the spouse would not encounter difficulties. From the five element theory, there is a conflict between the resource and output elements. This conflict is one of the causes to misfortunes. For example, the resource of the self is water while the eating god and the hurting officer is fire; water would douse the fire, preventing it from increasing the strength of the wealth. This explanation found in many Chinese texts is based upon logic. Using the logic of the Five Element Theory can produce many variations and differing degrees of the strength of the self when it faces against the wealth element.

As mentioned earlier in this segment, having wealth exposed in the stems is not good since the wealth tends to be vulnerable to 'robbery' by a sibling rivalry if encountered in the luck cycle. One of the prime example comes from the great golfer, Tiger Woods. Eldrick Tont Woods, or Tiger Woods, was born on December 30, 1975. He is a Yang Metal (庚) self sitting on top of the Dog (戌), but as you can see in his chart below, he has his direct wealth element sitting in the Year stem, the Yin Wood (乙). In addition, the Yin Wood (乙) is rooted in the branch of the Rabbit (卯).

Hour	Day	Month	Year
丁 Yin Fire	庚 Yang Metal	戊 Yang Earth	乙 Yin Wood
亥 Pig	戌 Dog	子 Rat	卯 Rabbit

67	57	47	37	27	17	7
辛 Yin Metal	壬 Yang Water	癸 Yin Water	甲 Yang Wood	乙 Yin Wood	丙 Yang Fire	丁 Yin Fire
巳 Snake	午 Horse	未 Goat	申 Mon-key	酉 Rooster	戌 Dog	亥 Pig

By looking at this chart without an understanding of the fundamentals of how flow works, most would use the 'strong' or 'weak' mechanism to determine a person's favourable and unfavourable elements. Traditional Chinese methods would label Tiger Woods as a "fake wealth follow" flow where his flow leans towards wood and water. This is exactly what Tiger Woods is, a "fake wealth follow", or in Chinese: "假從財格". Since he was born in the month of the Rat, the wood in the Year pillar takes the water from the Rat (子) while the Yang Metal (庚) self surrenders to the wood.

Encountering metal can be devastating for Tiger Woods as metal can easily cut through wood. How can we tell that Tiger Woods benefits from wood? At the age of 27, when his luck cycle moved onto the Yin Wood (乙), his career started to take off as extra wealth entered his flow. We can look back to 1999, the year of the Rabbit (卯), to determine the benefits of wood in his birth chart. In 1999, he began a sustained period of dominance in the history of golf. In 2003, the year of the Goat (未), it combined with the Rabbit (卯) to strengthen the flow of wealth and led to his engagement with Elin Nordegren. Looking at more recent history, in 2007, he won many major endorsement deals with companies such as Gillette and Gatorade. In 2007, the year of the Pig (亥), the wooden pig combined with the Rabbit (卯) in his year pillar, solidifying the wealth flow.

Since metal is his unfavourable element, to confirm this, we can look into the Rooster cycle which began for Woods at the age of about 33 and lasts for 5 years. Tiger Woods turned 33 on December 30, 2008. Since the Rooster (酉) and the year of the Ox (丑) in 2009 combines to form a half metal alliance, it should be evident that the metal is his most disliked element. With the additional metal in 2009, Tiger Woods was exposed for extramarital affairs. The problem with a chart like Woods is that when wealth is heavy in a chart, it is quite often that men will have affairs outside of the home as wealth in a chart symbolizes the spouse or partners. In addition, his day pillar is the Yang Metal

Dog (庚戌). This special pillar is often labelled in Chinese texts as the 'bossy self' and 'love addicts', and as a result, Tiger Woods always had the urge within him to have affairs. The special pillars and stars will be covered later in this book. His case serves as a great example of how the changing of a cosmic flow in the luck cycle can alter one's life and relationship.

Below is a different case where the self and the spouse are not negatively harmed by the sibling rivalry. This is example by a famous Four Pillars practitioner Tsui Lok Ng (徐樂吾), 滴天髓徵義 page 305.

Hour	Day	Month	Year
癸 Yin Water	丁 Yin Fire	乙 Yin Wood	丁 Yin Fire
卯 Rabbit	酉 Rooster	巳 Snake	未 Goat

Luck Cycle (starting age not provided)			
辛 Yin Metal	壬 Yang Water	癸 Yin Water	甲 Yang Wood
丑 Ox	寅 Tiger	卯 Rabbit	辰 Dragon

This person is a Yin Fire (丁) self, born in the month of the Snake (巳), when fire is burning bright. This chart seems to be an unfortunate case where the two Yin Fires (丁) in the stems are competing for both wealth (metal) and resources (wood). The wealth in this chart is considered quite heavy due to the fact that the Rooster (酉) and the Snake (巳) combine to form half a metal alliance. There is competition for wealth amongst the two Yin Fire (丁) in this chart – but fortunately, the competition is pacified by the Yin Water (癸) found in the hour stem. In addition, the Rabbit (卯) is subjected to a clash with the Rooster (酉), preventing the wood in the Rabbit (卯) from reducing the effects of the Yin Water (癸) and feeding the two Yin Fires (丁). This is also a great illustration of how a clash works in favour of the chart. The key in this clash is that the Rooster (酉) and the Snake (巳) are both united, making it difficult for the Rabbit (卯) to pose a threat to the metal. If a Pig (亥) comes around in a luck cycle or in the year, it will create a conflict between metal and wood.

During the first Yin Water (癸) period, this person was in school and was quite successful with his studies; this can be attributed to the Yin Water (癸), preventing the two fires from fighting. In the Yang Water (壬) period, the Yin Fire (丁) was combined, nullifying the effectiveness of the fire rival. He was married and made a substantial amount of money. It can be said that without the Rooster (酉) sitting in the day pillar, it would be difficult for him to get married since the other hidden metal is beneath the Snake (巳). The advantage of having the Rooster (酉) is two-fold. Firstly, the Rooster (酉) possesses the wealth element of the self and it is well protected as it sits beneath the self. It is considerably difficult for a 'sibling rivalry' to take his possession because of where the wealth element belongs in the chart. Secondly, pure metal makes it easy for the Rooster (酉) to combine with the Snake (巳) in solidifying the metal team. The example of Tsui Lok Ng (徐樂吾) illustrates how a 'sibling rivalry' in a chart is not always negative as long as it is under control. It is also important to keep in mind that as long as the wealth is sitting below the self, the wealth and the spouse is usually well protected

The next chart demonstrates the self surrendering to the wealth, a pure 'wealth follow' flow. The former Chairman of the Chinese Communist Party, Deng Xiaoping was born on August 22, 1905, a Yang Earth (戊) self.

Hour	Day	Month	Year
壬 Yang Water	戊 Yang Earth	壬 Yang Water	甲 Yang Wood
子 Rat	子 Rat	申 Monkey	辰 Dragon

85	75	65	55	45	35	25	15	5
辛 Yin Metal	庚 Yang Metal	己 Yin Earth	戊 Yang Earth	丁 Yin Fire	丙 Yang Fire	乙 Yin Wood	甲 Yang Wood	癸 Yin Water
巳 Snake	辰 Dragon	卯 Rabbit	寅 Tiger	丑 Ox	子 Rat	亥 Pig	戌 Dog	酉 Rooster

When looking at a chart, the first step is to determine the cosmic or leading flow. For Deng Xiaoping, it is straight forward, since water is leading the flow, as seen by the two Yang Waters (壬) in the stems and the water trio of the Rat (子), Monkey (申) and the Dragon (辰). This is a pure 'wealth' flow in which water is the most important element along with the significance of metal, the provider of water. The Yang Earth (戊) has no power or strength to block the tide of the water. His chart must surrender to the water flow. From a relationship standpoint, Deng stands to benefit from his spouse, but on the other hand, his relationship is vulnerable to external factors that can take his spouse away due to the fact that wealth is shown in two of the stems.

How the Cosmic Flow of Wealth Supersedes the Spouse Palace

There is no set rules defining the spouse palace as the only determining factor of what type of spouse a man can expect. Certain elements and symbols within a birth system can provide a different picture. The leading flow can change the way in how the character and nature of the spouse is viewed, and whether she would be helpful or not to her husband. This next example illustrates how the wife was helpful and supportive, despite the spouse palace possessing an unwanted element. Famous director, Ang Lee, born on October

23, 1954, in Taiwan is a perfect example of how the leading flow provided him with a very helpful and supportive wife. Below is his birth system.

Hour	Day	Month	Year
X	壬 Yang Water	甲 Yang Wood	甲 Yang Wood
X	子 Rat	戌 Dog	午 Horse

58	48	38	28	18	8
庚 Yang Metal	己 Yin Earth	戊 Yang Earth	丁 Yin Fire	丙 Yang Fire	乙 Yin Wood
辰 Dragon	卯 Rabbit	寅 Tiger	丑 Ox	子 Rat	亥 Pig

Ang Lee was born in the month of the Dog (戌), a period when hard lava from the earth was ignited by the Horse (午), located next to his birth month in the year branch. The Dog (戌) and Horse (午) created a half fire alliance and was constantly fed by dry logs of wood as represented by the two Yang Woods (甲) on top of them. It can easily be established that fire is the main flow of his chart. As a result, Ang Lee's cosmic system partially surrenders to the fire. The partial surrender classification is caused by the Rat (子) found in the day branch. Since the Rat (子) is located in the spouse palace, it is easy to quickly assume that his spouse would not be helpful or supportive of Ang Lee. This is where cosmic flow and the lead of the wealth element supersede the spouse palace. From evaluating Ang Lee's life history, after graduating from school, he remained unemployed for more than six years during the Rat (子) period in his luck cycle. Obviously, the Rat (子) is proven to be a cause of misfortunes and difficulties in his life. On the other hand, his wife, Jane Lin (林惠嘉), was with him every step of the way and supported the entire family of four. Since the 'wealth' in Ang Lee's birth chart can also represent his spouse, it superseded the 'spouse palace' in determining the importance of his wife.

In order to determine the importance of fire in his birth system, any one of the Horse (午), Tiger (寅) and Dog (戌) can be used for testing, as all three of them together would form a complete fire team. By having a complete fire trio, the flow of fire would be solidified. A screenplay competition was organized by the People's Republic of China's Information Office in 1990 where Ang Lee submitted two of his films, "Pushing Hands" and "The Wedding Banquet". 1990 was the year of the Horse (午), and as a result, the fire catapulted both his movies respectively to first and second place. It was at this event that a movie producer invited Lee to direct "Pushing Hands" with a full-length feature. To verify the effects of the Tiger (寅), evaluating the events during the Tiger (寅) cycle in Ang Lee's life would be the best way to confirm the fire flow, as he had a complete fire trio during his early to late 40s. With an entire fire alliance, it is no surprise that success was imminent and his rise to fame began with the movie "Sense and Sensibility" in 1995. To carry on his momentum, he filmed "Crouching Tiger, Hidden Dragon" and it won multiple Oscars and other film awards in the year 2000. Some of his success can also be attributed to the earth found in his luck cycles, accompanied by the Tiger (寅). Since earth controls water, the earth entering his life at the age of 38 suppressed the water rivalry found in the Rat (子). Ang Lee's drive and determination during his bad cycles helped him succeed when his luck cycle turned positive. In addition, with the help and support of his wife, he was able to live and pursue his dreams. Even though his "spouse palace" in the day branch had an unfavourable symbol, the fire wealth flow was the true indicator of his wife's support.

Direct (正印) and Indirect (偏印) Resource and the Self

Intentions: Disperse the controlling elements, feed the self element, control the output elements, support the Rivalries.

Direct and indirect resources are the element that feeds the self. For example, a wood self is fed by the water; therefore, water is considered resource for the wood. To be more specific, the direct resource is the opposite polarity to the self element. For a Yang Wood (甲) self, the direct resource would be the Yin Water (癸). On the other hand, the indirect resource to the Yang Wood (甲) would be the Yang Water (壬). The indirect resource shares the same polarity as the self.

Having resources is good as long as the self is not overwhelmingly strong. Charts that belong to a strong classification would dislike the resource element, especially if it is not enough to push the self towards a dominant self. Dominant selves are able to enjoy the resource element as the resource element would solidify its dominant classification. If the resource element sits underneath the self stem, again, it is important to determine whether it is go-ing with the flow of the chart or against the flow of the chart. This is always the first factor to look at in any chart when trying to understand the importance of the spouse or partner. Usually, if the spouse palace possesses the resource element in relation to the self, and assuming that the resource element goes with the flow of the chart, the spouse or partner tends to be friendly, nice and helpful to the breadwinner.

Example: Resource			
Hour	Day	Month	Year
X	戊 Yang Earth	X	X
X	午 Horse	X	X

For the chart above, the Horse (午) possesses fire, which is the re-source element to the self. The resource element is particularly useful for those who are a weak self and in need of the resource element. Charts classified as a weak self tend to have a very supportive partner or spouse if the resource element sits underneath the self. For the example above, if the Yang Earth self was born in the spring season where wood is strong, the earth energy would be trapped, depending on the rest of the chart's elements. Utilizing the resource element in this chart, which is fire generated from the wood in the spring season, can feed the earth self. As long as the resource element is not subjected to the control of the wealth element, the spouse would be very supportive of the self. As mentioned earlier, the wealth element is also used to determine the type of spouse one would have; we will go into further detail about the wealth element later, but for now, the focus is on the spouse palace.

If the self is strong and sits on top of resources. If it cannot become a dominant self, the partner or spouse cannot come to the aid of the person. He will most likely have to work hard on his own without the support of his spouse. It is often said that the indirect resource often represents a godmother-like figure, while the direct resource equates to the real mother. From a Four Pillars point of view, both types of resources serve specific functionalities. An overdose of direct resources in a birth chart can lead to becoming overweight, while an overdose of indirect resources can lead to malnourishment. Charts yielding or surrendering to the flow of resources would not have this problem. Therefore, understanding the flow of the birth system is imperative prior to making any assumptions.

When children are upset by their mother, most tend to directly voice their opinion in some form. Whereas, those with godmothers tend to be quiet and less outspoken. This analogy can be used on Direct and Indirect Resources. Later on, we will explore how Indirect Resources can create problems for those possessing the Eating God (output element) in their chart.

Friend(比肩), Rob Wealth(劫財) and the Self (Sibling Rivalries)

Intentions: Assist the self, rob wealth, disperse the resources, tend to the controlling element (比劫敵官殺), allow output.

Friend and Rob Wealth refer to the same element as the self. The only difference is that Friend has the same polarity as the self element. For example, the Friend of a Yang Wood (甲) self is Yang Wood (甲). On the other hand, the Rob Wealth of the Yang Wood (甲) is the Yin Wood (乙), an opposite polarity of the same element. The Rob Wealth or Friend can also be referred to as a RIVALRY.

For the charts that are not placed in a special classification or do not have a well-defined flow, the Friend or the Rob Wealth in the spouse palace can be either be helpful to the self, or it can be an obstruction to the self. Weak self charts that lack resources with a Friend or the Rob Wealth under the self stem tend to have a favourable spouse or partner. The characteristics of the Friend aids the weak self, and the spouse is beneficial if the Friend sits in the spouse palace. Both the Friend and Rob Wealth are often labelled or referred to as "Sibling Rivalry". In life, rivalries can easily turn into friends as they would enjoy working together. Charts classified as weak would require the aid of the same element as the self. Charts belonging to the Dominant classification can benefit from the same element as well. On the other hand, when the flow does not enjoy having another Friend or Rob Wealth in the birth system, the rivalry can turn into competition. Such competition can lead to tragedy in some cases. Birth systems classified as feeble would not enjoy the same element as the self, since the Rivalry would take away some of the benefits that the feeble self is enjoying. By strengthening the feeble self with the same element as the self, the person would become rebellious.

Dominant self charts tend to have a Friend or Rob Wealth sitting in their spouse palace. These people tend to have a very pleasing, attractive and helpful partner; this is also a result of having a favourable element in the spouse palace. Of course being in a good cycle would be an added bonus. These people usually have good taste and like to attract the attention of people around them. The President of France, Nicolas Sarkozy, serves as a prime example. Nicolas Sarkozy was born on January 28, 1955, a Yin Earth (己) in the month of the Ox (丑). Below is a chart of Nicolas Sarkozy.

Hour	Day	Month	Year
乙 Yin Wood	己 Yin Earth	丁 Yin Fire	甲 Yang Wood
亥 Pig	丑 Ox	丑 Ox	午 Horse

52	42	32	22	12	2
癸 Yin Wa-ter	壬 Yang Water	辛 Yin Metal	庚 Yang Metal	己 Yin Earth	戊 Yang Earth
未 Goat	午 Horse	巳 Snake	辰 Dragon	卯 Rabbit	寅 Tiger

On the surface, interpretations and methods would label his chart as a strong self, and that he requires metal and wood. If this was the case, how would one explain his rise to power during the Horse (午) cycle in his late 40s? The fire and earth in the Horse (午) strengthened the self and allowed him to become a true dominant self. The Horse (午) cycle coincided with his appointment into the Minister of the Interior office. If we go back a bit further to the Dragon (辰) cycle, in 1983, he was appointed as Mayor of Neuilly-sur-Seine, a commune bordering the western edges of Paris. He was Mayor from 1983-2002. Having tested his favourable flow in his system which is fire and Earth, we can come to a conclusion that it is highly possible that his partner would be attractive and supportive of him. Nicolas has married 3 times already and three of his wives are people of prominence. His latest relationship is with Carla Bruni, an Italian-born songwriter, singer, and former model. We will investigate further into their relationship later. For now, it is important to understand that when the spouse palace contains the same element as the self, which is beneficial to the flow of the chart, it is most often the case that their partners tend to be attractive, pleasing and influential.

Franklin Roosevelt was born on January 30, 1882, 8:45pm.

Hour	Day	Month	Year
丙 Yang Fire	庚 Yang Metal	辛 Yin Metal	辛 Yin Metal
戌 Dog	午 Horse	丑 Ox	巳 Snake

Source: 命理一得, 徐樂吾 p.40

Franklin Roosevelt serves as a good example in terms of Friend/Rob Wealth. At first glance, it looks like Franklin has quite an abundant amount of the same element and resources since he has wet earth from the Ox (丑). In addition, there are two Yin Metals (辛) found in his system while the Snake (巳) in the year branch, combining with the Ox (丑) month to form a half metal team. The chart seemingly wants to go with a dominant metal flow, but unfortunately, the hour pillar and the day branch prevents this from happening. The Dog (戌) in the hour branch contains heavy earth and fire while the Horse (午) also combines with the Dog (戌) to form half a fire structure. Essentially, Roosevelt can only be classified as a strong metal and the other metal needs to be curbed. Adding more metal would cause more problems to his chart as the battle of the rivalries in his chart would intensify. The rivalry can be competing for many factors in his life, which includes: wealth, relationship and health.

To test this case, we can look at 1921, the year of the Yin Metal Rooster (辛酉). In 1921, Franklin Roosevelt suffered from paralytic illness which left him permanently paralyzed from waist down. Since we are looking at the relationship aspect of this chart, with so much metal in his chart competing for wealth in his life, it would be difficult for him to be in a prolonged relationship. It was well documented that Franklin had affairs outside his marriage. Again, this is another example of cosmic reality based on the truth, not on chance. Could this be avoided? For Four Pillars consultants, recommendations or advice would be to tell the client that he is probably better off staying single, but if he has to get married, he will need to choose a partner or spouse who possesses a chart that has a cosmic flow that is in his favour. He would benefit from women who possess fire in their birth system.

Each element has a main rival and whether the rival is good or bad depends on the classification of the birth system. Most often, a dominant self enjoys having rivals in the chart or encountering rivals in the luck cycle. The rivalries would help to maintain the dominant flow of the birth chart. On the other hand, as explained with Roosevelt's system, the rivalry was working against him, which could be counted for his disabled condition. A charts that surrenders to a leading flow of an element different than the self needs to be careful of the rivalry, as the rivalry can compete with the self and disrupt the flow. Below is a chart of the ten heavenly stem and their key rivals.

Heavenly Stems	Key Rival
Yang Wood 甲	Rabbit 卯
Yin Wood 乙	Dragon 辰
Yang Fire 丙	Horse 午
Yin Fire 丁	Goat 未
Yang Earth 戊	Horse 午
Yin Earth 己	Goat 未
Yang Metal 庚	Rooster 酉
Yin Metal 辛	Dog 戌
Yang Water 壬	Rat 子
Yin Water 癸	Ox 丑

When looking at a chart and determining whether the rivalry is favourable to oneself, identify the self element, then verify what has transpired in the year the key rival appeared. Verification can also be conducted in the luck cycle where the key rival was encountered. For example, a Yang Wood (甲) self encountering a Rabbit (卯) should have triggered some negative key events if the Rabbit (卯) and the wood is not favourable to the birth composite. If the Yang Wood (甲) self sits on top of the Tiger (寅) in the day pillar for a chart classified as strong, there is a high possibility that wood is unfavourable and the relationship may become challenging. Going back to Roosevelt's birth system, he is a Yang Metal (庚) self. 1921 was the year of the Yin Metal Rooster (辛酉), and the Rooster (酉) is the key rival to his Yang Metal (庚) self element. Since Roosevelt's birth chart is considerably strong, as he entered a year with more metal, misfortunes would occur. Coincidentally, Roosevelt was paralyzed in the year of the Rooster (酉).

Birth charts with "rivalries" are easy to spot. The "rivalries" can be found in the branches, or in the heavenly stem. The same symbol as the day stem found in the month, year or hour can create problems for charts classified as being feeble. There can be many variations of the rivalry, depending on the classification of the birth system. Weak selves are in need of some assistance to hold on to money while strong selves need to rid themselves of the rivalry. Then there are the systems that surrender to the leading flow, or have the possibilities of surrendering, and these systems fear the appearance of another rivalry. In 2007, I encountered a system on the borderline of surrendering. One of my clients, Tom, came to see me and he mentioned that he was devastated by what had transpired in his life. Tom was born on January 15, 1978 in

Vancouver, Canada. Although he does not know his birth hour, I was able to deduce what was happening with his birth system.

Hour	Day	Month	Year
X	丁 Yin Fire	癸 Yin Water	丁 Yin Fire
X	丑 Ox	丑 Ox	巳 Snake

33	23	13	3
己 Yin Earth	庚 Yang Metal	辛 Yin Metal	壬 Yang Water
酉 Rooster	戌 Dog	亥 Pig	子 Rat

Tom is a Yin Fire (丁) self born near the end of the winter season where the strength of fire is almost non-existent. There was a half metal team in the branches formed by the Ox (丑) and the Snake (巳). He is definitely well-loved and cared by his family as he surrenders to the metal and water. The Yin Fire (丁) in the year may pose problems in his life but it is under the control of the Yin Water (癸) in the month stem. As long as Tom's birth system remained loyal to the flow of metal and water, he will continue to benefit and live a happy life. Wealth was neatly tucked into his branches as he had hidden metal in each of the three branches in his system. In order to unearth the wealth from him, a powerful sibling rivalry has to enter the system. By evaluating his luck cycle, Tom enjoyed more than 28 years of metal and water and during this period. He did not really need to work as his parents provided him with financial support. When he looked for a job, it was handed to him quite easily.

In 2006, his good fortunes took a drastic turn ever since he met a foreign exchange student from Japan. Her name was Izumi. It was also at this time where his system transitioned into the Dog (戌) cycle, an animal hidden with predominantly hard molten earth. Coincidentally, from looking at the Chinese lunar calendar, 2006 was the year of the Yang Fire Dog (丙戌); the Yang Fire for the year erected the fire out of the Dog (戌). The earth stemmed the tide of the water while the rivalry of the fire suddenly became stronger. The first sign of things to come was when Tom decided to get engaged with Izumi after knowing her for less than 6 months. The engagement ring was quite expensive. After their engagement, he flew to Tokyo to meet with her family. Tom's family then began to plan for the wedding which was supposed to happen in 2007.

His family continued to spend money preparing for the wedding and they have given Tom's fiancé a sum of money as a gift. Their family also purchased jewellery for Izumi. Three months before the wedding, Izumi suddenly disappeared and left Vancouver without leaving a trace of her belongings. The jewellery and engagement ring that were given to Izumi were also taken away. Tom and his family were shocked and in denial. They later realized that Izumi was only after their money but it was too late.

From analyzing the cosmic energy of 2007, the Yin Fire Pig (丁亥) brought about a rivalry in Tom's system. Not only did the rivalry of the Yin Fire (丁) unearth his personal wealth and belongings, the Pig (亥) also played a damaging role in breaking up his cosmic system. The Pig (亥) clashed with the Snake (巳) in the year branch, weakening the team of metal. The Snake (巳) being combined by two of the Ox (丑) suddenly lost its strength and his wealth was suddenly vulnerable to robbery. With the clash transpiring, the Yin Fire (丁) in 2007 was able to rob Tom's wealth in his cosmic system.

Officer (正官), Seven Killings (七殺) and the Self

Intentions: Control the rivalry, protect the wealth, support the resources.

The officer or seven killings is the element or star that controls the self. For example, a Yang Wood self would be controlled by the Yin Metal-辛 (officer) or Yang Metal-庚 (seven killings). If the self is strong with very few officers and it encounters the wealth of that luck cycle, the spouse or partner of this person tends to be attractive. On the other hand, if the Friend/Rob Wealth also appears within the wealth luck cycle, challenges and difficulties are faced by the person's spouse. Order and discipline are two major characteristics of the controlling element.

When a vast amount of officers or seven killings are found in the chart or rooted in the branches, this can pose to be a problem for the spouse if there are no hurting officers or eating gods present. Remember that the wealth element is often considered the spouse or partner. Officers or seven killings being strong in the chart would reduce the wealth element. When the self encounters resources, most often the spouse would tend to get sick or be physically weak.

If the seven killings is the useful god or the most favourable symbol in the chart, the spouse or partner tends to be very influential in the household. Birth charts which are considerably strong or classified as strong would be favourable to the controlling element. Once the controlling element is encountered for a specific year or cycle, possibilities of an increase in salary wages and promotions are high. With the controlling element for in the spouse palace, the spouse tends to be attractive and can provide sound advice for the household. The controlling element is a complicated topic of discussion. The positioning, usefulness, and strength are all matters. For the evaluation of relationships, the controlling elements are the key components for a women's birth system. The discussion of the controlling elements will be explored further in the next chapter.

Analyzing a Female's Chart

1.
Finding the "Husband Star"

From the previous chapters, it is evident that analyzing a female's chart differs greatly from analyzing a male's chart when it comes to relationships. The simplest method of finding the 'male' or 'husband' star in a female's chart is by looking for the officer or controlling element. From my experience, I find that many middle-aged women in Asia—especially women from Hong Kong and Taiwan—are quite concerned with having a Four Pillars chart that has a proper makeup to benefit and ensure prosperity for their husband. The strength of the officer in the female's Four Pillars chart is vital in determining whether the husband will be successful. Utilizing wealth in a chart to support the officer or controlling element can aid the husband. One the other hand, having too much of the output element can damage the controlling element, as explained earlier in the section regarding the hurting officer and the eating god.

Eating God (食神)/Hurting Officer (傷官) and the Self

Numerous Chinese books have mentioned that if a woman has too many 'Hurting Officers' or elements that reduce the self, they can cause misfortunes to their husbands. The Hurting Officer is the output element in relation to the self element; it is the opposite polarity of the self element. For example, the Hurting Officer of the Yin Wood (乙) self element would be the Yang Fire (丙). For many cases, this is true but we also must look at the entire chart. If the birth chart possesses wealth elements in the stems, the 'Hurting Officers' may actually be used to feed the wealth element. As a result, the female's chart can use 'wealth' as their spouse. So why do people consider the 'Hurting Officer' a cause to a husband's misfortune? This can be attributed to the fact that the 'Hurting Officer' controls the 'Officer' or 'Seven Killings'. In the Four Pillars system, the controlling element is often considered the spouse. With an abundance of 'Hurting Officers', the woman can cause misfortunes to her spouse. It is not their choice to cause misfortunes. The misfortunes are a result of their energetic makeup in the cosmic system. Below is an example taken from p. 161 of the author Master Yeo "尤達人" in his book 'Forty Years of Life' or "知命四十年", and it explains why it is difficult to actualize dreams when a woman possesses a heavy amount of 'Hurting Officers'.

Hour	Day	Month	Year
壬 Yang Water	辛 Yin Metal	壬 Yang Water	戊 Yang Earth
辰 Dragon	巳 Snake	戌 Dog	寅 Tiger

Her spouse is considered to have a fire chart since fire controls the Yin Metal (辛) self. The chart illustrates a case where the 'husband star' has no power or authority in a relationship with this person. The reason why the 'husband star' is weak is because of the two Yang Water (壬) controlling the fire. Being born near the end of autumn makes the fire weak, and by adding Yang Water (壬) on top of the fire, it actually hurts the spouse. When women have too many Hurting Officers controlling the officer in a chart, it is said that the husband usually have no authority in the household. Since this person already possess quite a few Hurting Officers, if she were to encounter more water in her luck cycle, her husband can run into possibilities of loss of wealth or accidents. The best remedy for this type of a chart is to use the wealth element to reduce the Hurting Officer. Since the wealth element is wood, the choice of colors, industry, career, and placement of plants can reduce the negative impacts when she runs into a water cycle.

Many Chinese texts mention that if a woman possesses too much Hurting Officer, the wealth can sometimes be considered as the spouse in the chart. Additional wealth can also be applied to dissipate the power of the Hurting Officer. Using wood will not only drain the strength of the water, but it can also strengthen the fire.

Hurting Officer with Wealth (傷官生財), For Females Expect a Prosperous Spouse

Master Yeo, '尤達人' mentioned in his book '傷官有財配合, 源遠流長', meaning that a chart having 'Hurting Officers' with wealth tends to live a long and happy life. The wealth must also be supported in the branches in order to maximize the dispersion of the 'Hurting Officers'. Having a Hurting Officer accompanied by wealth in the stem is very beneficial as it results in a complete cycle of three elements flowing harmoniously from the self to the Hurting Officer, then to the wealth.

For charts of females, if the wealth element is not present, the spouse would be negatively affected as the Hurting Officer will control the Officer of the chart. By having the wealth present, it can reduce the negative impact of the Hurting Officer and feed the Officer, thereby ensuring a continuous cosmic flow in the chart. Women possessing the wealth and the Hurting Officer in the heavenly stems will definitely enjoy a better marriage life. In Chinese, we say, "傷官有財, 源遠流長". If the Officer, meaning the controlling element, is not present in the female's chart, the wealth can bring about a prosperous spouse when she encounters the controlling element in the luck cycle.

Below is another example from 尤達人 (知命四十年, p.150), where the Yang Metal (庚) self is surrounded by water.

Hour	Day	Month	Year
癸 Yin Water	庚 Yang Metal	辛 Yin Metal	甲 Yang Wood
未 Goat	子 Rat	未 Goat	申 Monkey

The 'Hurting Officer' in this chart has been strengthened in reaction to the combination between the Rat (子) and the Monkey (申), which forms a half water team. Not only is the foundation led by the water team in the branch, the heavenly stem also presents a Yin Water (癸) in the hour stem. The water in this chart is very important as it serves as a mechanism to weaken the sibling rivalry or 'Rob Wealth' found in the month stem represented by the Yin Metal (辛). The metal and water in this chart can be described as clear and bright, and in Chinese: "金白水清". The earth found in the Goat (未) is too dry and hard to support the metal. By utilizing the Yang Wood (甲) in the Year stem, it can reduce the impact of the 'Hurting Officer' to provide a harmonious flow from the metal to the water, then from the water to the wood. The Yang Wood is considered rooted in this situation as a result of the Goat (未) and the combination between the Rat (子) and the Monkey (申). In her mid-life, her luck cycle headed towards South and Southeast, two directions represented by fire and wood; it was the best period of her life as the cosmic flow was continuous and uninterrupted.

Officer (正官), Seven Killings (七殺), and the Self

For further discussion on the controlling elements from the previous chapter, there is a major difference between men and women who possess the controlling elements. For women, the controlling element is often associated with their partner or spouse, while the Officer and the Seven Killings have different qualities. To reiterate, the Officer is the controlling element of the polarity opposite to the self element while the Seven Killings, sometimes referred to as 'Tyrant', is the controlling element of the same polarity. In order to illustrate

the difference between the two, here is a story about the two types of controlling elements.

One day, a group of people decided to go camping. In the evening, a
couple of the campers washed the vegetables, while others sliced meat. The
rest of the group prepared the stove and placed the charcoal into the pit. The
group worked together in tandem and the entire process was cooperative and
harmonious. At dinner time, the 'Officers' arranged all of the food onto a plate.
The 'Seven Killings', seeing a lot of leaves left over from the vegetables, came
up with the idea to use dried leaves for tea. This posed a problem: the campsite
lacked fresh water, which is needed for boiling and making tea. The river that
they were using to wash their hands with did not have clean water. The Seven
Killings decided to hike to the waterfall for clean water. This is the nature of the
Seven Killings—they will choose to go out of bounds just to obtain fresh water.

See the difference between the Officers and the Seven Killings? Officers
behave in an orderly conduct. Officers represent order, stability and discipline.
On the other hand, the Seven Killings represent instability, hidden order, and
they tend to think outside of the box to accomplish an objective. From a relationship aspect, women with officers in the birth system tend to have a stable
husband and they would become very loyal to the husband. Women with seven
killings would often want more in their relationship. Affairs and divorces are
much more probable with these women. Having a mix of Officers and Seven
Killings can be disastrous as the two types of controlling elements may create
disorders in the birth system. When a female has both types of controlling

elements in the birth chart, men are often present in their lives but the female may have trouble deciding between her choices of men. This is not their fault. The cosmic energy in their birth system attracts the men to their lives. The theory of the mixed controlling elements will be explained later with examples.

Alexandra Manley, Countess of Frederiksberg, serves as a great example of what may happen when a female has the officer sitting below the self. It also goes to show how a relationship can easily turn sour with an existence of a sibling rivalry in the chart. Alexandra was born on June 30, 1964, a Yang Metal (庚) self.

Hour	Day	Month	Year
X	庚 Yang Metal	庚 Yang Metal	甲 Yang Wood
X	戌 Dog	午 Horse	辰 Dragon

48	38	28	18	8
乙 Yin Wood	丙 Yang Fire	丁 Yin Fire	戊 Yang Earth	己 Yin Earth
丑 Ox	寅 Tiger	卯 Rabbit	辰 Dragon	巳 Snake

Alexandra has a very favourable spouse palace, as the Dog sits in her spouse palace. Why? Because the Dog (戌) combines with the Horse (午) to form a team of fire to control not only the self, but also the sibling rivalry of the Yang Metal (庚) in the month stem. The best way to nullify the effect of the sibling rivalry is to use Yin Wood (乙) since it will combine away the competition. Utilizing the Yin Wood will ensure a harmonious relationship. In 1995, Alexandra announced her engagement to Prince Joachim of Denmark and was married the same year. Coincidentally, 1995 was the year of the Yin Wood Pig (乙亥). Looking at her luck cycle, from the ages of 43-47, it should be a period of happiness in terms of relationship but again, the problem lies in the month pillar, where the Yang Metal (庚) is constantly looking for ways to take away her spouse. The Tiger (寅) during the period between the age of 43 and 47 completes the fire trio, and it should continue until the end of the Yin Wood (乙) cycle starting at age 48.

If the cosmos were perfect, it is better served that women should have only one Officer placed in the spouse palace. Unfortunately, we do not live in a perfect world. The instability, variations and changes in the cosmos creates boundless possibilities—that is why everyone is presented with challenges in life. The Ten Gods is just another important measuring stick used within the entire Four Pillars system. The next set of theories will try to bring together some and all of the gods, utilizing examples and logical approaches to explain how they interact with each other.

Other Theories

Aside from all of the different types of methods used in the analysis of relationships, there are other theories involved in evaluating a female's Four Pillars chart. These theories have many variations and differ in degrees and levels but they serve as guidelines that should be considered when doing consultations for women. They have been tested and verified in many different situations and have been proven to be quite accurate. There are factors which may change some of the readings, such as: one's education, where they were born, and whether they choose to get involved in a relationship. Those who remain single may not be affected by the theories presented as it would not be possible to cause harm or benefit to a spouse if they don't have one.

The theories in this section are put together from a logical standpoint. Birth systems must be looked at from a case by case basis and some of the theories here may not be suitable or applicable for certain birth charts. Charts that are classified in a different category such as surrender, transformation or a Dominant self may not be affected by some of these theories. A deeper understanding of the Four Pillars, accompanied by critical thinking, is required in order to utilize some of the theories. I will include some of my own analysis and experience with some of my clients in this section. The theories I present may be overwhelming for those who do not have a fundamental understanding of the five element theory. By practicing and envisioning the cycles, this hurdle can be overcome. Do not fret—these theories are considered advanced in the Four Pillars practice.

Weak Self With Lots of Wealth (財多身弱)

A female with an abundance of wealth in her chart may appear to be destined with wealth and fortune. Women who are classified as a weak self with a lot of wealth have opportunities of marrying into a rich family. But is it really their money and fame that goes along with it? They are usually physically beautiful from an appearance standpoint. Most often, after marriage, they will be subjected to the control of their husband or the elders. This type of individual tends to be obedient and patient with the husband, even when he misbehaves. If they had their own opinions, they will remain reserved about them. They may also indirectly affect the well-being of their husband's career and public opinion. Sadly, if they were to marry a man with high social status, it is advisable that they remain hidden from the view of the public.

I understand the harsh extremity this scenario presents, but this is cosmic reality. In Chinese, a weak self with a lot of wealth is said to be a person of "富屋貧人", and in English: "Poor person residing in a wealthy residence"—in other words—a servant. In many traditional Asian societies, some women would not have issues with this and may actually cherish such a predicament

"WEAK SELF WITH LOTS OF WEALTH "

This is a very common term used by the Chinese to label rich people who are often sick. It is often used colloquially as a joke to describe friends who may have lost money in gambling or on the stock markets. Within Four Pillars, it can be a serious matter depending on the degree and level of weakness."

as some women believe marrying into a rich family ensures a prolonged period of subsistence and wealth. The common negative outcome, however, could be divorce or the married men engaging in extramarital affairs. They are generally too weak to stand up for their own rights and opinions. Weak selves are usually in need of resources and the resources can easily damage the reputation of their husband. This is because resources reduce the strength of the controlling element. Not only does the resource damage the reputation of the husband, but also, the woman may find that they may no longer rely on the husband. This sort of quandary is brought upon the husband by the cosmic inequality of the female's Four Pillars chart. In chaotic times, it is probable that the birth chart of the husband is also engaged in a bad cycle. There will be a few case studies on "weak self with lots of wealth" later in this book.

Aiding the Husband (幫夫命)

Marrying into a rich family is certainly no guarantee to happiness, but what if a person's Four Pillars chart has the cosmic energy that is in favour of helping the husband succeed? About 30 years ago, many women were curious about whether they would be able to help their husband prosper after marriage. Even today, I am often asked this same question. The most ideal trait to look for is the wealth in the woman's Four Pillars chart. Remember that wealth in a chart feeds the Officer (controlling element). For example, earth would be the wealth of a wood self element; as a result, the earth would feed and support the metal (officer) in the birth chart. Whether the wealth is beneficial or not makes a difference. In cases where the self element is weak while being surrounded by the wealth element, the person's marriage life will take a downturn if this person encounters the officer/controlling element cycle. The controlling element is suddenly strengthened and women who are married may be abused by their spouse.

From my experience and practical applications of analyzing Four Pillars, it is safe to say that a woman who has a strong self with a lot of wealth can help the husband prosper once she encounters the controlling element cycle. Utilizing wealth to support the officer is auspicious in the case of a strong self. Even if she is in a wealth cycle, the husband can stand to benefit tremendously in his career and endeavours. On the other hand, if a woman possesses a weak self, it does not mean that the woman will lead a life of misfortunes. The Four Pillars chart of a woman who has resources that aid the self can stand to benefit the spouse as well. If she encounters an officer/controlling element cycle, the cycle can feed the resource and in turn, the resource can disperse the energy of the officer and feed the self. Charts like this can produce many benefits to the husband.

Since the key ingredient to having a successful husband in a female's chart is the strength of the controlling element, focus should be primarily placed upon that element first if clients are interested in learning about it. Women who possess a weak controlling element do not always mean that they would have a weak husband. If the female was to get married within a period where the controlling or wealth element comes into the luck cycle, the female's cosmic energy can indirectly support the husband. Charts having many of the same elements as the self can pose relationship issues due to possible competitions between these same elements and the self for the husband. Simply put—

the chance of the husband involving in extramarital affairs are high. These elements can be contained as long as there are controlling elements with enough strength in the right season. They can also be contained if there are output elements feeding the wealth element. Similarly, the wealth elements come to the aid of the controlling elements. This may seem complicated, but if a birth system is logically evaluated, the strength of the controlling element can be determined. Having determined the strength of the controlling element provides the Four Pillars practitioners with an understanding of how each of the luck cycles can harm or support the spouse.

Rivalry in the Chart Results in Hurting the Husband? (羊刃劫旺 剋夫?)

Rivalry, found when the same element appears simultaneously in the birth chart, more often or not have detrimental effects within a relationship. The issue with rivalries is that they are constantly lurking near the self, waiting to take what is most precious, whether it is money or relationship. If you refer back to the key rival table of each of the elements, having the key rival present in the birth system can cause anxiety and unrest. Most often, the Yang self element encountering the cardinal symbol would feel a greater effect. For example, for a Yang Fire (丙) self with another Horse (午) in the system, moving into a fire cycle can create greater discomfort as more fire battles with the self. The exception is that if the self is classified as Dominant, this person may actually reap more benefits than harm from the additional fire. Birth systems that want to become dominant but cannot tend to suffer a great deal of distress in their relationship. When they are in need of help, assistance may not be readily available for them. These people tend to be competitive and are able to withstand problems of varying degrees throughout their lives. They usually find a way to get through issues on their own. Weak selves, on the other hand, do not mind having a rivalry in their birth chart since they are in need of help in strengthening themselves.

Below is an example of a rivalry sitting in the branch beneath the day stem.

Hour	Day	Month	Year
癸 Yin Water	丙 Yang Fire	辛 Yin Metal	庚 Yang Metal
巳 Snake	午 Horse	巳 Snake	子 Rat

Example taken from: 王姿尹, 八字實錄, 女命專論 *(P.68)*

This person is a Yang Fire (丙) self born in the beginning of the summer. The heat is intensified by the Horse (午) beneath the self as the the birth hour moves near the middle of the day. Although this chart is hot, it cannot become a dominant fire due to the water and metal that surrounds the self. The direct officer, represented by the Rat (子), is located quite far from the self and is easily subjected to the attack of the Horse (午) in the branch. Fortunately, the Snake (巳) in the month branch is separating the two. Having the direct officer in the branch is more favourable than having it exposed in the stems. Unfortunately for her, she also has a Yin Water (癸) found in the stems, which can easily be taken away. This birth system is better served with the water as it can provide the cooling for the self while curbing the uninvited attacks from the hidden fire in the branches. Both her controlling officer and the wealth elements are vulnerable to the rivalry. If she were to encounter more fire in her luck cycle, mishaps will definitely occur. Let us now take a look at the luck cycle.

35	25	15	5
丁 Yin Fire	戊 Yang Earth	己 Yin Earth	庚 Yang Metal
丑 Ox	寅 Tiger	卯 Rabbit	辰 Dragon

Things look bleak for her after evaluating her luck cycle. Problems began occurring in her late 20s as the Tiger (寅) entered the picture. The Tiger (寅) combines with the Horse (午) in the spouse palace to empower the rivalry. During this period, she began to run into financial difficulties with her husband and they started borrowing money from many different sources. With two of her wealth elements, the Yin and Yang metals, exposed in the stems, money issues would come to the forefront when she runs into a bad cycle. Then came the Yin Fire (丁) cycle and the problems compounded as people began to sue them for their debts. The husband decided to free himself of the situation and filed for a divorce. Although the husband left his wife, he still provided partial monetary support to her and hoped to reunite with her one day. It is quite unfortunate that this couple did not have their birth chart evaluated. With prior knowledge to problems that can transpire in their life, those problems could have been avoided.

This example seems to be much more forgiving. Fortunately, she does not possess too much resource elements that may overpower the self. What would happen if the self had resources in the chart in addition to the rivalries? The circumstances can worsen for a marriage life and the next example illustrates the calamity.

Hour	Day	Month	Year
己 Yin Earth	戊 Yang Earth	乙 Yin Wood	丁 Yin Fire
未 Goat	子 Rat	巳 Snake	未 Goat

Example taken from: 王姿尹, 八字實錄, 女命專論 *(P.70)*

This female is a Yang Earth (戊) born in the month of the Snake (巳). Many earth symbols are both hidden and present in the stem surrounding the self but the Rat (子) in the day branch. This, of course, keeps the soil wet and prevents the earth from becoming dominant. In addition, the Yin Wood (乙) found in the month stem is controlling and loosening the earth like a plant with extending roots. Similar to the previous example, the self element cannot be strong enough to be dominant. The other earth in the birth system must be curbed and controlled by the wood in order to avoid a rivalry battle. The next item to evaluate would be her luck cycle.

35	25	15	5
己 Yin Earth	戊 Yang Earth	丁 Yin Fire	丙 Yang Fire
酉 Rooster	申 Monkey	未 Goat	午 Horse

By looking at her luck cycle, the fire and earth created more trouble in her life. This person was married once in her early 20s and remarried at the age of about 30 during the Yang Earth cycle. Three months into her marriage, her husband found a few medical receipts and payments for her former spouse. He immediately filed for a divorce. After her divorce, she returned to the former in-laws and resided with them. Her mental health was very unstable due to the amount of fire and earth cycles that she had been through.

The examples presented in this section explains what rivalries can do if the self cannot follow a leading or dominant flow in the chart. This is the brutal reality of having key rivals in the chart. Rivalries in the system are difficult to avoid. The I Ching tells us that it is always better to yield to difficult situations rather than combat against it. By following some of the rules in the I Ching, many tragedies can be avoided. Avoiding conflict is the best way to avert danger. Unfortunately, there are always birth charts that possess rivalries, leading to conflicts. The conflicts of the rivalries can translate into conflicts for spouse, money or other valuable possessions in one's life. Trying to remove oneself from competition would create less conflict in life.

Let's take a look at one exception. In the next example, the rivals have no strength whatsoever to fight the self element. The self element surrenders to the leading flow and enjoys a harmonious life.

Hour	Day	Month	Year
乙 Yin Wood	乙 Yin Wood	乙 Yin Wood	辛 Yin Metal
酉 Rooster	巳 Snake	未 Goat	丑 Ox

Example taken from: 王姿尹, 八字實錄, 女命專論 *(P.77)*

This female is a Yin Wood (乙), born near the end of the summer when the energy of wood is dissipating. Although there are two Yin Woods (乙) flanking both sides of the self, the two other rivals don't have the power to fight with the self. Looking at the branches, there is a complete metal alliance where the Rooster (酉), Snake (巳) and Ox (丑) unite. In the Year stem, the Yin Metal (辛) is located next to the rivalry, constantly cutting it and preventing it from growing. Her chart surrenders to the controlling element—which is metal. The metal flow of her birth chart can be confirmed by understanding how her husband had prospered after she was married. Since birth, she has been blessed with more than 30 years of metal and earth cycles and have not ran into any major difficulties in life. Cosmic systems that surrender to the leading flow with the cycles supporting the flow tend to ward off any rivals in their birth chart. Empowering the self with the same element—wood in this case—can lead to misfortunes.

Women with rivalries found within a strong birth system can still enjoy a wonderful marriage. Unlike weak charts, a chart classified as strong can easily withstand the control of the controlling element. Rivalries are often known to create discomfort to a person when they move into a wealth cycle. As long as there are controlling elements in a birth system, the controlling element can prevent the rivalry from fighting the self for the wealth. In this sense, the controlling element can serve as a security guard to protect the wealth. Within this process, the wealth can also support the controlling element. Also, it is not always true that rivalries would create problems within a birth chart. As long as the rivalries are being monitored and controlled by the controlling element, the cosmic disorder can be kept in check.

"HURTING HUSBAND, OR IN CHINESE '剋夫'"

This is a commonly used term amongst women in Hong Kong when they meet with Chinese astrologers. They would want to know whether they can help their husband, or hurt their husband. More than 95% of my female customers in China and Hong Kong would ask me, 'do I have a hurting husband life?' The degree and level of how one can hurt the husband depends on many factors within the birth chart. Some may accept this reality and enjoy living alone.

Indirect Resource and the Eating God (論梟神奪食)

The combination of the Indirect Resource and the Eating God can be problematic if found in the birth chart. Remember that both of them are of the same polarity: if one of them is Yang, the other is Yang, if one is Yin, the other is Yin. Since the Eating God is of the output element, indirect resources can damage the output element, preventing the output from having the ability to express itself. For example, a Yin Earth (己) self, the Yin Metal (辛) would be the Eating God (output) of the self while the Yin Fire (丁) would be the Indirect Resource. In this situation, the Yin Fire (丁) would damage the output, Yin Metal (辛), by constantly burning it with a light flame. On the other hand, the Direct Resource, Yang Fire (丙) would not pose damages to the Yin Metal (辛) since it combines with the Yin Metal (辛). In addition, the Yang Fire (丙) is like the sun; it would shed its sunlight onto the metal by providing it with warmth and brilliance, rather than burning it.

So how does this analogy translate into real life? Here is another story. Uncle Tom is a nice and pleasant person who enjoys helping out his neighbours whenever they decide to look for him. One day, Uncle Bob decided to ask Tom for assistance to fix a leak in an old roof. Uncle Bob not only knew he could take advantage of the free labour, but he also had other ideas brewing in his mind, aside from the free assistance. Uncle Bob told Tom to climb onto the roof for an inspection. When Tom did so, the roof started to tremble and he heard a few snaps and cracks. To his surprise, the roof started to cave in. The next door neighbour, John was watching from afar and noticed the collapse and went over to Bob's house. Bob was furious and told Tom to pay for the damages. John came by and asked what had happened. Bob said "Tom just took apart my roof! I just asked him to take a look and he damaged the entire roof!" Tom, the weak and innocent, knowing that he was only evaluating the roof was speechless. Bob told Tom to pay for the damages or be ready to go to court. John saw what had happened and was willing to be a witness. Unfortunately for Tom, he was setup by Bob and he had to pay for all the damages on the roof. Little did he know that Bob already knew that he needed a new roof but was not willing to pay for his own expenses, so he took advantage of Tom's good will.

This is an example of what can happen when the Indirect Resource contains the Eating God (output element). Tom did not have the courage to speak up for himself. These people think or believe that by being speechless, they are innocent by default. They tend to attract people who are constantly waiting to take advantage of them. If there is an opportunity to take advantage of them, bad events will transpire. Their enemies strike when the opening is there. The end result may be just as devastating as having rivalries in a birth chart. As long as the birth system does not encounter more indirect resource, bad events may not transpire. On the other hand, if the birth system possesses Indirect Wealth, the Indirect Wealth can prevent the Indirect Resource from damaging the output element. Since wealth controls resources, it can deflect scheming individuals like Uncle Bob away from getting too close. Obviously, Bob has been looking for opportunities to lure Tom into this predicament. Had Uncle Tom been in an Indirect Wealth cycle, Bob will not have the opportunity to make his move.

Most often, women are more vulnerable to the Indirect Resource than men. Why? Females classified as being strong tend to be more confident in themselves. Their overconfidence makes them think aggressively, rather than shielding themselves from any pitfalls or dangers. A strong self chart that does not favour Indirect Resources often attracts bad people in their lives. Strong self women are often independent, but during bad cycles, their independent nature can lead to uninvited attacks. When they are cosmically attacked by the Indirect Resources, their mental state can become very unstable. This situation can be compounded by the addition of the controlling element, which would feed the Indirect Resources. The nature of these attacks can involve rape and sexual abuse. The structure of these birth systems is different from females who have a mix of Officers and Seven Killings without the presence of Indirect Resources. In the latter case, they tend to attract men who are actually interested in marrying them, instead of a pull towards short term encounters. Below is an example of what can transpire with a female who has an abundant amount of Indirect Resources.

Hour	Day	Month	Year
己 Yin Earth	辛 Yin Metal	辛 Yin Metal	己 Yin Earth
亥 Pig	丑 Ox	未 Goat	丑 Ox

40	30	20	10
乙 Yin Wood	甲 Yang Wood	癸 Yin Water	壬 Yang Water
亥 Pig	戌 Dog	酉 Rooster	申 Monkey

Example taken from: 王姿尹, 八字實錄, 女命專論 *(P.134)*

It is obvious that this birth chart has no shortage of Indirect Resources. The self is a Yin Metal (辛) surrounded by Yin Earth (己), while the month stem presents another Yin Metal (辛) which is the rivalry. The Indirect Resource of Yin Water (癸) is found in the Ox (丑). During the Rooster (酉) luck cycle, at the age of about 28, it was the year of the Yin Fire Snake (丁巳). There was a possibility of having her boyfriend taken away from her by another person. It was at this time that she had a mental breakdown and had to go to the hospital. She was not able to remember her friends. To make matters worse, her friends betrayed her during the time she was ill. Her bad luck can be attributed to the bad cycle that she was in. The additional metal coming from the Rooster (酉) attracted bad energy into her life. The next cycle was the Yang Wood (甲), also the Direct Wealth to the self in her case. Unfortunately, the wealth was not able to suppress the earth around the birth system due to the combination of the Yin Earth (己) and the Yang Wood (甲) creating more earth into the system. It was another period of suffering until she reached the age of 40. Her life became better as the Yin Wood (乙), the Indirect Wealth, was able to neutralize the earth surrounding her birth system. Every aspect of her life became smooth including her mental state. This example illustrates the tragedy that can transpire to a person where there is a heavy amount of Indirect Resources uncontrolled in the birth system. Once the Indirect Resources were subjected to the control of the Indirect Wealth element, the cosmic instability was no longer present.

Again, going back to a remedy for the Indirect Resource, a birth system possessing the Indirect Resource and the Eating God can avoid invited attacks as long as the Indirect Wealth is present. Since the Indirect Wealth controls the Indirect Resource, the Indirect Resource has no means to damage the Eating God. Think of it this way: if there are enemies lurking around a female, they would observe the situation and see if her voice or opinion has any authority. With a group of supporters defending the female, the enemies would think twice prior to attacking. In addition, the group of supporters and authorities may already know who the enemies are so it would be difficult for the female to become vulnerable to attacks; that is the power of the Indirect Wealth. Direct Wealth can also serve to protect the self—but to a lesser degree.

Hurting Officer Hurts the Husband? (傷官剋夫?)

It is often said in many classic Four Pillars texts that women with birth systems that have too many output elements can hurt the credibility and stability of the husband. This is even more evident if the output element is the Hurting Officer. Rest assured, this is not always the case—it depends on whether the self is strong or weak. Charts surrendering to the output element are one of the exceptions. There are some who may have wealth in the system to disperse the energy of the output element; And as the wealth dissolves the output element, it can support the controlling element in the chart. On the other hand, there are some who may decide to never marry. Females with birth systems composed of a strong Hurting Officer are usually very meticulous when it comes to their choice of marriage partners. Since a useful Hurting Officer in a person's system represents intelligence and expression, these people set higher standards for the type of partner that they want. The following example is the birth system of a famous East Asian female singer, Teresa Teng (鄧麗君), born on January 29, 1952, hour of the Dragon in Taiwan.

Hour	Day	Month	Year
庚 Yang Metal	庚 Yang Metal	癸 Yin Water	壬 Yang Water
辰 Dragon	辰 Dragon	丑 Ox	辰 Dragon

38	28	18	8
己 Yin Earth	庚 Yang Metal	辛 Yin Metal	壬 Yang Water
酉 Rooster	戌 Dog	亥 Pig	子 Rat

By looking at her birth system, it is apparent that there is a lot of water with sufficient wet earth to support the Yang Metal (庚) self. Her Four Pillars chart looks very pure from an elemental perspective: the flow of metal and water is smooth. The water, her output element, allows her to claim fame with ease and express herself with clarity. Water is her most favourable element and since she was born in the winter, when water is exceptionally strong. The use of her voice as a singer brought her fame and glory in throughout Asia. She is a talented artist, as the output element in her chart would symbolize. There is an absence of fire throughout her chart. Even if she had encountered fire in her luck and annual cycles, it can easily be dashed away by the amount of water that she possessed in her system.

Finding a suitable partner was very difficult for her. Life can be strange sometimes: the more we desire something, the harder it is to obtain it. Teresa's birth system has the absence of fire, the controlling element for her system, which made it difficult for her to meet someone suitable. In addition, the strength of her Hurting Officer made her set higher standards in terms of who she was willing to be with. Some may conclude that she would marry more than once because of the reappearance of her spouse palace (day branch) symbol three times in her birth system. The Dragon (辰) in her day branch is found also in the year and the hour branches. With all the metal and water in her birth chart, and being born in the winter month of the Ox (丑), her birth system lacks the existence of fire. The problem with the injection of fire into her system is that it can cause health issues to her throat. Recall from chapter one that metal in Four Pillars represents the throat, lungs and tongue. Additional fire encountered in the luck or annual cycle can create conflicts between the water, metal and fire, leading to misfortunes on her part.

Turning to her luck cycle, she had enjoyed more than twenty years of water flow in her luck cycle, which provided her with the fame and fortune throughout East Asia. The metal within her birth system and in the luck cycle created a competitive environment for her—a situation that forced the young singer to work hard. In order to identify her flow, we can focus on the pure water element of the Rat (子) and observe what had happened during the Rat (子) cycle. Her first claim to fame came in 1968, the year of the Monkey (申), when her performance on a popular Taiwanese music TV show led to a record contract. The Rat (子) in her luck cycle united the Monkey (申) year with her Dragon (辰) in the day branch to form a complete water trio. Since water provides her with a harmonious flow, anything that impedes or pollutes her system, which would be wet or hard earth, can cause misfortunes.

On May 8, 1995, Teresa had died from a severe respiratory attack while vacationing in Thailand. There are a few factors that could have triggered this unfortunate event. First, 1995 was the year of the Yin Wood Pig (乙亥), a time when Teresa's birth system had two Yang Metals (庚) competing for the Yin Wood (乙). From perspective of natural cosmic laws, this contention led to a discomfort that jeopardized her health. Second, she was in the Yin Earth (己) cycle and the Yin Earth (己) is composed of wet and

soggy materials that polluted her birth system. Vacationing in the heat of the summer in Thailand deteriorated her condition as her cosmic system dislikes fire and hot weather. The combination of the negative factors resulted in her tragic death. Can this incident be avoided? If she understood the leading flow of her birth system, she may have been able to avoid the tragedy. Travelling during hot summer months should have been ill-advised in her case, especially when she has a history suffering from asthma. Perhaps she would have lived longer had she understood the nature of cosmic flow.

Theoretically speaking, women who are weak selves with strong output elements in the birth system, especially if it is the Hurting Officer, often work hard and spend tremendous effort in earning a living. They need to make money to support their spouse. By working hard and expending the energy, they can fight off the heavy amount of the output that they possess. If the energy is not spent, however, the output element can easily cause relationship issues within the house. On the other hand, a woman with a strong self and a Hurting Officer can get by without expending as much energy, because the man of the household can adopt the role of being the sole breadwinner.

Hurting Officer Attacking the Direct Officer (傷官見官, 為禍百端)

If the hurting officer sees a direct officer in their annual cycle, they tend to hurt others indirectly. Their intentions and actions can be damaging to all the people involved, including themselves. Here is a story that can shed light onto this theory. Uncle Jim was laid off from Company XZY and he was bitter. In order to free himself of his anger, he sent an anonymous email ridiculing the boss and his treatment of employees. It was obvious to the executives in the company that Uncle Jim sent off the email. His email was also traced by Mr. Void, the network administrator of the company. Since he was associated with Robert, who was currently working for the company, Robert was given a warning despite his innocence, and was shafted of a pay raise. At the end of the entire episode, Uncle Jim pretends to be the blameless one. To keep a long story short, whenever birth systems with Hurting Officers encounter a Direct Officer in the luck cycle, they may do something out of line and indirectly hurt others in the process. Having both Direct Officers and Hurting Officers in the chart can be even more troublesome as the two elements can hurt others on a consistent basis.

In 2007, I was presented with a female's birth chart by the name of Angela. From an initial reading, I noticed that this was not an ordinary birth system, since the self was surrounded heavily by earth elements.

Hour	Day	Month	Year
癸 Yin Water	戊 Yang Earth	辛 Yin Metal	己 Yin Earth
丑 Ox	戌 Dog	未 Goat	未 Goat

43	33	23	13	3
丙 Yang Fire	乙 Yin Wood	甲 Yang Wood	癸 Yin Water	壬 Yang Water
子 Rat	亥 Pig	戌 Dog	酉 Rooster	申 Monkey

Angela's mother came to me and asked me about her daughter's character and wanted to know more about her future. From a logical standpoint, this Four Pillars chart has a Yang Earth (戊) self born in late summer, when the weather still considered hot. Angela was sitting on top of four earth elements, as represented by the Dog (戌), Ox (丑), and Goat (未) in the branches. In addition, there was another Yin Earth (己) found in the stem. The overall makeup of this birth chart made me believe that this can be classified as a Fake Dominant self. The reason why it is classified as a Fake Dominant self was because of the Yin Water (癸) in the hour stem and the Yin Metal (辛) in the month stem. The biggest issue with her birth chart is that the Yin Metal (辛) in the month stem is constantly cutting the Yin Wood (乙) hidden in the two Goats (未).

This is a good example of the Hurting Officer attacking the Direct Officer. She is obviously self-centered and very selfish. She would do many things to hurt others without taking any blame or guilt. It is quite often that she would back stab and cause grief within the household. She enjoys spreading rumours and lies to disrupt order while hoping to benefit from the confusion and disagreements. Weakening the psyche of others is the key to her game. Unfortunately, her mind games are easily discovered and she would act innocent throughout the entire episode. This sort of event usually transpires whenever the Direct Officer is under attack. Like a country with its leaders and government in disarray without order and control, the country would often end up in chaotic turmoil. The greater the disorder, the better it is for a new de facto government to take control of the country through a well-timed rebellion. The worst part about the Direct Officer being controlled by the Hurting Officer within a birth system is that these people do not even know what their goal or purpose is in creating such disorders. They just want others to suffer and become miserable.

The other problem in her birth chart lies in the day pillar where the Yang Earth Dog (戊戌) is considered a bossy pillar (explained later). When a bossy day pillar experiences a clash, the probability of injuries or illnesses is high. For this example, she experienced pneumonia in the year of the Yang Metal Dragon (庚辰) in 2000 and was hospitalized. Prior to that year, she had just stolen her sister's boyfriend for the sake of competition. That was another example of the Hurting Officer attacking the Direct Officer in 1999. The Rabbit (卯) in 1999 was in conflict with the Hurting Officer (Yin Metal) of her birth chart. After enjoying the misery of her sister, she had moved on and left her boyfriend in 2000. This is a result of the Dragon (辰) and the Dog (戌) clash.

This female, being classified as a 'Fake Dominant Self', has little hope of finding a spouse that meets her requirements. This can be seen in 'Fake Dominant Selves.' They must be willing to accept a weaker partner or someone who is willing to obey her orders. These types of people always think they are better than everyone else and deserve the best. Angela is constantly comparing herself with others. It is very difficult for people who are classified as a 'Fake Dominant Self' to be satisfied with what they have. This is not a problem in life as long as these people do not harm others to achieve their objectives. With the Hurting Officer in Angela's month stem, it makes her very ambitious and cunning; she would hurt others to achieve her goals. As of the writing of this book, she has just been married to a man who can be classified as a 'Weak Self with Lots of Wealth.' Even though she is married, she will still be on the look out for other men.

"FAKE VS REAL (DOMINANT SELF)"

The difference between 'Fake' and 'Real' in Four Pillars is like owning a real Louis Vuitton bag vs a replica. People who are classified as 'Fake' do not mean that they are pretentious in real life. They just want to belong in the category of Dominant. By being dominant, they are like a powerful king or queen commanding their soldiers. By being classified as Fake Dominant, when they encounter bad cycles, they would try to attain their goals in whichever way they can even if it means hurting others.

Mixed of Officer and Seven Killings (官殺混雜)

Females with birth systems possessing both the Direct Officer and Seven Killings in the stem may engage in activities that are against the social norms of society. In good cycles, they would stand up for a good cause and may attempt to change social rules. These people would have opportunities to get involved in politics or fight for women's rights. During bad cycles, they may take an extreme approach and entangle themselves in illegal activities; such activities may include taking drugs and prostitution. Many famous porn actresses possess charts where they would want to surrender to the flow of the controlling element but fail to do so. The flow is considered to be volatile as they are constantly being thwarted by certain elements in the birth system, and as a result, they may engage in unlawful activities or activities that are unpleasing to the eyes of the public. They also believe that they can be above the law.

There are, of course, exceptions to this theory as those with Guide and Guard stars can avoid a troubled life. The Hurting Officer and Eating God can control the mix of Officer and Seven Killings. In addition, resource elements by the side of the self element can disperse the strength of the controlling element. Below are examples of two porn actresses who have controlling elements in their birth charts, but cannot surrender to the controlling element.

Hour	Day	Month	Year
X	己 Yin Earth	乙 Yin Wood	丙 Yang Fire
X	卯 Rabbit	未 Goat	辰 Dragon

Hour	Day	Month	Year
X	甲 Yang Wood	庚 Yang Metal	癸 Yin Water
X	戌 Dog	申 Monkey	丑 Ox

Both examples illustrate a strong amount of controlling elements, but they cannot surrender to the flow due to the fact that the resource element is strongly present in the year stem. Unfortunately, the resource element is not by the side of the day stem to disperse the controlling element. Their lives can become much more volatile, leading to misfortunes, depending on the luck cycle that they are in. Both of these examples lack the output element. The output element can put these charts back in harmony as it can prevent the controlling element from causing instability in their birth systems.

Here is another example whereby this female wants to offer a new face to democracy and lead political rallies.

Hour	Day	Month	Year
X	庚 Yang Metal	丁 Yin Fire	丙 Yang Fire
X	申 Monkey	酉 Rooster	寅 Tiger

This Four Pillars chart is partially different than the first two as the self is strong. The Month and Year stems each present a Direct Officer and a Seven Killings respectively in the system. In addition, a pure rival is found buried in the month of the Rooster (酉). Such a powerful rivalry tends to create a volatile life. It was said that she worked in a nightclub as a summer job after breaking up with her boyfriend during her teenage years. There were sources claiming that she took money for physical intimacy—but she made it clear that she did not offer sex for money. The self can benefit from the controlling elements as the fire can curtail the rivalry in her birth chart. The previous two examples did not have the luxury of utilizing the controlling elements to control the rivalry.

For this theory of 'Mixed of Officers and Seven Killings' to hold true, the birth chart must be weak enough so that the self would not surrender or require extra resources to disperse the controlling element. If the resources are nowhere to be present, extreme problems and misery can occur. For the first two examples in this theory, they were fortunate that there are resources found where the controlling element did not take full advantage of the self element. Consequently, they were able to avoid illegal activities. For the third example, the rivalry causes her discomfort, leading to her move towards politics. A special note to highlight in the third example emphasizes the fact that both the self and the controlling elements are just as strong. She is at a greater advantage than the first two examples since the controlling elements can be utilized in this chart to curtail the rivals in the branches. On the other hand, the other two examples present a weak self where they are controlled and trapped by the Direct Officer and Seven Killings.

It is not all too bleak with mixed controlling elements in a birth system. Charts surrendering to the flow of the controlling elements with a luck cycle loyal to the flow are the most fortunate. Those who require a blend of controlling elements in their birth systems would also benefit from the control. Having one of the two controlling elements combined away can also solve the problem. Consider this scenario: the self element under the control of the Direct Officer and the Seven Killings. Evidently, it would create a "two-headed" pull without a specific officer taking the charge. This can lead to undisciplined behaviour in the public and society. If the birth system encounters an element that combines one of the controlling elements away, the self will finally have a "boss" or "manager". It is just like going to work with two managers, having two people to report to would make the job difficult and miserable because of the conflict in assigned priorities and tasks. Removing one of the bosses would allow one to prioritize work and properly schedule tasks.

Here is another porn actress who possesses a distorted birth system where there is no clearly defined flow. To compound the problem, there is a mixed of both the Yin and Yang controlling elements. She was born on February 22, 1982.

Hour	Day	Month	Year
X	丙 Yang Fire	壬 Yang Water	壬 Yang Water
X	子 Rat	寅 Tiger	戌 Dog

26	16	6
甲 Yang Wood	乙 Yin Wood	丙 Yang Fire
申 Monkey	酉 Rooster	戌 Dog

The Yang Fire (丙) self in this example cannot surrender to the amount of water in her system, nor can she become a dominant fire self even with the fire combination between the Tiger (寅) and the Dog (戌). Her system is constantly being frustrated by the conflict between fire and water. One of the ways to quell the water is to use earth. Unfortunately, her luck cycle does not present much earth early in her life. Another way for the water and fire conflict to be stopped is through the use of wood. The wood in the Tiger (寅) had no strength as it is combined by the Dog (戌) to form fire. Her luck cycle needs to move towards the spring, meaning the Tiger (寅), Rabbit (卯) and Dragon (辰), which would bring about harmony between the fire and water in her chart.

She grew up with divorced parents and had dropped out of high school at the age of 15. At the age of 19, she was introduced to a porn director and accepted an offer to become a porn actress. Her cosmic system basically lost a sense of direction; with the mix of controlling elements, she became easily accessible for men. From a cosmic point of view, she had multiple bosses yet these bosses were only there to use and abuse her. Generally speaking, this person can belong on any part of the line graph between strong and weak but may never have a chance to become 'Feeble' or 'Dominant'.

Overly Distorted System:
Lost of direction with a mix
of controlling elements.

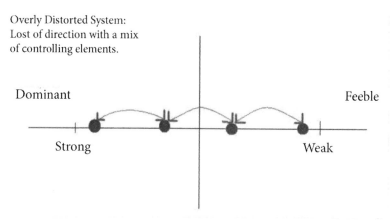

Since these people usually belong in between the 'Strong' and 'Weak' area on the line graph, there are two elements that can prevent problems from occurring. For a strong self with lots of controlling elements, like the most recent example, if they encounter the output element in the luck cycle, the multiple controlling elements lose its strength. On the other hand, weak selves require the aid of resources, which can strengthen the self and weaken the controlling element. Both the resource and output element has its own advantages, depending on the degree of strength the self element possesses.

Greed for Wealth Harming Resources (貪財壞印)

Before moving on to more charts and analyses, I would like to talk more about wealth and its influence on birth charts. Wealth throughout mankind has created disharmony from a micro to a macro level. Many of the wars throughout history were about disputes over territory, and such territorial disputes have come with monetary gains. The Japanese in World War II expanded throughout Asia in search of resources. Military expansions have led to brutality and hardships for those who are involved. Dating back to China's warring period, for those who are familiar with the Three Kingdoms, Cao Cao's expansion and greed led to his failure at the Battle of the Red Cliff. Hitler's need for oil and resources in the Caucuses region led to the failure of his army in taking Moscow and Stalingrad. He had diverted some of his divisions to focus more on the wealth of the Caucuses region and depleted the front line of sufficient troops to win the war in Stalingrad. Hitler's breech of the Nazi-Soviet Non-Aggression pact can also be related to the "Greed for Wealth Harming Resources". The Soviet had a neutral stance towards the Nazi regime and vowed never to get involved in Germany's invasion of Poland. Dragging the Soviets into World War II brought about a two-front war where Germany had very little hope in winning. Had the Germans allied with the Soviets, they may have received supplies and ammunition to support the war on the Western Front. It may have led to the defeat of the British and French.

Stories can be told from reading a Four Pillars chart and the stories can be related to the demise of political leaders who have personal agendas. The hunger and greed for wealth by individuals in the society has led to misfortunes. The wealth element within the Four Pillars of Destiny can also create disharmony within individual birth systems. Greed, laziness, and vanity are characteristics that often lead to mishaps. It is not always a 'money-making' period when one encounters the wealth element. The entire structure of the birth chart and flow must be evaluated first prior to making any judgements about the wealth element. The theory "Greed for Wealth Harming Resources" is sometimes used in Chinese classical texts. Trying to explain and reading it through a Four Pillars chart can be quite difficult. Here is another story that can clarify how this theory can be applied.

Peter is interested in making money from stocks. So Peter decides to look for a stock broker. Peter meets a stock broker (Johnson) and asks for advice. Johnson presents Peter with two types of stocks. The first stock, XYZ, has a lower return, yet the stock is less risky with limited volatility. On the other hand, the second stock is an oil services company, ABC, which is more volatile with higher risk but greater returns. It is common for high risk stocks to come with greater rewards. Peter decides to put money into XYZ with less risk. One week later, XYZ rises 10% on an upbeat earnings report while ABC has yet to move. Peter calls up Johnson and says "I knew XYZ was a better investment, I don't need investment advice." Two weeks later, ABC explodes and goes up 40% because of sudden rise in oil prices. Peter suddenly becomes furious with Johnson and tells him, "I wanted to buy ABC all along but you talked me into buying XYZ." Johnson felt disgusted as he only presented Peter with the risk reward analysis of the stocks. A month has passed and Peter approached Johnson for more stock tips. Johnson replied on the phone and said, "since you are so good at predicting the movement of stocks, why do you need my advice? You can go buy a stock of your choice and make 40% gains within two weeks if you wanted to. I don't think I am capable of satisfying your requirements." This is how the theory "Greed for Wealth Harming Resources" works.

Before crossing a bridge, such individuals would burn their bridges, cutting off others—and at times, their own—opportunity to get to the other side. The wealth element must be an unwanted element in the birth chart in order to satisfy the criteria of this theory. The level and degree of harm done to the resources depends on the strength of the wealth element. Weak selves relying on resources for assistance would not want to encounter a wealth cycle. Here is an example from a five element perspective. The resources for a Yang Wood self would be water and the wealth element would be earth. Again, earth controls water, making a weak wood self lose the ability to utilize the resources. This theory is about how the wealth element can damage the resource element, which can also translate into the loss of wealth in real life. Let's take a look at a Four Pillars example.

In 2009, a lady by the name of Ada came to me for a Four Pillars consultation. From looking at the chart, Ada came across to me as a person who prioritizes money. Where there is money to be made, she would want to be part of it as long as hard work is not involved. Below is her Four Pillars chart.

Hour	Day	Month	Year
戊 Yang Earth	甲 Yang Wood	丁 Yin Fire	丙 Yang Fire
辰 Dragon	申 Monkey	酉 Rooster	申 Monkey

62	52	42	32	22	12	2
庚 Yang Metal	辛 Yin Metal	壬 Yang Water	癸 Yin Water	甲 Yang Wood	乙 Yin Wood	丙 Yang Fire
寅 Tiger	卯 Rabbit	辰 Dragon	巳 Snake	午 Horse	未 Goat	申 Monkey

Ada is a Yang Wood (甲) self born in the month of the Rooster (酉). The next thing that we want to look for is to see whether there are any combinations found in the branches. For Ada's birth system, there is a half water combination between the Dragon (辰) and the Monkey (申). Although the Rooster (酉) and Monkey (申) wants to join together to form a directional/seasonal combination, it is not possible without the Dog (戌). As mentioned earlier, directional/seasonal combinations require the existence of all three symbols in order for the combination to form an elemental structure. With the half water combination seen in Ada's birth chart, the flow is led by both metal and water. This birth chart is feeble and follows the flow of water.

To confirm my assessment, I noticed that she had a long run of water and metal cycles, which began from the age of 32 all the way to age 57. Let us first look at the Snake (巳) cycle between her ages of 37 and 41. Although the Snake (巳) possesses fire and is considered a summer seasonal animal, it combines with the Rooster (酉) to form half a metal combination. The Snake would also want to combine with the Monkey (申) in her day and year branches. It was during that period that she had a divorce. This is explainable through the fight to combine amongst the elements within her branches. In addition, she has a duplicated spouse palace which is found in the year branch. When the symbol in the spouse palace is duplicated within the chart, it would increase the probability of re-marriage. Aside from her issues with marriage, she has had a long period of "easy money" due to the water found in her luck cycles. Ada has never worked for anyone in her life and the majority of her income still comes from her ex-husband. She was born in Hong Kong but travels to Vancouver quite often.

The problem with her chart comes from the Yang Earth (戊) in the hour stem. The earth prevents the water from reaching her, especially at times when she encounters more earth and fire. Her birth chart fits the category of "Greed for Wealth Harming Resources". When I was conducting a reading with Ada, she was constantly asking me about when she would become rich. Ada was a very sly person who would try to manipulate people for her own benefits; her manipulative tactics would often lead to a loss of friends. Ada called me one morning and mentioned to me about how opportunities came about for her after I had given her some Feng Shui advice. The unfortunate part is that she did not want to follow through with her opportunities as it was too much work to wake up in the morning at 10am. She said working six hours a day would interfere with her Mah-jong lifestyle.

Ada did not mention the reasons for her divorce, but it is not be difficult to decipher possibilities from evaluating her Four Pillars chart. The double Monkey (申) tends to create movements and instability in her life, especially since one of them resides in her day branch. Another reason is due to her

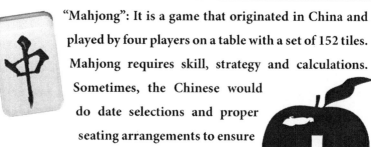

"Mahjong": It is a game that originated in China and played by four players on a table with a set of 152 tiles. Mahjong requires skill, strategy and calculations. Sometimes, the Chinese would do date selections and proper seating arrangements to ensure that they can capitalize with their energy to enhance their chances of winning.

attitude and laziness. From the analysis, this type of person often wants the easy way out in life. Charts being labelled with the theory of "Greed for Wealth Harming Resources" are often looking for ways to make money without contributing much work in return. They are not always considered dishonest people, nor do they have evil intentions. They enjoy bargaining for deals yet they do not see the big picture in collaboration and friendship. The best remedy for these people is to understand their birth chart and change their mentality. Feng Shui cannot change one's mentality and greed over money, it must come from the mind. They have to be honest with themselves.

2.
No Flow? Not A Problem

It is not possible that every birth chart has a leading flow. Some birth systems may require certain elements to ensure harmony. An element within a birth system may be critical in providing a stable growth cycle. The stable growth cycle can be brought about by one element feeding another in a cyclical pattern. Sometimes, three or even four elements would need to be involved. For example, a wood self can support the fire while the fire can then feed the earth and so forth. The birth system of the famous actress starring in the sitcom Friends, Jennifer Aniston, serves as the perfect example of where a single element is vital to ensure a smooth and stable growth. The growth and stability of the elements would ensure harmony in her cosmic system to bring about great success in her acting career. She was born on February 11, 1969 in the hour of the Pig (亥).

Jennifer Aniston is a Yin Fire (丁) self born in the month of the Tiger (寅). She is sitting on top of a Snake (巳) where it provides

Hour	Day	Month	Year
辛 Yin Metal	丁 Yin Fire	丙 Yang Fire	己 Yin Earth
亥 Pig	巳 Snake	寅 Tiger	酉 Rooster

48	38	28	18	8
辛 Yin Metal	庚 Yang Metal	己 Yin Earth	戊 Yang Earth	丁 Yin Fire
未 Goat	午 Horse	巳 Snake	辰 Dragon	卯 Rabbit

roots for the fire to burn brightly. The Yang Fire (丙) sitting in the month, representing the sun, seems to be overshadowing her brightness. The most impressive part about her birth system is the presence of the Yin Earth (己) sitting in the year stem as it is constantly weakening her rivalry, the Yang Fire (丙). This allows her Yin Fire (丁) to burn brightly without worrying about others overshadowing or outperforming her as the Yang Fire (丙) is entangled by the Yin earth (己) next to it. The Yin Earth (己) for Jennifer Aniston is known as the "Useful God", an element that is critical to her birth system, allowing her to succeed. In Chinese, it is called "用神" (Yong Shen). Do not confuse the "Useful God" with the "Ten Gods"—the Yin Earth (己) from a Ten Gods perspective is the Eating God of this birth chart.

"USEFUL GOD"

This term is used many times within this book. It is often used to define the favourable elements or specific symbols within a birth chart that is the most important. By determining where the Useful God is located, and its relations to the self element, more information can be extracted from a birth chart. (Book two will go into further details about the Useful God)

Although Jennifer does not belong to either a 'Dominant' or a 'Feeble' classification, the Yin Earth (己) is the key to her success as it curtailed the fire rivalry in her cosmic system. She belongs to the strong end of the spectrum where her birth system needs cooling from the earth. The graph below illustrates her position on the line where she is located near the edge of dominance—but unfortunately, she will never have a chance to cross the border. Even though she is placed near the border of dominance, she was still able to become famous whenever the luck cycle was in her favour.

Classification of Jennifer Aniston

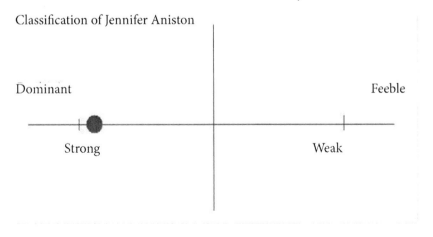

Dominant   Feeble

Strong   Weak

As it has been mentioned earlier, birth systems with a Hurting Officer or Eating God may harm the husband or create an unhappy marriage life. With the Yin Earth (己) as the most favourable element in her chart, it would prevent her from having a good relationship with her partner or spouse, since the Yin Earth (己) controls water. Water, being her controlling element, has no strength to control the self. According to the New York Times, during her marriage with Brad Pitt, Pitt was allegedly cheating on Aniston (The New York Times. Retrieved 2010-06-23). Whether it is true or not, there is a great possibility as she was in the Snake (巳) period of her life where the Yang Fire (丙) hidden in the Snake (巳) was acting as her rivalry. The fire rivalry had taken away her spouse within the birth system. In essence, the earth had brought her fame, but it was also her 'Achilles heel' in her cosmic system when it came to relationship matters.

Identifying and understanding the Ten Gods can provide Four Pillarspractitioners with more details about a person's birth chart. The qualities and characteristics of the Ten Gods and how it can be applied to one's success and failure would be explored with further details in my second book. The proper application of the Ten Gods cannot be possible within a Four Pillars chart analysis without classifying a birth chart. After a chart has been classified, practitioners can determine the usefulness of the specific God within the birth chart, and how they are affected by the luck cycle. In the next section, we will explore how 'Special Stars' influence a Four Pillars chart and what they mean.

"TEN GODS APPROACH "

Many people who are new to Four Pillars may be fearful of certain 'Gods' or 'Stars' in their chart because of the name. The 'Seven Killings' may not sound as good as 'Indirect Wealth'. When people think about 'Indirect' or 'Unconventional' Wealth, they may think about winning the lottery. Each of the 'Gods' have their advantages and disadvantages. Having a useful Seven Killings is much better than having Indirect Wealth that is always taken away. Think about this! The second book will explore the Ten Gods in greater detail.

Part Three

Special Stars

1.

When evaluating a Four Pillars chart, determining the cosmic flow and the energy makeup of the birth system is of vital importance. If the cosmic flow cannot be verified, an inaccurate consultation and recommendation can become damaging. Once the big picture of the birth system is evaluated and understood, there are other tools that a Four Pillars consultant can utilize to expand their interpretations. Those tools include the use of special stars. Below is a list of special stars that can be extrapolated out of a birth system, assuming that the stars are present in the Four Pillars chart.

As shown on the next page, the top row represents the self element while the left column represents the name of the star. The chart is primarily based out of the self element; therefore, references to the stars should only be made by using the self element. Of course, within the practice of Four Pillars, there are countless additional special stars that can be included into an analysis, but since the major focus of this book is on relationships, the stars presented in this section should provide enough information for the readings

	甲 Yang Wood	乙 Yin Wood	丙 Yang Fire	丁 Yin Fire	戊 Yang Earth	己 Yin Earth	庚 Yang Metal	辛 Yin Metal	壬 Yang Water	癸 Yin Water
Yang Guide	未	申	酉	亥	丑	子	丑	寅	卯	巳
Yin Guide	丑	子	亥	酉	未	申	未	午	巳	卯
Study	亥	午	寅	酉	申	酉	巳	子	申	卯
Scholar	巳	午	申	酉	寅	酉	亥	子	寅	卯
Red Light	午	午	寅	未	辰	辰	戌	酉	子	申

of this scope. Each of the stars serves different purposes and functions depending first and foremost on the cosmic flow and the positioning of the stars in a Four Pillars chart.

To keep things simple, the Yin Guide Star for a Yang Wood (甲) would be the Ox (丑) while the Yang Guide Star would be the Goat (未). What is the difference between a Yang and Yin Guide Star? From the name of the star itself, it points directly at a male and female, therefore, a Yang Guide Star tends to be male while the Yin Guide Star is female. In Lily Chung's book, "Easy Way to Harmony", she mentions that the Guide Star:

> "*Functions like an invisible hand guiding us to success and good fortune. To have such a star is to be extremely blessed; one usually succeeds easily. The person with a guide star is also likely to be kind and bright. The particular blessing given depends on the strength of the star. However, even a powerless (those in a void position) guide makes a happy and decent person. (Lily Chung, Easy Ways to Harmony, P.39)*"

'Void' star or position will be discussed later. Of course, if the Guide star is found in the spouse palace, accompanied by the correct flow, the spouse would be very useful and helpful in the success of one's career and ambitions. There is also a high possibility that one's spouse is well educated if the scholar or study star sits in the day branch. . Some people may wonder why they are not blessed with an "easy life", despite having a Guide star in their birth system. Remember that easy life, fame and fortune are all subjective. Here is another simple story illustrating what a 'Guide' is. One day, a young boy was playing by the park and one day, he dropped his toy into the well. As he tried to reach for the toy, he fell into the well. Fortunately for the little boy, an old worker who was mowing the lawn by the park saw him fall into the well. The old man rescued the little boy and quickly rushed him to the hospital. Eventually, despite the pain he initially suffered, the little boy recovered from the accident. The old man who saved the little boy served as his "Guide". Essentially, this "Guide" is more than a helping hand as he was able to help the boy get out of trouble.

We cannot create our own guides or sit still in hope of having "Guides" fall miraculously from the sky. Just because a Four Pillars chart may have guide stars, these guide stars do not magically appear at our front door. People with guides in their system would also need to work hard with an objective or goal in life. Think about this: how can guides be of any assistance to us if they do not know what we want? Just like the little boy falling into the well, the old man's objective was to save the little boy. Remember that the Guide star is there to provide a helping hand. Once a person has an established objective or goal in life, there will be others along the way to provide support and advice in terms of how to achieve those goals and objectives.

The scholar and study stars are also two auspicious stars and they are mainly focused on education. Education provides people with confidence and the ability to achieve great things in life. Having this star in your system puts you at a greater advantage in the academic field. Those who have the scholar star in the day branch tend to spend their entire life studying, going to school and most likely belong to the academic field. In general, having a scholar star in the birth system makes one focused in their education and these people are civilized – or at the very least – appears to be civilized. They are very artistic, intelligent, and focused on academic success. Even during bad cycles, they are well protected by the scholar star, which is similar to the guide star. Many successful scholars and professors possess the scholar star. The same can be said about having the study star in one's birth system. The study star, however, is not as powerful as the scholar star. The study star can quite possibly lead one to constant studying without great results, whereas the scholar star can bring about greater achievements in the academic field.

The "Red Light" star (also referred to as the Peach Blossom star) is a problematic star for those who possess it in their cosmic system. This star can lead to relationship troubles and instabilities. It also depends on where the star is located. Having such a star located in the day branch almost ensures that traumatizing relationship issues are bound to occur. The exception is that if this star is voided, the impact and effect of the "Red Light" star could be nullified. We can refer back to the Four Pillars chart of Tiger Woods here.

Hour	Day	Month	Year
丁 Yin Fire	庚 Yang Metal	戊 Yang Earth	乙 Yin Wood
亥 Pig	戌 Dog	子 Rat	卯 Rabbit

The "Peach Blossom" star of Tiger Woods is the Dog (戌) and it sits right in the day branch. There was trouble waiting to occur in his relationship life. In late 2009, it was allegedly reported that Tiger Woods had affairs and relationships with many different women. Many women approached the media to confess about their relationships with him in the past five years. These relationships were said to have been constantly occurring while he was already married. These issues are most likely caused by the "Red Light" star sitting in the day branch. The effect of the "Red Light" star is weaker if it is located in the year branch but the relationship troubles may occur much earlier in life. The month and hour branch can also pose problems to the self in terms of relationships if the star is found in either of those two positions in the birth chart. If the star is found in the luck cycle or for a specific year, relationship issues are possible during that period.

2.
Peach Blossom and Red Light Pillars

Aside from "Red Light" stars, there are also "Red Light" pillars. Here is a list of the "Red Light" Pillars.

甲午	乙未	丙寅	丁未	庚戌	辛未	癸未	辛酉

A list of the "Red Light" Pillars.

These "Red Light" pillars are considered to be much more powerful than the "Red Light" stars. They have to come as a complete pillar in order to affect one's relationship life negatively. Having the pillar located in the year would not have any effect but if the birth system has another "Red Light" pillar or star, the person can experience difficulties in finding a suitable partner. They also tend to worry more about their relationships, and as anxiety kicks in, these people can also become suicidal at times. They may have the tendency to use drugs or get into affairs to satisfy their sexual needs and desires.

The effect of the "Red Light" pillar can become the most detrimental if it is located in the day. People having the "Red Light" pillar in the day tend to have volatile mood swings and emotional setbacks within their relationship, which can affect their career and goals in life. The cosmic effect of the "Red Light" pillar affects the mind; therefore, the best solution is to relieve the mind from worries and anxieties. Thinking outside of the box, reading constructive materials and exercise are good remedies for those having the "Red Light" pillar in their birth system. The "Red Light" pillar can also be found in one's month or hour pillar, but the effects of the pillar is not as powerful as the day pillar. Again, just like the other stars, if one of the symbols in the pillars is a 'void' star, the effects of the "Red Light" pillar would be reduced. The next example presents a more comprehensive look at the "Red Light" pillars.

Life with a Red Light Star and Wealth, Money and Relationship

The 'Red Light' star can create relationship issues or unwanted desires. Those who have this star would place a greater emphasis on their relationship life and may be troubled by their relationship. Their careers may also be affected by their personal life as it is difficult for them to separate love from work. The 'Red Light' Star affects both men and women. The next example illustrates how a middle aged woman has desires for young men.

Hour	Day	Month	Year
庚 Yang Metal	丁 Yin Fire	己 Yin Earth	乙 Yin Wood
戌 Dog	丑 Ox	亥 Pig	酉 Rooster

Example taken from 知命四十年, 尤達人, *p.107*

The above chart presents a Yin Fire (丁) self born in the winter, where the fire energy is trapped or non-existent. In addition, the fire self is surrounded by metal as represented by the metal combination between the Ox (丑) and the Rooster (酉), and the two metals in the stems. The self almost surrenders to the wealth but the fire support lies in the Dog (戌) and the Pig (亥). The Dog (戌) possesses fire while the Pig has wood to support the fire. This can be classified as a "Weak Self With Lots of Wealth". The Useful God comes from the wood in the Pig (亥), therefore, if the self encounters the Rabbit (卯), she should be able to prosper from the cosmic combination.

In addition, the chart has two 'Red Light' pillars in the hour pillar and the year pillar. It is certain that this person will get into affairs or relationship issues. When she reached the Yang Water Tiger (壬寅) and Yin Water Rabbit (癸卯) cycles, she began making money as the Rabbit (卯) combined with the Pig (亥) to form a wood team to support the self. In addition, the Tiger (寅) strengthened the fire, and as a result, it led to a 20 year period of prosperity. The following cycle was the Yang Wood Dragon (甲辰) and the Yang Wood (甲) also supported the self leading to another period of prosperity. As she made money her desires turned towards younger men – an anomaly led by the two Red Light pillars. The Dragon (辰) also increased the likelihood of her involvement with men as the Rooster (酉) in the chart signifies the Peach Blossom of the Dragon (辰). This woman was involved in many relationships with younger men but she never chose to get married.

This example illustrates how a weak self can accumulate wealth by utilizing resources to aid the self. In addition, it showed the influence of the Red Light stars in her relationship life. Once wealth was amassed, a person with Red Light stars will have other desires and will get involved in love affairs with men of all ages.

Another group of pillars that can affect one's relationship life is the "Relationship" pillar. Below is a list of the "Relationship" pillar.

辛卯	壬辰	癸巳	丙午	丁未	戊申	壬戌	癸亥	丙子	辛酉	戊寅	丁丑

A list of the "Relationship" Pillars.

Lily Chung writes in her book, Easy Ways to Harmony (p.18), that:

> *"People having these pillars are likely to have problems with in-laws or with getting the right marital partner. They are more likely to encounter some odd marriages. The magnitude of the effect depends on the position and the number of such pillars one possesses. One of these as a day pillar is the worst. If you are trapped in a tangle of frequent, bitter fights with your in-laws or step children, you most likely have two or more such pillars, and one of them as the day pillar. What can you do? Try to detach yourself from the tangle. Knowing this truth saves you trouble of seeing a counsellor."*

Of course, there is no a guarantee that a relationship life will suffer if a birth system has one of these pillars in the day pillar. There are some cases where the spouse can become supportive as the day branch may very well serve as a key symbol to the leading flow of the birth chart. If problems exist with the in-laws, learn how to cope with the issues and accept the fact that the relationship will not be smooth. Avoid putting up a stand against the in-laws as it will often be a futile fight. Patience and tolerance can go a long way in pacifying the problems. Below is an example of the Relationship pillar sitting in the month pillar of French President, Nicolas Sarkozy.

Hour	Day	Month	Year
乙 Yin Wood	己 Yin Earth	丁 Yin Fire	甲 Yang Wood
亥 Pig	丑 Ox	丑 Ox	午 Horse

The Yin Fire Ox (丁丑) is found in the month pillar in his birth system. He has been married three times and this could be a result of the cosmic effect of the "Relationship" pillar. In addition, his spouse palace represented by the Ox (丑) in the day branch is also replicated in the month branch, hence, being married more than once for such a birth system is highly likely. Coincidentally, Carla Bruni, his wife, also possesses a "Relationship" pillar, as represented by the Yin Metal Rooster (酉). For Carla Bruni, the effects of this pillar are much greater since it is sitting in the day pillar.

Hour	Day	Month	Year
丁 Yin Fire	辛 Yin Metal	壬 Yang Water	丁 Yin Fire
酉 Rooster	酉 Rooster	子 Rat	未 Goat

For Carla Bruni, getting into odd relationships is a regular routine for her. She's been involved in a relationship with the following people: Louis Bertignac, Mick Jagger, Eric Clapton, Léos Carax, Charles Berling, Arno Klarsfeld, Vincent Perez, former French Prime Minister Laurent Fabius, Raphael Enthoven, and Nicolas Sarkozy (Source: Time Magazine). This is her take on it: "love lasts a long time, but burning desire would be two to three weeks." (BBC News)

2.

Void Stars

The "Relationship" pillar, just like the other stars can have its effects reduced or nullified by the Void Stars. So what are Void Stars and what are their effects? A list of Void Stars are shown on the next page.

To determine what the void stars are for a birth system, look at the self pillar only. We can use Sandra Bullock's birth system as an example.

Hour	Day	Month	Year
庚 Yang Metal	丙 Yang Fire	辛 Yin Metal	甲 Yang Wood
寅 Tiger	子 Rat	未 Goat	辰 Dragon

Since her day pillar is the Yang Fire Rat (丙子), search for the Yang Fire (丙) row in the Void Star chart, and search for the Yang Fire Rat (丙子) pillar. Once you have found the Yang Fire Rat (丙子) pillar, match it up with the two Void Signs on the bottom row. For Sandra Bullock, it is the Monkey (申) and the Rooster (酉). Since the Monkey (申) and the Rooster (酉) are her Void Stars, any positive attributes that these symbols may have possessed have been reduced, according to the laws of the Void Stars. Since it was determined earlier that Sandra Bullock needs to use metal and water, the Monkey (申) and Rooster (酉) still had a positive impact on her life. Why? The reason why both the Monkey (申) and Rooster (酉) benefited her career was because of its

	1	2	3	4	5	6
甲	甲子	甲戌	甲申	甲午	甲辰	甲寅
乙	乙丑	乙亥	乙酉	乙未	乙巳	乙卯
丙	丙寅	丙子	丙戌	丙申	丙午	丙辰
丁	丁卯	丁丑	丁亥	丁酉	丁未	丁巳
戊	戊辰	戊寅	戊子	戊戌	戊申	戊午
己	己巳	己卯	己丑	己亥	己酉	己未
庚	庚午	庚辰	庚寅	庚子	庚戌	庚申
辛	辛未	辛巳	辛卯	辛丑	辛亥	辛酉
壬	壬申	壬午	壬辰	壬寅	壬子	壬戌
癸	癸酉	癸未	癸巳	癸卯	癸丑	癸亥
Void	戌,亥	申,酉	午,未	辰,巳	寅,卯	子,丑

A list of the Void Stars

combinations with the branches in her birth system. The Monkey's (申) combination with the Rat (子) and the Dragon (辰) superseded the Void Star rule.
In addition, the Rooster (酉) has a harmonious combination with the Dragon
(辰), as found in her year branch.

From experience, I find that when the Void Stars are combined within
the birth system, the effects of the void are often nullified; it means the stars
are no longer voided.

Sandra Bullock's birth system illustrates that it is not always a bad sign
to have Void Stars or Signs, nor negative events always occur when there is a
clash. For example, the Ox (丑) in 2009 granted her an Academy Award as the
Best Female Actress when the Ox (丑) clashed with the Goat (未), weakening
the symbol that was blocking her water flow. Some Chinese texts do mention that if the Void Stars are a symbol of a Trio combination, Six harmonious
combination or the Directional combination, the positive impacts are magnified. This explanation may require more verification and testing. In the case of
Sandra Bullock, the Monkey (申) year did in fact give her a role in the movie
Crash (2004), which claimed three Oscars for its outstanding performance.

If the Void Stars are combined with a symbol that has an unfavourable
element for the birth system, the negative effects will be magnified. Having a
Void Star in the month branch can mean that the person may not have any
siblings, or their relationships with their siblings are usually not harmonious.
They may lack the support of their siblings. If the Void Sign is found in the day
branch or the controlling element for a female's birth system, finding a

good marriage partner can become difficult. Special stars like the scholar stars that are voided in one's birth system may nullify the positive effects of one's studies and educational capabilities. The Guide star on the other hand can still be effective as the Void Star cannot completely nullify its effects. A birth system possessing a voided "Red Light or Peach Blossom" star would reduce the negative effects that can hamper one's relationship life. In summary, Void Stars can show up in a luck cycle, annually, monthly or daily. Every birth system has two Void Signs. The most fortunate cases are the birth systems with Void Stars that cancel out the negative symbols so that harmful effects can be reduced.

The structure of the Four Pillars chart can also be evaluated using the Void Stars chart. If three of the four pillars are located in the same column, these people are considered very lucky (Easy Ways to Harmony, p.14. Lily Chung). Lily mentions that "these people are destined to quick wealth and fame without much effort. For example, we can look again at the birth chart of Princess Diana, born on July 1, 1961, Dog Hour.

Hour	Day	Month	Year
丙 Yang Fire	乙 Yin Wood	甲 Yang Wood	辛 Yin Metal
戌 Dog	未 Goat	午 Horse	丑 Ox

Her Year, Month and Day pillars are all found under the same column, in column 4 of the Void Star Chart. In addition to having three or all of the pillars in the same column, one must also be reminded that the cosmic flow can override such success and fortune. If the cosmic flow and luck cycles are not in one's favour, wealth and fame may not be able to come about. Fortunately for Princess Diana, her wood self element was never very often empowered by water and other wood elements in her luck cycle. As a result, she benefit from not only the fire flow that was leading her chart, but also by the combination of the flow pillars where she had three of the four pillars in the same column.

Trying to spot a birth system with three pillars located in the same column is a difficult task when confronted by a customer on the spot. It requires the recognition and memory of the patterns. Based on experience, I have noticed many people who have three or more pillars located in the same column to be very intelligent, knowledgeable, and successful. People who possess a chart classified as feeble accompanied by the special pattern, and the addition of the luck cycle going with the flow, are extremely powerful and intellectual. They have a high status in society and are usually well respected.

3.
Other Stars

The next table presents four different stars, the Romance, Mobility, Solitude and Anxiety stars. These stars are determined by using the Year branch in a birth system.

Year Branch	Romance	Mobility	Solitude (m/f)	Anxiety (m/f)
Rat 子	Rooster 酉	Tiger 寅	Tiger 寅, Dog 戌	Tiger 寅, Dog 戌
Ox 丑	Horse 午	Pig 亥	Tiger 寅, Dog 戌	Pig 亥, Rabbit 卯
Tiger 寅	Rabbit 卯	Monkey 申	Ox 丑, Snake 巳	Rat 子, Dragon 辰
Rabbit 卯	Rat 子	Snake 巳	Ox 丑, Snake 巳	Snake 巳, Ox 丑
Dragon 辰	Rooster 酉	Tiger 寅	Ox 丑, Snake 巳	Tiger 寅, Horse 午
Snake 巳	Horse 午	Pig 亥	Dragon 辰, Monkey 申	Rabbit 卯, Goat 未
Horse 午	Rabbit 卯	Monkey 申	Dragon 辰, Monkey 申	Dragon 辰, Monkey 申
Goat 未	Rat 子	Snake 巳	Dragon 辰, Monkey 申	Snake 巳, Rooster 酉
Monkey 申	Rooster 酉	Tiger 寅	Pig 亥, Goat 未	Horse 午, Dog 戌
Rooster 酉	Horse 午	Pig 亥	Pig 亥, Goat 未	Pig 亥, Goat 未
Dog 戌	Rabbit 卯	Monkey 申	Pig 亥, Goat 未	Rat 子, Monkey 申
Pig 亥	Rat 子	Snake 巳	Tiger 寅, Dog 戌	Ox 丑, Rooster 酉

Romance, Mobility, Solitude, and Anxiety Stars.

For example, if a person was born in the Year of the Rat (子), the Romance star would be the Rooster (酉), the Mobility star would be the Tiger (寅), the Solitude star – if the person is female – is the Dog (戌), while the Anxiety star for a male would be the Tiger (寅). Each of these stars has special effects on the cosmic system. Birth systems that possess the Romance star tend to attract people easily and it does not always have to be people of the opposite sex. The effect of the star depends on the positioning within the Four Pillars chart. A Romance star located in the day branch can bring about many friends and romance. In addition, if the Romance star is supportive of the leading flow, it can become very auspicious especially when it comes to meeting people and business partners. If the Romance star is located in the year, month or hour branch, the effect is still there but not as pronounced as having it reside in the day branch. Birth systems that do not have the Romance star can also experience its positive benefits when the star is encountered in the luck cycle or once every twelve years, months or day. During bad cycles, however, this star can bring about traumatizing and unwanted relationships.

Going back to the birth chart of Princess Diana, her Romance star is located in the month branch, represented by the Horse (午). The Horse (午) was supportive of the leading flow of fire, rendering her a charming individual who attracted others with ease. People with this star in their birth system can also be said to be attractive, smart and easy going. Again, as with any other stars, the Romance Star has to in tune with the individual's flow for the positive effects to take place.

Hour	Day	Month	Year
丙 Yang Fire	乙 Yin Wood	甲 Yang Wood	辛 Yin Metal
戌 Dog	未 Goat	午 Horse	丑 Ox

Below is another example with Carla Bruni's Romance star – the Rat (子) – as she is born in the year of the Goat (未). It is obvious that the Rat (子) is supportive of the leading flow in her birth system as verified earlier in this book. Carla Bruni is widely considered as an attractive model and she has a great number of fans who love her music. Three of her albums were all ranked number one in France when they were first released.

Hour	Day	Month	Year
丁 Yin Fire	辛 Yin Metal	壬 Yang Water	丁 Yin Fire
酉 Rooster	酉 Rooster	子 Rat	未 Goat

Both examples of Carla Bruni and Princess Diana illustrates how having the Romance star can support the main cosmic flow of a birth system, allowing individuals to gain fame from their attractive and sociable characteristics. Lily Chung mentions that "people with a Romance star falling in a void sign need help in getting married." (Easy Ways to Harmony, p.50) Movie stars, actors, singers and members of the royal families have a greater chance of possessing a Romance star in the month or day branch. This is evident in Carla Bruni's and Princess Diana's case.

Hour	Day	Month	Year
X	壬 Yang Water	丙 Yang Fire	丁 Yin Fire
X	申 Monkey	午 Horse	巳 Snake

The Princess of Sweden and Duchess of Västergötland Victoria, also has a Romance star located in her month branch seen above represented by the Horse (午). She is also considered to be very attractive, bright and well-loved. The Romance star is easy to remember. Every birth system has a Romance star and it is one of the four cardinals, the Rat (子), the Rabbit (卯), the Horse (午) and the Rooster (酉). Birth charts possessing more than one of the four cardinals may also experience many unexpected romances. For those who do not have a Romance star, you can still take advantage of such a star since it appears every twelve days, months or years.

Brad Pitt is a perfect example of a Four Pillars chart possessing more than one of the cardinals in his branches. He was born on December 18, 1963 in the hour of the Rabbit (卯). It is no doubt that Brad Pitt is classified as a Dominant self as his birth chart possesses mainly wood and water. The Yin

Earth (己) found in the hour is the only element that is not aligned with the flow. He has a powerful wood team where the Goat (未) and the two Rabbits (卯) join forces in the branch. This is also supported by the Rat (子) month where the water is feeding the wood.

Hour	Day	Month	Year
己 Yin Earth	乙 Yin Wood	甲 Yang Wood	癸 Yin Water
卯 Rabbit	未 Goat	子 Rat	卯 Rabbit

Going back to the Romance stars, with three cardinals in his branches and a true Romance star in his chart as represented by the Rat (子), it is very easy for him to attract members of the opposite sex. Brad Pitt was named the 'Sexiest Man' Alive twice by People in 1995 and 2000. In 2006, 2007, and 2008, he was on Forbe's annual Celebrity 100 list, ranked No. 20, No. 5 and No. 10 respectively. Of course this was no coincidence as he was in the Monkey (申) cycle which empowered the water in the Rat (子) as it fed the self.

There are other stars within the table that may affect one's relationship life. The Mobility star, sometimes referred to as the 'Travel star' or 'Travel Horse', represents movement. Those having a Mobility star in the birth system tend to be more mobile. It does not always mean that one has to be constantly travelling. They can also be unsettled within one job and would switch jobs frequently throughout their lives. If the Mobility star is in the spouse palace (day branch), there is a very high possibility that the person's spouse will travel for his career. Of course, if the Mobility star is an auspicious symbol in the birth chart, movements or migrations tend to be good. If a person encounters the Mobility star during a specific year or within a specific luck cycle, multiple changes should be expected. The changes are usually positive if the elements required for a chart is found within the Mobility star. Businessmen, army personnel, the homeless, sailors and flight crews have a higher possibility of possessing the Mobility star in their birth chart due to their high level of movements.

Other stars that can affect relationships include the anxiety and solitude stars. These two types of stars are self explanatory from their names. Those who possess anxiety stars often worry about many issues and aspects in their lives. Issues that could be very minor may be exaggerated due to the anxiety star within the birth system. With solitude star, it can mean loneliness but this interpretation can be quite vague. Some individuals actually enjoy being lonely. Great scholars and scientists may possess this star as they require a tremendous amount of time to be alone thinking and researching. So just because a person may possess the solitude star, it does not immediately result in loneliness or sadness; if these stars are in the spouse palace (day branch), these people may worry more about their relationship. The positioning and placement of the stars may tell a different story.

4.

Guard Stars

The next series of stars is the Guard stars. These stars are determined by the month branch.

Month Branch	Guard
Rat 子	Yang Water 壬, Snake 巳
Ox 丑	Yang Metal 庚
Tiger 寅	Yang Fire 丙, Yin Fire 丁
Rabbit 卯	Yang Wood 甲
Dragon 辰	Yang Water 壬
Snake 巳	Yang Metal 庚, Yin Metal 辛
Horse 午	Yang Fire 丙, Pig 亥
Goat 未	Yang Wood 甲
Monkey 申	Yang Water 壬, Yin Water 癸
Rooster 酉	Yang Metal 庚, Tiger 寅
Dog 戌	Yang Fire 丙
Pig 亥	Yang Wood 甲, Yin Wood 乙

A list of "Guide Stars".

The Guard stars are similar to the Guide stars in the sense that both stars provide protection. The Guide, as explained earlier, provides an individual with sound advice and assistance if you are in need of advice. In order for the Guide to be fully utilized, it is better to know your objectives and what you want to achieve. On the other hand, the Guard star provides greater protection, especially when one is in a difficult situation. The Guard would be there to protect and also prevent troubles from increasing. The most ideal situation is to have the Guard star found somewhere in the day pillar, as it is the most powerful position for bringing about great fame and fortune. Jennifer Aniston's birth chart possesses the Guard stars in the day and month stem.

Hour	Day	Month	Year
辛 Yin Metal	丁 Yin Fire	丙 Yang Fire	己 Yin Earth
亥 Pig	巳 Snake	寅 Tiger	酉 Rooster

She is born in the month of the Tiger (寅) and she possesses two Guard stars, one in the day, as represented by the Yin Fire (丁), and one in the month, as represented by the Yang Fire (丙). Aside from having good luck cycles, and work ethic, the Guard stars within her birth system provided her with additional assistance in her career when she needed it. The Guard stars helped her attract good connections and helpful people within her life. In addition to the two Guard stars, Jennifer Aniston's birth composite possesses a few other auspicious stars which include two Guide stars, the Pig (亥) and the Rooster (酉). The Rooster (酉) is also both her Study and Scholar star.

5.
Commanding Pillars

Similar to other stars and special pillars, the commanding pillars has its greatest effect on the day pillar. The effects of this pillar are reduced if it is only found in the Year, Month, or Hour pillar. Having these pillars in more than one pillar would magnify the effects. People possessing this pillar tend to be authoritative and demanding to themselves and the people around them. When these individuals enter a bad cycle, their authoritative nature may become dictatorial and oppressive. During good cycles, they would work very hard and strive for perfection. They would take the "do what it takes" approach to get the job done. It does not mean that they would cause harm to others just to achieve their objectives. Cosmic flow plays a big part in the characteristics of the commanding pillars. In general, people with the commanding pillars have key objectives and goals in mind and can become very successful if they are in good cycles. From a relationship standpoint, they can become very sceptical about their partner and others around them during bad times. Below is a list of the 'Commanding Pillars'.

戊辰	戊戌	庚辰	庚戌	壬辰	壬戌

A list of "Commanding Pillars".

Liliane Bettencourt's Four Pillars chart illustrates the number of 'Commanding Pillars' found in her system.

Hour	Day	Month	Year
X	壬 Yang Water	庚 Yang Metal	壬 Yang Water
X	戌 Dog	戌 Dog	戌 Dog

With the possession of three 'Commanding Pillars' in her birth system, the combination of luck, opportunities, and hard work made her one of the richest women on the planet. This pillar does not always guarantee success; in the next chapter, an example of the misfortunes will be examined.

6.
Summary

With the use of special stars, it provides practitioners with more information about the fortunes or misfortunes of a birth system. Having "good stars" is always a blessing in disguise. For those who do not have any of the good stars in the birth system, there is nothing to be afraid of. Birth systems having all the best stars imaginable also do not guarantee success. It is more important for a Four Pillars chart to have a consistent leading flow aided by the luck cycles. There are many more stars in the Four Pillars system that can be analyzed but I will not go into detail with those stars in this book since the prime focus is on relationships. If you are inexperienced as a Four Pillars practitioner, you can still have fun and evaluate the stars and try to notice whether they play a prominent role in a birth system. Be aware that the use of stars is not a method used to classify birth charts; they are only an additional tool to evaluate one's fortunes. Classifications of a cosmic system require much more analysis and logical thinking.

"SPECIAL STARS"

Their functionality and effectiveness can only be determined after the Four Pillars chart has been classified. The principles of the five element theory in the practice of Four Pillars supercede the qualities of a star. Imagine a chart possessing guide stars but the guide stars are unfavourable elements. The symbols representing the guide stars may do more harm since they are unfavourable to the birth chart."

Putting It All Together

1.
Case Studies

Now that we have evaluated the different methods of evaluating the birth chart, examples from my personal experience and research will be explored in greater depths. The most efficient and effective way to classify the birth system is to start by determining the flow. By determining the flow, a 'Useful God' or a 'useful element' can be found in a birth system. Once the birth chart has been classified, the possibilities in expanding an analysis are unlimited—from relationships to health, career, wealth, personality characteristics and so forth.

Piecing together and presenting a detailed analysis of a birth system could be your ultimate goal. For others, solving the issues at hand may be much more critical. There are specific reasons why people seek Four Pillars practitioners; Therefore, understanding every aspect of a Four Pillars chart would be ideal. In this book, you have learned how to evaluate relationships, from a classification and characterization point of view. The use of special stars has also equipped you with more details of a birth system. This chapter will provide an in depth look at specific cases explaining why some relationships workout while others just seem to fail no matter what happens.

2.

Remarriage

Going back to one of the examples in the book, Tom Cruise, evidence can be found within his birth chart highlighting possibilities of remarriage. One of them mentioned earlier was the duplication of the spouse palace represented by the Tiger (寅) in the day branch and the year branch.

Hour	Day	Month	Year
丙 Yang Fire	壬 Yang Water	丁 Yin Fire	壬 Yang Water
午 Horse	寅 Tiger	未 Goat	寅 Tiger

The other factor that causes the instability in his marriage life is the Yin Fire (丁), presented in the month stem. The Yin Fire (丁) in his chart, which is his wealth and spouse, is constantly competed against by the other Yang Water (壬) found in the year stem. In order for the competitor in the year stem to be put under control, wood must be utilized. Symbols such as the Rabbit (卯) and Pig (亥) can help weaken the competitor. Both animals would strengthen the wood in the chart due to their combinations with the Goat (未). By strengthening the wood, the energy of the competitor, water, would be reduced and the flow would enjoy a smooth transition from water to wood producing fire.

Nevertheless, it would be difficult for Cruise to maintain his relationship for a long period of time because the two Tigers (寅) in his birth system are constantly duelling to combine with the Horse (午) to form fire. The fight to combine would usually upset the spouse within his system. The best approach to take for his cosmic system is to accept reality and try to choose a spouse who had been married before. People who have been married may not want to go through another divorce and they may want to maintain a marriage with their partner. Finding a partner who travels for work often is another remedy. The reason for having a partner who travels is because the Tiger (寅) in his birth chart represents the mobility star. Since there are two Tigers (寅) in his birth chart that wants to combine with the Horse (午), a lot of movement is expected from the spouse.

Hour	Day	Month	Year
辛 Yin Metal	庚 Yang Metal	丁 Yin Fire	己 Yin Earth
巳 Snake	寅 Tiger	卯 Rabbit	酉 Rooster

63	53	43	33	23	13	3
庚 Yang Metal	辛 Yin Metal	壬 Yang Water	癸 Yin Water	甲 Yang Wood	乙 Yin Wood	丙 Yang Fire
申 Monkey	酉 Rooster	戌 Dog	亥 Pig	子 Rat	丑 Ox	寅 Tiger

Shown on the previous page is an example of a male's Four Pillars chart born on March 16th, 1969 in the hour of the Snake (巳).

The special feature of this birth composite is the fact that both the self element, Yang Metal (庚), and the wealth element, wood, are equally as strong. Regarding the metal, it is not only supported by Yin Earth (己) in the year stem and the Yin Metal (辛) in the hour stem, but also, the branches has a Snake (巳) and Rooster (酉) half metal combination. On the other hand, the wealth is just as strong due to the fact that this person is born in the month of the Rabbit (卯) when wood is in full bloom. The wood is also found in the Tiger (寅) in the day branch.

Having both the self and the wealth being strong in a chart would result in dissatisfaction with the status quo in terms of money and spouse. To compound the issue, the birth chart possesses a clash between the Rooster (酉) and the Rabbit (卯). Since the Rabbit (卯) is the wealth of this chart, it also represents the spouse, which is often under the stress of the clash. With so much metal in the chart, he would need to utilize fire to reduce the strength of the rivalry, metal, and protect the wealth which is wood. Unfortunately, fire is not found in the luck cycle aside from the first luck pillar. There is some fire in the birth chart but it does not have the strength to control the metal as the earth in the year stem is dissipating the strength of the Yin Fire (丁) from controlling the rivalry.

He was married at an early age in his late teens—as seen from the combination between the Yin Wood (乙) and the Yang Metal (庚) self. Note that the combination does not result in a transformation because he was born during the spring season. As he reached his late 20s, relationship issues began to transpire. At the age of 23, when he moved into the Yang Wood (甲) cycle, the urge to meet other women occurred and this resulted in a competition for women as seen through the rivalries in his chart. As the water became stronger in the luck cycles, it had strengthened the wood creating an intense battle within the chart for the wealth. In 2002, the year of the Horse (午), it combined with the Tiger (寅) to form half a fire team controlling the metal. Within the same year, he had divorced and married another woman.

The main problem with the above birth composite is the metal rivalry found throughout the chart competing for the wealth. Birth charts possessing rivalries, meaning the same element, tend to cause problems to a person financially and also in their marriage. The rivalries are constantly competing with the self for the wealth, which can be unnerving at times. Rivalries must be controlled in order to prevent them from causing financial and relationship difficulties. Translating rivalries into real life, they can come in the form of competitors in business, career, and for the spouse. The strength and effects of the rivalries also depends on the luck cycle and the specific year that is being analyzed. If the rivalry encounters more resources, both the self and the rivalry would compete for the resources. If a wealth cycle is encountered, the battle becomes increasingly fierce as both the self and the rivalry would engage in a fight for money.

Remarriage can come in many forms within a Four Pillars chart. The most apparent case is the reappearance of the spouse palace in another branch in the birth chart, as illustrated with Tom Cruise. Another is from charts possessing rivalries—although of course there are no guarantees. Charts having rivalries are more difficult to detect and evaluate in terms of remarriage and divorces. Rivalries that are weak stand a lesser chance of fighting the self for the spouse or money. Rivalries apply to both male and female. If the self is born in a prosperous season where rivalries are present, assuming that the birth chart is not classified as being Dominant, divorce is very likely. Why? If the rivalries are fierce and strong, they are ready to attack at any moment. When these strong self birth systems encounter more resources or wealth in the luck cycle, the fight will become increasingly vicious.

3.
Affairs

Today, affairs are quite common. The Internet is one of the causes of affairs. Believe it or not, "Facebook and other social networking sites have been utilized by more unhappy individuals to seek out and have an affair and cheat on their partner. Facebook is being cited in almost one in five of online divorce petitions, lawyers have claimed. (The Tech Journal Dec. 6, 2010.)" As some people become frustrated with their own relationship life, they may want to seek new adventures or companions. Others may have grown tired of their relationship but are unable to get out of their relationship because of certain commitments. Both men and women are guilty of getting themselves into affairs. Affairs within a birth system can be identified within the branches.

By looking at the day branch, if there is more than one combination for the day branch with other symbols in the birth system, there can be multiple possibilities. One of those possibilities is that the partner may have an affair with someone else. Another possibility is that the partner may have been married, divorced, but may need to tend to his/her children from his previous relationship. This is only one way to identify affairs. Another method is by evaluating the stems to see whether there is a fight to combine, or if there are transformations creating wealth elements in a male's chart. For a women's birth chart, a fight to combine with the officer or controlling element can also create unsettling and unwanted affairs. This next example illustrates the combinations of branches and stems bringing about affairs.

Hour	Day	Month	Year
丙 Yang Fire	己 Yin Earth	甲 Yang Wood	癸 Yin Water
寅 Tiger	亥 Pig	子 Rat	卯 Rabbit

45	35	25	15	5
己 Yin Earth	庚 Yang Metal	辛 Yin Metal	壬 Yang Water	癸 Yin Water
未 Goat	申 Monkey	酉 Rooster	戌 Dog	亥 Pig

The above is a birth system of a male born in Hong Kong on December 2, 1963. His birth chart was brought to me by his wife in the mid-1990s during my early days of practice in the Four Pillars. The leading cosmic flow found here is wood. This is the result of the combination between the Tiger (寅), Pig (亥), and also the Rabbit (卯) and the Pig (亥). The Pig (亥) within this birth chart is always temped to cross the month branch and unite with the Rabbit (卯). He was married in 1986, and he had an affair with another woman in 1988. In 1992, he was troubled by rumours and gossips about him having an affair with yet another woman. This brought about a lot of misery and tension within his marriage life.

During the same time, his wife never felt secure and she was constantly checking on her husband. The affairs were caused by the combination between the Yin Metal (辛) in the luck cycle at age 25 and the Yang Fire (丙) in the hour stem. The combination formed water, creating more wealth for the self. Wealth also being women in his life, brought about temptations for him to get involved with other women. In the meantime, his wife also had opportunities to meet other men but fortunately, she chose to stay loyal to her husband.

I sensed that something negative will transpire at the period of age 35 to 50 since he was in the metal and earth cycles. The metal would disrupt the leading flow of his wood while the Yin Earth (己) served as his rivalry. Age 50 to 55 would be a very positive turnaround as the Goat (未) enters his life and creates a complete wood alliance in his branches. Luck cycles that go against the flow of a birth system is often problematic. The problems depend on many different factors. Rivalries from the same element create the greatest cosmic disorder to birth systems that surrender to a leading flow.

Birth systems teetering on the borderline between a leading flow (feeble) and a weak self are even more problematic as these people may suffer a prolonged period of unhappiness. They have many illusions as they always believe they can get what they want. This is a result of being on the borderline. When they are in good cycles, their goals and objectives are easily achieved. When things do not go their way in life, they would create problems for others. They become greedy, lazy and also possessive. In 2010, when I was consulting in China, I met Phyllis. She was born on April 26, 1984.

Hour	Day	Month	Year
壬 Yang Water	庚 Yang Metal	戊 Yang Earth	甲 Yang Wood
午 Horse	寅 Tiger	辰 Dragon	子 Rat
37	27	17	7
甲 Yang Wood	乙 Yin Wood	丙 Yang Fire	丁 Yin Fire
子 Rat	丑 Ox	寅 Tiger	卯 Rabbit

Phyllis was introduced to me by a friend and she called me up one night to make an appointment for a consultation. After writing down her birth details, I looked at the birth system and felt a little distraught. I did not know whether I wanted to deal with this person or not, because the birth system is classified as a borderline chart. People with this type of chart tends to not listen to advice. I suspected that this person is rebellious, unhappy and self-destructive. Out of curiosity, I decided to meet with Phyllis.

The first thing that came to my attention with this chart is the fire and water combinations in the branches. The water was led by the Dragon (辰) and the Rat (子) while the fire was led by the Horse (午) and the Tiger (寅). Wood in this instance can neutralize this conflict. Even though she has a Yang Wood (甲) in the year stem, it may not be enough to solve the problem. After questioning her, she was most successful academically during the Rabbit (卯) cycle between the ages of 12 and 16. The strength of the Rabbit (甲) can force the Tiger (寅) and the Dragon (辰) to combine into a complete Directional trio. Only water and wood can push this cosmic system into a complete surrender. Again, as mentioned in the earlier chapters—it is better to have both feet in the door rather than having just one.

Ever since she moved onto the next cycle, she has experienced many issues within her relationship life. The Yang Fire (丙) cycle, being the seven killings to the self, was problematic as men entered her life on a consistent basis. None of the men were loyal to her. In 2005, Phyllis' relationship with her boyfriend turned into a nightmare as her boyfriend was cheating on her. She was considering suicide as an option to escape the debacle. 2005 was the year of the Rooster (酉) and it is the key rival to the Yang Metal (庚) self.

Throughout the consultation, she was concerned with her relationship life and status. Phyllis questioned me on her future spouse and when she would be able to get married. From a cosmic point of view, the water combination in the branches will never allow her to have a happy marriage. Since fire is her controlling element, it is constantly under the scrutiny and attacks of the water. She will always want someone of high status but she will never be able to sustain a relationship with such a person. Affairs in her life are bound to happen whether she or her partner takes the initiative; this is the brutal reality of her birth system.

The borderline classification of her system places her in a difficult predicament. She lacks love and care from not only the family but also from friends. Phyllis' cosmic system makes her sceptical and insecure, and as a result, her only way of comforting herself is to date multiple men hoping to ensure that there is someone to love her constantly. Prior to meeting her, I had predicted that she is rebellious and unhappy quite often. This is a person who would create office politics and spread rumours just to try and get ahead of the game. During our meeting, she admitted to her rebellious nature and her desire for more all the time. Unfortunately, Phyllis' petty games cost her job in 2009. She did not learn from her misfortunes and continues to behave the same in her new job. Borderline systems are often entangled in misery and conflicts. These conflicts often translate into brutal punishments in life. During bad cycles, people like Phyllis should seek advice and counselling to prevent her from repeating the same mistakes that led her to devastation. The best Feng Shui remedy for her has to come from the heart. Changing her attitude and reminding herself to be unselfish can help her avoid problems in the workplace.

4.
Divorce

Sometimes, the wife's birth chart indirectly harms the spouse cosmically through the birth composite. Harming the spouse does not always mean that a divorce is bound to happen. Quite often, it can be unavoidable. For instance, a female's chart with too many output elements would damage the officer element in the chart as mentioned many times throughout this book. From a five element theory point of view, a female with a wood self and an abundant amount of fire as the output would harm the metal. Metal for a wood self is the officer. Having too much fire would suppress the strength of the metal, and as a result, there may not be an opportunity for marriage or perhaps the marriage may not last long. For men, having too many symbols of the self element can rob them of their wife and wealth, hence the term Rob Wealth. The output elements for women and the sibling rivalries for the men are often recipes for disasters when it comes to relationships.

Rivalries are generally problematic for both men and women especially if those rivalries are not on your side. In 2009, as I was in search of research data for this book, I stumbled upon an interesting birth chart while I was getting a haircut. The owner of the hair salon was a female in her mid-40s and she started a conversation with me about her life. Her name is Christina. During our conversation, I had this uncomfortable feeling that something bad had happened to her recently and she sounded very sceptical after finding out about my profession. Nevertheless, she provided me with her birth details. Christina was born on November 21, 1963, in the hour of the Snake (巳).

Hour	Day	Month	Year
丁 Yin Fire	戊 Yang Earth	癸 Yin Water	癸 Yin Water
巳 Snake	辰 Dragon	亥 Pig	卯 Rabbit

56	46	36	26	16	6
己 Yin Earth	戊 Yang Earth	丁 Yin Fire	丙 Yang Fire	乙 Yin Wood	甲 Yang Wood
巳 Snake	辰 Dragon	卯 Rabbit	寅 Tiger	丑 Ox	子 Rat

Christina is a Yang Earth (戊) self inundated with water in both the month and year stems. The water is particularly strong since she is born in the winter. Observing the branches, the Rabbit (卯) and the Pig (亥) combine to form wood. This birth system becomes a little unclear with the Dragon (辰) sitting in the day branch while the Yin Fire (丁) and Snake (巳) in the hour pillar warms and strengthens the self. Since the earth is born in the winter, the likelihood of Christina surrendering to the water and wood flow is probable. Before evaluating the luck cycle, there is one more combination that should be noted: the Yang Earth (戊) combining with the two Yin Waters (癸) in the stems.

With the water feeding the wood combination in the branches, if she were to encounter additional wood or water in her luck cycles, her cosmic system would benefit her spouse. Yang Earth (戊) on the other hand would create an arduous situation for Christina as it would fight with her for the wealth element, Yin Water (癸), by combining it away. Since she is in the hair styling business, I quickly had a look around her neighbourhood. Judging by the abundance of other salons on the same block, competition is fierce. This is the result of the Yang Earth (戊) coming into her life at the age of 46. There was a combination of her cosmic system inviting competition and attracting competition. Her life was clearly going towards a downturn.

The rivalry coming from the Yang Earth (戊) at the age of 46 not only created an environment of competition within her neighbourhood, but also took away her husband recently. She reported to me in our conversation that there was a high possibility of an affair between her husband and another woman. Christina's cosmic system creates a strong energetic flow of the controlling element; with the Rabbit (卯) cycle between the ages of 41 and 45, her husband must have made a tremendous amount of money. The controlling element during that period was in full bloom. Coincidentally, once money was made, her husband left her for another younger woman. Could this have been prevented? Possibly, but a thorough analysis of her husband's Four Pillars chart may shed more light into the situation, unfortunately, Christina did not provide me with his details.

Her scepticism and reluctance to accept reality was caused by her day pillar, the Yang Earth Dragon (戊辰). This 'Commanding Pillar' has been explained in the previous chapter and Christina serves as a perfect example to what can happen during bad cycles. The pillar often creates a mentality of apprehension and doubt. If this pillar encounters a clash by the Dog (戌) or a rivalry by the Yang Earth (戊), she would want to place a protective barrier around herself and fight to the bitter end.

The contending forces of the Yang Earth (戊) got the better of Christina. Christina's upcoming cycles are not favourable to her. She will have to endure the next 20 years of earth cycles that will bring about misery and misfortunes. Some of these misfortunes are reduced by the profession that she is in, where she utilizes metal scissors to reduce the earth energy. Being physically around metal objects is beneficial to her. Christina has to learn not to compete and yield to the competition. Her misfortunes will come from financial issues and taking care of her rent payments. When she was cutting my hair, she had mentioned to me that her beauty salon was the only one in the neighbourhood that has lasted longer than 6 years. Recently, about 5 to 6 more beauty salons has opened up nearby. From the conversation that we had, she was not so much interested in remedies and what is in store for her in the future, instead, she was much more keen on the accuracy of what I had to say about her past. It is better to move on and look forward to a brighter future than to grasp onto the pain that she suffered through her divorce. Her stereotype about Feng Shui practitioners had created a barrier between superstition and reality. This is also a result of the makeup of her birth system and the luck cycle that she was in.

Birth systems encountering the rivalry cycles tend to bring about greater competition in many aspects of life, assuming that the same element as the self is unfavourable. Adversity and difficulties may last for a certain period of time. People who have favourable rivalries in the birth system tend to suffer considerably more. The rivalries are implanted in their Four Pillars chart for life. Typically, birth systems wanting to become dominant but cannot, would fear the existence of the rivalry. They would want to compete over anything even if it means ruining others who get in their way. Recently, the former husband of a woman came to me with her birth system. When I was talking to him, I had an eerie feeling that something was bothering him. For confidentiality purposes, only the birth system of the woman will be looked at here. Her name is Angie and she was born on December 8, 1972 (birth hour not supplied) in Hong Kong.

Hour	Day	Month	Year
X	癸 Yin Water	壬 Yang Water	壬 Yang Water
X	酉 Rooster	子 Rat	子 Rat

31	21	11	1
戊 Yang Earth	己 Yin Earth	庚 Yang Metal	辛 Yin Metal
申 Monkey	酉 Rooster	戌 Dog	亥 Pig

Angie's cosmic system is overwhelmed with water but the makeup of her birth chart does not allow her to become a fully dominant self. This is a difficult chart to classify due to the absence of her birth hour. If she was born in the hour of the Monkey (申) or the Dragon (辰), there could be a possibility of her becoming fully dominant. The reason why I concluded that Angie is not dominant is the due to the way she behaves and the information that I was provided with. Dominant selves are often possessive yet they have a strong presence in the public. They are often intelligent, hard working, and have the abilities to command a large group of people. Donald Trump is a perfect example as explained earlier in this book.

The first item that I discussed with my client was about her relationship with her parents. I was told that her parents left her and she grew up in a very poor neighbourhood as an orphan. By evaluating her luck cycles and the month and year pillars, it is easily concluded that both water and metal were not beneficial to her birth system. Dominant selves usually benefits from the same self element and resources; Angie's system did not demonstrate any benefits from those elements. Charts that are classified as Dominant would want to maintain the dominant flow in their birth system. Throughout her childhood days, she had suffered from the lack of education and proper parenting. From the age of one until age 16, she had a period of metal and water cycles, if metal and water were good for her, she would have benefited from the energy in the luck cycle. Unfortunately, she did not receive proper education and lived in a very poor neighbourhood in Hong Kong.

This system needed Yang Earth (戊) to curb the flow of water. The water which is unchecked in her system makes her very volatile, rebellious and evil. Angie was a very possessive woman and she took sole control of her husband's bank account. After having two children, she decided it was time to move on so she filed for a divorce in her early 30s. Angie lacked education and did not have the capabilities to raise two children, yet the court has ordered the two children to remain with her while her ex-husband provides financial aid to them for the next 15 years. The Yang Earth (戊) was able to quell the water in her system allowing her to get what she wanted without competition. The entire episode is a very unfortunate event for my client. He asked me if his children will ever live together with him again one day; but with such a possessive and selfish birth system, I am afraid that it is going to be very difficult.

The worst part of the court decision is that he has to continue to pay his ex-wife monthly childcare support. So what does Angie do with all this money? She hops on a boat to Macau on weekends to gamble while leaving the children at home unsupervised at times.

Rivalries have been a recurring theme throughout this book. People with birth systems possessing unfavourable rivalries can become brutal and selfish at their most inopportune or opportune time depending on how the situation is interpreted. With Angie's birth system, she will never be satisfied in terms of what she has; this is a result of many factors aside from the system that she was provided with at birth. Lack of education and care from parents played a major part in her life, making her suspicious of others at all times. Angie has to take as much as she can because of her insecurity.

5.
Case Studies: Weak Self with a lot of Wealth

In the previous chapter, the theory behind the "Weak self with a lot of Wealth" was discussed. Many birth systems fall into such a category but the degree of weakness has to be explored on a case by case basis. Charts classified as being on the borderline of becoming feeble requires more testing to determine whether wealth is favourable to them or not. Those who surrender to the wealth flow would definitely enjoy additional wealth in their luck cycles. Others who are classified as being strong should be capable of amassing a fortune during wealth cycles. In general, those classified as a weak self with a lot of wealth in their chart can run into major problems when they encounter a wealth cycle. The problems would include health issues and financial difficulties. If these people see more wealth in the luck cycle, they may have illusions about getting rich. In 2005, a lady came to my office and approached me with a Four Pillars chart of a man who has a somewhat of a weak self chart. I had to be careful with my words as always and we started off discussing about his financial well-being. This man was born in Guangzhou, China, on December 10, 1949 (hour not available).

Hour	Day	Month	Year
X	甲 Yang Wood	乙 Yin Wood	己 Yin Earth
X	戌 Dog	亥 Pig	丑 Ox

61	51	41	31	21	11	1
戊 Yang Earth	己 Yin Earth	庚 Yang Metal	辛 Yin Metal	壬 Yang Water	癸 Yin Water	甲 Yang Wood
辰 Dragon	巳 Snake	午 Horse	未 Goat	申 Monkey	酉 Rooster	戌 Dog

He was a Yang Wood (甲) self while he has a Yin Wood (乙) by his side in the month stem. The year pillar caught my attention immediately as I see the wealth, 'earth' as being "rooted" because of the Ox (丑) in the year branch. There is a stem combination between the Yang Wood (甲) and the Yin Earth (己) in the year but the problem lies in the month stem where the Yin Wood (乙) is standing in between them from combining. The day branch also presented more earth found within the Dog (戌). There was definitely no shortage of wealth found in this birth system. The next step in evaluating this birth system was to see whether he can surrender to the earth, or if he was strong enough to control the earth as his wealth. Since he was born in the month of the Pig (亥), surrendering to the earth is not an option. It did not matter if he was strong enough to control the earth, for the wood was born in the first month of winter while there was a lack of support from the branches aside from the Pig (亥). This birth system needed more wood, the Rabbit (卯) or the Goat (未) in order to be strong enough to control the earth. It looked like a weak self with a lot of wealth but I wanted to confirm this with the lady by questioning her.

At the time, this person was in the wealth cycle in the luck pillar of 51-60. If this is a weak self, obviously, wealth must have been a major issue with this person as more wealth is introduced into his system. The highlight of his life was probably during the Goat (未) cycle as it teamed with the Pig (亥) in the month pillar to form more wood supporting the self. At his late 30s, he probably made a fortune in what he was doing. I also believed that the Horse (午) cycle was inauspicious as the Horse (午) took away the wealth that he had tucked into the day branch, as it combined with the

Dog (戌) to form fire. This looked like a sad story waiting to be unfolded.

The lady then began to speak up and agreed with my assessment and told me that during his late thirties, he made a lot of money gambling at the casinos in Macau. He amassed over one million Hong Kong Dollars at one point in the 1980s. As quickly as he had built up the fortune, it all disappeared. The latter began as soon as he entered the Yang Metal (庚) period. The Yang Metal (庚), combined with the Yin Wood (乙) and took away his remaining support. It was at the same time that his brother had immigrated to Canada while leaving him a sum of money. His money quickly evaporated at the casinos as he continued to gamble. He thought the money that he lost—the money that once belonged to him—would return one day. The lady said he always thinks that "if I can do it once, I can do it again."

Macau: A former Portuguese colony that is now one of the two special administrative regions of China. The other special administrative region is Hong Kong. Macau's economy is based on tourism and is well known for many of its casino resorts. Travelling between Macau and Hong Kong by ferry takes approximately one hour."

As he moved into the wealth cycle at the age of 51, his situation became increasingly bleak as his wife and daughter deserted him. At the time of this consultation, he was supported by his brother on a monthly basis through a payment as long as he behaved himself. Everything regarding this person was bad news.

Recently, I met with the lady again, and she told me that he was taken into custody for throwing a cigarette onto the streets (there is a 3000 Hong Kong Dollar fine for littering and he was charged with that offense). Things turned for the worst as he started sleeping in the parks or under a bridge. Every month, he would continue to bother his brother for more and more money. The money he was given was used for a return ticket from Hong Kong to Macau, and undoubtedly, he was off to the casino again, trying to gain back what he thought was "rightfully" his.

It is unfortunate that he came to such a predicament, but it could have been avoided if he knew when to stop gambling and decided to find himself a job. Laziness and greed are two of the greatest evils written in the I Ching and this man bear these two traits. The lady who brought his birth information to me was his sister in law and she is constantly frustrated over this man, bothering her family for money. She asked me when he will stop bothering them. From looking at the luck cycle, it is going to last until his mid 70s, which would probably be until 2020. The only advice that I could give her is to "stop having money lent to him and make him work his way out of laziness".

This birth system illustrates a perfect example of what can happen to weak selves with lots of wealth. Not only did he lose all his money, but also, his wife and daughter had left him. It can be attributed to the fact that he had wealth exposed on the stem and the wealth being the Yin Earth (己) in the year stem. His birth chart became weaker as he moved into the wealth cycles.

Imagine this: a weak man needs to carry bags of coal on his back to heat his furnace. Instead of making three or four trips to the coal pit through steep hills and valleys, he decides to carry it all at once. Halfway through his journey back, the load felt heavier and heavier. Thinking that he can make it all the way back, he kept on going and eventually slips, injures his back, and drops the load. The pile of coal rolls down the hill into a river and he is left with nothing. Carrying more than the amount one can handle is the main theme of a weak self with a lot of wealth. In bad cases, these people would have illusions of becoming rich and jealousy would set in. They believe they can become wealthy with limited knowledge and hard work. For men, this invites the dangers of losing fortune and the entire family.

Now that we have taken a look at a weak self from a male's perspective, we can bring on another example of a female. In early 2009, I received a phone call from a female inquiring about a consultation of her destiny and she asked about her career and relationship with her husband. So I requested for her birth details, but she was apprehensive about providing me with her birth hour. Nevertheless, I was able to obtain that information from her and scheduled her into my office. This lady was born on April 24, 1977, in the hour of the Rabbit. When she entered my office, I could tell that she was uneasy with a Four Pillars reading. She was eager for good news, but was partially sceptical about the methods I practice. I believed she came for a reading out of curiosity, rather than to try and understand what can happen in the future. Shown next is her Four Pillars chart.

Hour	Day	Month	Year
辛 Yin Metal	辛 Yin Metal	甲 Yang Wood	丁 Yin Fire
卯 Rabbit	亥 Pig	辰 Dragon	巳 Snake

64	54	44	34	24	14	4
辛 Yin Metal	庚 Yang Metal	己 Yin Earth	戊 Yang Earth	丁 Yin Fire	丙 Yang Fire	乙 Yin Wood
亥 Pig	戌 Dog	酉 Rooster	申 Monkey	未 Goat	午 Horse	巳 Snake

For confidentiality reasons, let's call her Cammy. Cammy is a Yin Metal (辛) self born in the month of the Dragon (辰) in the Spring. Although Spring is considered heavy in wood energy, the month of the Dragon is dominated more so by wet earth, which is trying to feed the Yin Metal (辛) self. The self element is also supported by Yin Metal (辛) in the hour stem. Looking at the branches, there is a team of wood underneath her in the day and hour branch between the Pig (亥) and the Rabbit (卯). Her year pillar had Yin Fire (丁) strongly rooted in the Snake (巳). Even though the self has support, it is surrounded by elements that are weakening its strength, and as a result, this birth chart falls under the classification of a weak self.

Classifying her as a weak self can be confirmed by looking at the luck cycles. From the age of four all the way to thirty four, Cammy experienced more than 30 years of fire. For a weak self, it is resulted in years of hardship and lack of success in school. Cammy mentioned that she started working as a waitress and other odd jobs since the age of 18. It was during the Yang Fire Horse (丙午) luck pillar where she met her first boyfriend. By looking at the luck cycles, I believe that she moved on to another man immediately when she transitioned into the Goat (未) cycle, which started at around the age of 28-29. The Goat (未) combined with the spouse palace while forming more wealth in her chart. At this period, she would have an illusion believing that this new man in her life would bring her more fortunes in terms of money and less work. The wood which is her wealth element, became stronger with the inception of the Goat (未) cycle.

At the time, the man was a Chinese restaurant owner and chef. Apparently, he seemed like a stable and successful man. Cammy thought it would be a wonderful idea to secure her relationship with him. Having been together for less than a year, Cammy was pregnant in 2006 and discreetly forced the man to marry her. After their marriage in 2007, she gave birth to another child in early 2009.

The difficulties within her cosmic system lie in the metal and the wood where the other metal in the birth hour is constantly creating insecurities for her over wealth. Secondly, having wood exposed in the month stem can easily lead to a loss of wealth. Her spending habits are practically uncontrollable as wealth is easily leaked from the birth system. Utilizing water in her system is a possibility since the water can push the birth chart towards a feeble self surrendering to the wood. The sad fact is that when she encounters water in the luck cycle or in the year, her husband would be negatively affected by the cosmic energy. Since water controls fire, and fire being her controlling element, her husband's strength would be weakened by her cosmic makeup.

This is a borderline system where the chart is classified as a weak self and a surrender to offspring and wealth. By evaluating her luck cycle, she would lead more towards a weak self most of the time. This is quite noticeable from the way she behaves and the enthusiasm she has over money. Most women who are classified as a weak self are powerless at home and would be berated by their husband. She was interested in starting a cosmetic business since she has been seeing a lot of people succeed in this field. I mentioned to her that she will be engaging in a lot of competition and stand a high probability of losing money in 2010 and 2011. After my consultation, she carried on and opened her business in 2009 and sales for her have been bleak. In the summer of 2010, her company continued to lose money and she is still waiting for a positive upswing in her business. It is unfortunate how people would seek advice but do not take the advice. Instead, they are drawn away by short-term temptations in life when they are presented with money making opportunities. This is a typical example of what weak selves with a lot of wealth can do. When they encounter a bad cycle, they would find others to blame; it would either be the economy or the people around them.

6.

Case Studies: Rivalries, Clash and Unhappiness

As I was writing this book in the summer of 2010, I received a call from a friend regarding her relationship issues. Let's call her Sandy. Sandy was emotionally trapped over a man that has repeatedly cheated on her. Sandy mentioned that this man, Robertson, was dating another woman while they were together. She found this out from her friends. Sandy is a Christian and did not believe in Feng Shui nor destiny but out of curiosity, I decided to ask her for her birth date to try and make light out of the entire situation. Sandy gave me both her birth details and Robertson's birth details. She did not provide me with the birth hours but her birth date presented enough information for evaluation. Sandy was born on April 12, 1980 in Taiwan and below is her birth chart.

Hour	Day	Month	Year
X	乙 Yin Wood	己 Yin Earth	庚 Yang Metal
X	卯 Rabbit	卯 Rabbit	申 Monkey

This birth system come of no surprise as one of the major themes in this book, rivalries, is in full bloom found in the branches. She is a Yin Wood (乙) with two Rabbits (卯) present in the branches. The Rabbit (卯) in Sandy's system creates many problems in her life, mainly related to relationships. It is almost unavoidable that she will continue to run into issues. Here is her luck cycle:

33	23	13	3
乙 Yin Wood	丙 Yang Fire	丁 Yin Fire	戊 Yang Earth
亥 Pig	子 Rat	丑 Ox	寅 Tiger

With the amount of wood found in Sandy's cosmic system, the best way to contain it is through the use of metal. Fortunately, the Yang Metal (庚) in the year stem is strongly rooted by the Monkey (申). Obviously, this is a strong wood self with wood that is not strong enough to become completely dominant. She is trapped on the strong side of the spectrum where she needs to deal with her problems on her own with limited help.

To make matters worse, Sandy is currently in the Rat (子) cycle, which strengthens the wood with an ample supply of water. That water is formed by the combination of the Rat (子) and the Monkey (申). For those with advanced training in Four Pillars, it is easy to spot the "punishment" between the Rat (子) and the Rabbit (卯). It seems like there is a lot of bad news found in her cosmic system at the moment. Yin Earth (己), being her wealth element, is fought for by all the wood in the chart. In addition, the wood in the chart is strengthened by the Rat (子), which enhances the conflict for wealth. With the conflict for wealth in her system, finding a job and identifying goals for the future becomes a tougher task for Sandy. Yang Metal (庚), her officer and controlling element, is also exposed in the stem where the man is being taken away by the rivalries.

Her situation did not get any better as 2010 is the year of the Yang Metal Tiger (庚 寅). The Tiger (寅) clashed with the Monkey (申) in her chart. The Monkey (申), being one of her Guide stars made the impact much more dreadful. In addition, the Yang Metal (庚) on the stem lost its roots and was powerless in controlling the self. The rivalries hidden in the branches began to compete with the self for the controlling element. Finding a suitable marriage partner is one of the most challenging aspects of her life and this can be attributed to the dual appearance of the Rabbit (卯) in her birth system found in the day and month branches. Sandy said she was emotionally attached to Robertson and cannot let go of her relationship. Robertson said he loved Sandy but continued to see other women in the meantime. It seemed like a case where Robertson wanted to use Sandy as a backup plan while he was busy courting other women. Let's take a look at the birth system of Robertson and evaluate what is going on. Robertson was born on September 17, 1983.

Hour	Day	Month	Year
X	戊 Yang Earth	辛 Yin Metal	癸 Yin Water
X	申 Monkey	酉 Rooster	亥 Pig

33	23	13	3
丁 Yin Fire	戊 Yang Earth	己 Yin Earth	庚 Yang Metal
巳 Snake	午 Horse	未 Goat	申 Monkey

He is a Yang Earth (戊) self born in the month of the Rooster (酉) where metal is in full bloom while the strength of earth is receding. Robertson is sitting on top of a Monkey (申), where there is metal present. The Yin Water (癸) in the year wants to combine with the Yang Earth (戊) self but is separated by the month pillar. Essentially, the Yin Water (癸) has its roots from the Pig (亥); therefore, the self is surrendering to two flows, both metal and water. On the one hand, the metal in the system is in full bloom. On the other hand, the water in the year pillar is being fed by the metal. Obviously, this man wanted to bite off more than he can chew. He is definitely a smart and intelligent person with the Hurting Officer strongly rooted in the month pillar.

The problem lies in the luck cycle as he was in the Yang Earth (戊) cycle at the age of 27. The Yang Earth (戊) is rivaling the self for the wealth found in the year stem. During this cycle, Robertson is rather insecure about his relationship life and financial well-being as his rivalry from the luck cycle is making him uncomfortable. The year of the Tiger (寅) undoubtedly made him miserable as it clashed his spouse palace. The cosmic flow was not in his favour and the Tiger (寅) compounded to the problem that he had been experiencing throughout the current luck cycle. Although the Tiger (寅) wants tocombine with the Pig (亥), it is constantly tempted into a fight with the Monkey (申) bringing about instability within his branches. Looking at the special stars, the Yang Earth Monkey (戊申) day pillar is a 'relationship' pillar that compounds the problems within his relationship life.

From what Sandy had told me, I was able to piece together the entire story and confirm what has happened by looking at their Four Pillars chart. Since Sandy did not believe in my practice, I was not able to help her or provide her with any advice. She was too emotionally attached to listen to what I had to say. Little did she know that 2011 would bring about even more suffering as an additional rivalry will come about in the year of the Rabbit (卯). What does natural law tell us to do in such cases? Avoiding competition and accepting defeat is the best approach. For Sandy, letting go of her relationship and not getting involved with men during this period would release the tension in her life.

"RIVALRY"

This term has been used throughout the book. It is another way of referring to the same element as the self. Other terms would include 'Friend' and 'Rob Wealth'. It is not always bad to have rivals. A birth chart requiring additional assistance from a friend or sibling would enjoy the 'Rivalry'. When is the 'Rival' good for the birth chart? Weak self with lots of wealth would need a helping hand. Birth charts surrendering to a leading flow or strong birth systems would not enjoy the 'Friend' or 'Rob Wealth' luck cycles.

7.

Case Study: Homosexuality and Bisexuality

Homosexuality and bisexuality have been topics of debate amongst many Four Pillars practioners. Are there patterns within a chart that can be derived from homosexuals and bisexuals? More research is required in order to verify specific patterns regarding this topic. I have encountered a number of homosexuals and did a number of studies on their birth charts. I have yet to derive any concrete conclusions out of my research as of this moment. What I have noticed is that many homosexuals and bisexuals have 'rivals' within their birth chart. But having rivals in their birth chart is not sufficient information to prove that one belongs to this category. As more data has been gathered from this area, I will present more materials in the future about my findings. Below are a few examples on homosexuals and bisexuals.

Recently, a female by the name of Sue contacted me for a Four Pillars consultation and was interested in taking some classes with me. Sue was also a practitioner and was still learning the systems and methodologies of the Four Pillars of Destiny. She wanted some additional advice in terms of how she should approach the next 5 to 10 years. Below is her Four Pillars chart:

Hour	Day	Month	Year
甲 Yang Wood	丁 Yin Fire	癸 Yin Water	丁 Yin Fire
辰 Dragon	丑 Ox	卯 Rabbit	巳 Snake

65	55	45	35	25	15	5
庚 Yang Metal	己 Yin Earth	戊 Yang Earth	丁 Yin Fire	丙 Yang Fire	乙 Yin Wood	甲 Yang Wood
戌 Dog	酉 Rooster	申 Monkey	未 Goat	午 Horse	巳 Snake	辰 Dragon

Sue was born on March 21, 1977 at 8:30am, in Vancouver, Canada. Sue's birth chart possesses two Yin Fires (丁) in the stems and both of them are competing for the wood resources found in the Rabbit (卯). When I was talking to her, she mentioned that her partner had just recently left her in 2010. She was very upfront with me during the consultation and told me that she was a lesbian. There are many things happening with her chart, creating the instability in her life. Her fire is considerably strong and her chart requires the use of the Yin Water (癸) in the month stem to weaken her rival and nourish the wood. The Yin Water (癸) is the Useful God in her chart. Unfortunately, the Yin Water (癸) is weak. The only support the Yin Water (癸) has comes from the hidden water in the Dragon (辰), as found in the birth hour. The water in the Ox (丑) is not easily extracted because of its combination with the Snake (巳) to form half a metal team.

The importance of the water comes from its abilities to curtail the fire rival, weakening the strength of the metal, and feeding the wood in her chart. If additional metal comes along in Sue's chart, conflicts and misfortunes will arise; evidently, in 2005, during the year of the Rooster (酉), her father had passed away. In 2010, the Yang Metal (庚) energy for the year created a conflict amongst the two Yin Fires for her possessions. Sue had difficulties coping with the absence of her partner. Her partner had most likely left her for another person.

Sue's sexuality likely has something to do with the rival. Rivals, when unfavourable, provide a sense of insecurity and perhaps the insecurity could have influenced the nature of her sexuality. This is only an assumption. There are very limited Four Pillars resources and texts that I have found in Hong Kong and Taiwan that deals with homosexuals and bisexuals. I have encountered masters in Hong Kong where they have utilized a different type of divination method that can determine one's sexuality. The method requires an abacus and the 24 books utilizing the I Ching. For those who are interested in this topic, the pattern should be identifiable with sufficient data and research. Angelina Jolie, Lady Gaga, Drew Barrymore, and Ricky Martin, who are homosexual or bisexual, have similarities in their Four Pillars chart. Just like Sue, they possess rivals in their birth chart. Below are their birth charts with the rivals highlighted.

Hour	Day	Month	Year
癸 Yin Water	辛 Yin Metal	辛 Yin Metal	乙 Yin Wood
巳 Snake	巳 Snake	巳 Snake	卯 Rabbit

Angelina Jolie (June 4, 1975)

Hour	Day	Month	Year
己 Yin Earth	辛 Yin Metal	辛 Yin Metal	丙 Yang Fire
亥 Pig	未 Goat	卯 Rabbit	寅 Tiger

Lady Gaga (March 28, 1986)

Hour	Day	Month	Year
庚 Yang Metal	己 Yin Earth	戊 Yang Earth	乙 Yin Wood
午 Horse	亥 Pig	寅 Tiger	卯 Rabbit

Drew Barrymore (February 22, 1975)

Hour	Day	Month	Year
辛 Yin Metal	癸 Yin Water	庚 Yang Metal	辛 Yin Metal
酉 Rooster	未 Goat	子 Rat	亥 Pig

Ricky Martin (December 24, 1971)

So does it really matter whether the Four Pillars method can determine one's sexuality? It is more important to understand the needs of the people who seek help from Feng Shui consultants. In the case of Sue, she was more interested in her career and financial goals rather than about her sexuality.

8.
Case Study: South American Expedition

In the summer of 2009, I spent three months living in Quito, Ecuador. Prior to arriving, I was excited over the prospect of obtaining more research data on the Four Pillars of destiny. I did not know what to expect and I was curious about whether there were any noticeable differences in the birth systems of those who are born near the Andes Mountains right on the equator. I was fortunate enough to learn to converse in Spanish, and during the three months in Ecuador, I have obtained more than 100 birth dates from locals and travellers within that region. People that I have encountered include Ecuadorians, Peruvians, Argentineans and Colombians. The data that I had collected ranged from lawyers, teachers, government officials, students and business owners. I wanted to further my investigation on cosmic systems in the Southern Hemisphere.

Out of all the people that I had met throughout my journey, there was one case that stood out. It was a lady named Maria, who was in her late 30s. Maria was a single mother of three children. While I was taking private Spanish lessons, my tutor mentioned to me that she had a friend who is interested in my services and would like to invite me over to dinner. My tutor was amazed by the accuracy of the Four Pillars reading she had received and she told her best friend, Maria, about it. I accepted the offer as I was curious to find out more about the people of Ecuador. The only demand I had was red wine and home made tamales for supper.

Tamales: A traditional Latin American dish corn steamed in a leaf wrapper. It looks very similar to Chinese sticky rice but is filled with meat, cheese, vegetables, chilli and corn.

Maria lived a few blocks away from Estadio Olimpico Atahualpa in Quito, which was a considerably nice suburb within the city. Prior to evaluating the Feng Shui of her living space, I did a Four Pillars analysis for her and her three children. Maria was born on December 7, 1971 at the hour of the Goat (未).

Hour	Day	Month	Year
乙 Yin Wood	丙 Yang Fire	己 Yin Earth	辛 Yin Metal
未 Goat	寅 Tiger	亥 Pig	亥 Pig

51	41	31	21	11	1
乙 Yin Wood	甲 Yang Wood	癸 Yin Water	壬 Yang Water	辛 Yin Metal	庚 Yang Metal
巳 Snake	辰 Dragon	卯 Rabbit	寅 Tiger	丑 Ox	子 Rat

Maria is a Yang Fire (丙) self born in the month of the Pig (亥). A few things happening with her birth system. First of all, the Tiger (寅) sitting in the day branch would like to combine with the Pig (亥) in the month branch but is constantly tempted to hop over to the Pig (亥) in the year. The chance of marrying more than once is very likely to happen.

The Goat (未) in the hour branch wants to hop over the Tiger (寅) and combine with one of the Pigs (亥) in the birth chart. The complexity of the combinations in the branches leads her to men who may get involved in affairs. This chart is a recipe for relationship instability and avoiding such a predicament is a daunting task. Nevertheless, Maria's birth system is very special as the branches are all led by wood. She surrenders to the 'resources' and can be classified as a feeble self. Some people may classify this as a strong self with a lot of resources. If it is a strong self with a lot of resources, she would not benefit from wood—but the opposite is true for her. Maria has been entitled to an abundance of benefits and fortune in life by surrendering to the 'resources'.

> ### "從格 and 破格"
>
> Chinese classics on the Four Pillars would refer a chart surrendering to a leading energy as '從勢' or '從格'. This means the combinations in the branches are leading the flow. There is power and momentum led by the combinations. When the elements in the luck cycles go against the leading flow, the chart loses its momentum. This is referred to as '破格'. The direct translation in English is 'Destroy' or 'Broken'. It may sound harsh but from an energetic standpoint, it means the flow is impeded and momentum is lost."

Her most favourable elements are water and wood. As I was talking to her, I noticed water and wood running through her luck cycles starting from the age of 21 until the present date. Throughout the water and wood cycles, she did not really need to work and many men supported her livelihood. She gave birth to her children in her late teens and early 20s; after giving birth, she was still very attractive and many men were pursuing her. Maria used to work at a radio station as a talk show host. Since she was a mother of three, she felt that she needed to remain at home to take care of the children. Nevertheless, even as she was unemployed, there were a few men giving her money to spend and they did not mind her having three children.

It was obvious that she is benefiting from all the water and wood in her birth system and she is very fortunate that her luck cycle is in tune with the flow. Maria was in her Rabbit (卯) cycle, and that gave her a complete wood team in her system. Most often, birth systems with so many resources would result in the person becoming either overweight or malnourished, depending on whether the resources are direct or indirect. She did not possess any of those traits, because her resources were favourable to her. If resources were unfavourable to her, aside from health issues, it would have been impossible for her to have proper shelter and food without working. When resources are in one's favour, shelter is always provided to the person.

Maria was troubled by her relationship issues as her boyfriend ignored her for six months although he continued to put money into her bank account. This is most likely caused by the Ox (丑) clashing with the Goat (未) in the hour pillar disrupting the wood flow in her birth system. Keep in mind that the hour pillar in her chart is also a troubling relationship pillar, and as a result, the clash had created more discomfort within her relationship life. Maria's birth chart possesses a powerful resource team, hence money and shelter was always provided to her. Even though her boyfriend had left her, she never had to worry about finding a place to stay. Since her chart follows the flow of wood, metal would create the most problems for her. During the month of the Goat (未) in 2010, Maria's boyfriend reunited with her. This was the result of the wood combinations between the Goat (未) and the Pig (亥) and also the Tiger (寅) and the Pig (亥). When cosmic flow is disrupted, a level of discomfort would be presented. The severity of the discomfort depends on the luck and annual cycles. Fortunately for Maria, she was in a wood cycle, therefore, her issues in 2009 quickly disappeared when the wood energy of the Tiger (寅) year came along.

During my stay in Ecuador, I had met numerous women with relationship issues. Some of the women know that their husband is involved in another relationship, yet they are powerless to stop them. Others just accept it as a commonality. One of the Spanish teachers that I encountered in class offered up her birth date to me during one of our lessons. As I got to know her better, she began to tell me more about her personal problems with her husband. Her name was Nieves and she was born on January 26, 1968. Below is her birth chart. (Birth hour not supplied)

Hour	Day	Month	Year
X	辛 Yin Metal	乙 Yin Wood	戊 Yang Earth
X	丑 Ox	丑 Ox	申 Monkey

47	37	27	17	7
庚 Yang Metal	辛 Yin Metal	壬 Yang Water	癸 Yin Water	甲 Yang Wood
申 Monkey	酉 Rooster	戌 Dog	亥 Pig	子 Rat

Nieves was born in the wet earth month of the Ox (丑) and she is a Yin Metal (辛) self. There was definitely no shortage of resources, as she had an abundant amount of resources. The metal self was swaying towards the strong side of the spectrum. As I looked at her birth system, I did not see any good news in her upcoming luck cycles. There was no doubt that relationship is a major concern for her since I did not see any fire elements in her birth chart, nor did I see any coming up in the next ten years of her luck cycle. Compounding to the problem was the metal cycles which competed with her in her cosmic system. Unlike the issues that Maria Teresa had with men, Nieves' situation was much more disheartening.

In the chapter of the ten gods, I mentioned that those with an overdose of Indirect Resources have a greater possibility of being malnourished, while the opposite occurs for those with an overdose of Direct Resources. For Nieves, it was a surprise that her stature and frame did not present any signs of malnourishment, especially when she has a wealth of Indirect Resources both in the month and day branches. As we looked further into her health, she told me that she has constant stomach and digestion issues. This is also another side effect of what can occur when Indirect Resources is a problem to the self.

The main dilemma at the moment with Nieves isn't her health, however, it is more so her relationship life. She is a mother of three children and her husband has been cheating on her for quite some time. Nieves' husband works as an administrator at a local hospital in Quito and apparently, he has been having an affair with one of the nurses working at the hospital. Nieves knows about it and she has seen flirty messages sent by the nurse to her husband's mobile phone. The exchanges of messages have been occurring for a few years already, and it came as no surprise as she was in the rivalry period.

In 2009, it became more and more apparent that her husband is cheating on her. This can be attributed to the Yin Earth Ox (己丑), which empowered the rivalry represented by the Yin Metal (辛). Nieves asked if the woman would be willing to back off anytime soon. Unfortunately, I did not have any good news to present to her—the best I could do was offer some thoughtful advice. The brutal reality of cosmic systems is that not all problems can be solved through Feng Shui. It has to come from the mind. Since she is in a prolonged period of rivalries in the next fifteen years or so, she has no choice but to cave in to the competition and let it be. Rivalries of the same strength would incur heavy losses. It is like going into a boxing ring where both combatants are of equal strength. Even the victorious would suffer major wounds. This is the essence of natural law. The natural laws of the I Ching tell us not to compete or contend. Birth systems with competing cosmic forces have a much more difficult time in life, especially when luck cycles are not in their favour.

Her birth chart also presents two Ox (丑) side by side, as the spouse palace is replicated in the month branch. Remarriage is also possible. Holding onto her current relationship is like grasping at straws where the straws are unreachable. Nieves mentioned that she wants to keep the relationship together until her children have completed school; this would mean another seven to eight years. She asked if I had some Feng Shui "magia" that I can perform like the shamans in the Incas that can preserve her relationship. I just told her to accept cosmic reality. Perhaps some Feng Shui masters may be able to perform some sort of a "cure", but trying to tie down a man who is disloyal requires more than magic.

9.

Case Studies: The Lewinsky Scandal

In the late 1990s, a major controversy in the United States had transpired between the President of the United States, Bill Clinton, and a White House intern named Monica Lewinsky. The House voted to impeach Clinton based allegedly on his lies about his relationship with Lewinsky. There is no doubt that the cosmic system of Clinton played a major role in what had transpired. Four Pillars chart that counters the leading flow would upset the bosses within a cosmic system; this usually leads to punishments in real life. The degree of punishment often would depend on the level of infraction that one has committed.

Hour	Day	Month	Year
庚 Yang Metal	乙 Yin Wood	丙 Yang Fire	丙 Yang Fire
辰 Dragon	丑 Ox	申 Monkey	戌 Dog

67	57	47	37	27	17	7
癸 Yin Water	壬 Yang Water	辛 Yin Metal	庚 Yang Metal	己 Yin Earth	戊 Yang Earth	丁 Yin Fire
卯 Rabbit	寅 Tiger	丑 Ox	子 Rat	亥 Pig	戌 Dog	酉 Rooster

Being born in the autumn, where metal energy is prosperous, Bill Clinton's Yin Wood (乙) has virtually no strength to fight the metal flow. His self element is surrounded by the hostile nature, including a mix of fire, metal and earth. Imagine a flower trying to survive the hostile chill in the Autumn. Clinton's birth system needs to yield to metal to satisfy the leading flow. Any introduction of additional wood into his cosmic system would upset the metal rulers. The Yang Fires (丙) in the month and year stem are acting like the sun shining brightly upon the metal. Yang Fire (丙) in his system poses no threat to the metal.

So what happened between 1998 and 1999 that created such misfortunes for Bill Clinton? 1998 was the year of the Tiger (寅) and Clinton's system was suddenly under pressure as the Tiger (寅) clashed with the ruler and leader of his cosmic system, the Monkey (申). The wood within the Tiger (寅) empowered his self element and he is no longer feeble. In addition, the Monkey (申) served as his 'Guide' star and the 'Guide' has been nullified by the clash.

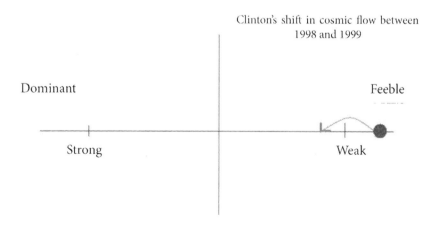

Clinton's shift in cosmic flow between 1998 and 1999

Dominant   Feeble

Strong   Weak

The previous line graph illustrates what had happened with Clinton's cosmic system. Evidently, empowering the self with more wood was not beneficial to his system. Adversity began creeping into his system and the momentum of the hardship increased in 1999, created by the Rabbit (卯). A system that was originally feeble was placed under a weak classification due to the changes of the annual energy; this shift in classification resulted in an impeachment trial of President Bill Clinton. From being a helpless baby, Clinton was turned into a reckless fifteen year old teenager. Unfortunately, mistakes were made and he had to pay the price for the cosmic shift. Could this predicament be avoided if Clinton knew ahead of time? The job of a Four Pillars practitioner is to recognize such a predicament and provide their clients with the knowledge of the possibilities of trouble. Perhaps the punishment that Clinton would have received could be avoided by knowing ahead of time.

10.
Case Studies: Google

Relationship analysis within the Four Pillars system can also be applied onto business partnerships. One of the most famous business partnerships in the past decade can be witnessed within the technology space. It is quite common for most people to go online and make use of Google's website in one way or another. The people behind the scenes who created Google have revolutionized the way we use the internet. There are two people who were instrumental in creating Google, which has turned into a household name.

Both Larry Page and Sergey Brin worked together and founded Google in 1998. So what was it that allowed the both of them to function together as a cohesive unit? Is there a specific cosmic flow that they benefited from? How did they amass such great fortunes in a short period of time? By looking at their Four Pillars chart, we can answer some of the questions. We can turn our attention first to Larry Page, he was born on March 26, 1973.

Hour	Day	Month	Year
X	辛 Yin Metal	乙 Yin Wood	癸 Yin Water
X	酉 Rooster	卯 Rabbit	丑 Ox

37	27	17	7
辛 Yin Metal	壬 Yang Water	癸 Yin Water	甲 Yang Wood
亥 Pig	子 Rat	丑 Ox	寅 Tiger

He is a Yin Metal (辛) self sitting on top of a metal rivalry, the Rooster (酉). In his month pillar, the wood is strongly rooted by the month of the Rabbit (卯), as a result, both the self and the wealth are just as strong. In such a scenario, the best element to use in his birth chart would be the Yin

Water (癸) found in the year stem where it can drain the strength of the rivalry, the Rooster (酉), and feed the wealth, the wood. Below is his luck cycle and as we can see, it comes to no surprise that his success came during the Yang Water Rat (壬子) pillar where water was most prosperous.

In 1998, Google was co-founded by Larry Page and Sergey Brin, then in 2004, it officially went public and became a huge success. So what is the reasoning behind his partnership with Sergey Brin that led to this success? There must be some sort of a cosmic harmony in order for such a successful partnership to come about. Sergey was born on August 21, 1973 and below is his birth chart.

Hour	Day	Month	Year
X	己 Yin Earth	庚 Yang Metal	癸 Yin Water
X	丑 Ox	申 Monkey	丑 Ox

Sergey himself is a Yin Earth (己) self born in the month of the Monkey (申) where the metal in the month stem is strongly rooted. The only symbol missing in Sergey's birth system that would allow metal to take control of the leading flow would be the Rooster (酉). If we take a look at their day branches, there is a half metal combination between Larry's Rooster (酉) and Sergey's Ox (丑). This combination makes a perfect team. By having Sergey's birth chart follow the lead of metal, essentially, his earth surrenders to the output element, which is very auspicious. This places Sergey's classification into the feeble category.

34	24	14	4
丙 Yang Fire	丁 Yin Fire	戊 Yang Earth	己 Yin Earth
辰 Dragon	巳 Snake	午 Horse	未 Goat

Coincidentally, Sergey's greatest luck came about in his late 20s and early 30s as he entered the Snake (巳) period. With the Snake (巳), it formed a half metal team with the Ox (丑) in his birth chart. Both Larry Page and Sergey Brin were in their best cycles at the time when Google was founded. Both Larry and Sergey formed a powerful alliance with proper timing, not only within their own cosmic systems but also together as partners. This example of business partnership demonstrates that relationship analysis can also be applied to businesses, sports teams, and any type of collaborative works.

10.
Possibilities of Marriage

After investigating the different scenarios in a relationship, there are probably some concerns amongst those who are single. Many single women that I consult tend to ask me this question, "will I ever get married?" They often ask whether there are requirements in a Four Pillars chart that will allow a smooth and happy marriage. In order to have a happy marriage and relationship, the requirements are minimal, but the unfortunate reality is that not a lot of people possess those minimum requirements. From the examples in this book, it seems like there is more bad news than good. Remember, however, that my examples are drawn from my own experiences, and that I belong in a profession where I encounter many people in difficult times.

From research, analysis and data collection, I have come up with a list of features for women who may experience marital problems. The marital problems vary in different degrees and levels depending on many of the factors that have been covered in this book. Here is the list:

1. Weak controlling element, or the controlling element hidden in one of the four 'earth' animals (Dragon, Goat, Dog, Ox), perhaps even the non-existence of the controlling element in the Four Pillars chart.

2. Birth system does not have a Useful God. In the past, some masters would mention that the Useful God can be considered a spouse star. If the Useful God is not found in the birth system, it could be encountered in the luck cycle allowing one to have a temporary marriage.

3. Self is too strong or dominant.

4. Self is too weak.

5. Output elements are too strong and located right in front of the day stem.

6. The controlling symbols are 'voided' or if there are two pillars voided in the birth chart.

7. Women surrendering to the output, or sometimes called 'Follow Offspring' (從兒格) with no wealth elements in the birth system or luck cycle.

8. Complete Yin birth system. Meaning all four pillars of the birth chart are Yin symbols.

9. Complete Yang birth system. Meaning all four pillars of the birth chart are Yang symbols.

10. Sibling rivalry next to the day stem. This has been a recurring theme throughout the book.

11. Birth systems possessing anxiety or solitude stars sitting in the day branch.

This list is by no means exhaustive. There may be other theories and principles that I have left out. The list provided here can be used for investigative purposes when examining a Four Pillars chart. 'Marital problems' does not mean divorce; there are possibilities where these people may choose not to be married at all. Testing and verification with real examples, combined with a logical approach are the best ways to increase one's capacity for making the proper prediction and analysis. If point number 9 was encountered in an analysis, having a complete Yang birth system does not conclude that this person will have marital problems. The strength of the controlling element may change the analysis. The same can be said of a strong chart. We have seen a proven fact with the birth system of Jennifer Aniston that a strong system may suffer from marital problems, hence her separation from Brad Pitt. The choice of marital partners may change the outcome. Imagine if she chose to be with someone who is a lot younger than her and possesses the elements that she requires, the analysis will take a different course. As mentioned many times in this book, nothing is absolute! Testing and the evaluation of one's background can slightly change the tide of a Four Pillars chart. Luck and the composition of the birth system does not change, it is how one approach life and how bad situations are dealt with that are more important.

Documenting your good days and bad days is the best way to identify your flow. We all possess a specific type of energy that can be determined through our Four Pillars birth chart. Why do we have good days and bad days? The energy around us is constantly changing thereby affecting our behavior and mind. When the energy is going with our flow, we are presented with fewer obstacles in life!

Concluding Remarks

The Four Pillars system in the past few decades has become tremendously popular in the West, and this universal system can be applicable to people all over the world, as proven by examples within this book. We are all interconnected within the web of cosmic flow. Examining our Four Pillars blueprint, capitalizing on our strengths and knowing our weaknesses can allow all individuals to live in harmony with the cosmos. It is the cosmic imbalance of nature that creates a set of life challenges that we all must face and confront. From the stories and case studies observed in this book, it is evident that going against the flow can result in misfortunes in relationships. Analyzing relationships is just one of many components that can be extracted from a birth chart. Wealth, career, scholastic and athletic potential, and weaknesses in health can also be determined through the Four Pillars system. Four Pillars is by no means the only astrological system that can provide such predictions. It is one of many systems that can be used. As mentioned in the preface, there are other widely practiced systems in China, such as "Purple Star Astrology" (紫微斗數), that can provide similar results if used properly. I believe the choice amongst various astrological systems should depend on how comfortable a practicioner feels with it in practice.

The Four Pillars divination method, if done properly, can help many people prevent problems from occurring, or at the very least, reduce the expected negative impacts. On the other hand, it can allow us to capitalize on what we were given from the cosmos. Determining the cosmic flow and understanding where a birth system may encounter problems or fortunes is only one part of a Four Pillars consultant's practice. The essential aspect of this practice is to provide remedies. Those equipped with Feng Shui training through the use of Flying Stars, Eight Mansions, and other methods can help solve some of the issues. Another method is through counselling and ensuring that those who are about to enter a bad period know what to expect. Exercising, studying something difficult, or travelling are some of the most natural ways to deal with cosmic stress. If you are about to encounter a bad cycle, it is best to create your own suffering. How do we create our own suffering? As mentioned, exercising and exerting energy by studying challenging courses are some of the ways to create our own suffering. We can also donate blood, give to charity or see a dentist during bad times. Meditation can also relieve stress from the cosmic system.

For relationship issues, if couples want to maintain their relationship, sleeping in separate bedrooms or travelling alone for an extended period of time could keep a relationship together. The duration of separation may depend on the luck cycles. In some cases, as we have explored in this book, marital problems are almost unavoidable. It could be the result of the luck cycle or the structure of the birth system. Remember: it is not the end of the world if you were to run into a bad cycle. It is more important for people to accept cosmic reality for them to do the right thing. There is no such thing as a "perfect" Four Pillars chart. The key ingredient to enjoying a long and prosperous life is to operate within the boundaries of what one is presented with. If those boundaries strip the chance for one to be in a harmonious relationship, there may be other options. Divorce may not always be such a bad idea. Some people may thrive or become even happier after a divorce. The Four Pillars of Destiny equips practitioners with the knowledge of one's cosmic boundary. It allows us to understand what we need to do at certain times and when we should stay low.

There are many dimensions and aspects that can be explored when using the Four Pillars system. The sages throughout Chinese history have left an incredible system that has yet to be understood by many people. This powerful system is not just meant to be used to untap the favourable and unfavourable elements, nor is it only used to predict when good luck is coming along. The Four Pillars system can help practitioners and enthusiasts explore their relationships with others as well as the relationships with people of the previous generation. This book has only explained a portion of what the entire Four Pillars method is meant to predict and analyse. I have yet to explore other factors including the determinination of: wealth, promotion, career, academic achievements, health, and many more. The concepts of the Ten Gods introduced in this book are only a portion of what the Ten Gods represent in a birth system. My next few books will explain the Ten Gods in greater detail.

The types of cosmic flow introduced are only from an 'elemental' perspective. I have yet to touch upon the characteristics of those 'elemental' perspectives, nor have I explained the types of flow pertaining to a specific 'surrendering' system. My next book will focus on the types of 'surrender' systems and their characteristics as a part of the foundation necessary in analyzing success and failures. Topics on the Four Pillars are endless – and so are its limitations.

Appendix

PLOTTING A FOUR PILLARS CHART

Putting together your Four Pillars birth chart takes only a few simple steps. The Four Pillars is composed of the Year, Month, Day and Hour and each pillar has a stem and branch. The first thing to do is to obtain a copy of a Chinese Thousand Year Calendar. Please note that there are many different versions of the Chinese calendar in the market but most of them should contain similar information. There are also computer programs and online calculators – but there may be vast discrepancies between an automatically generated plotting and manually calculated chart.

The best way to illustrate how to plot a chart is to use an example. Let's pick a date: January 1, 2010, born at 11:30pm. You would still use 2009 since the birth date is still in the lunar year of 2009. It is important to remember that the Chinese New Year does not begin until February 4th/5th. Looking at the Year pillar first, we see that it is a Yin Earth Ox (己丑) as circled by the marker in the image.

西曆二〇〇九年 己丑	農曆月	正月大	二月大	三月小	四月小	五月大	潤五月
	月柱	丙寅	丁卯	戊辰	己巳	庚午	
	九星	五黃	四綠	三碧	二黑	一白	
節氣		立春 雨水 初0廿20 十時四時 子50戌44 時分時分	驚蟄 春分 初19廿19 九時四時 戌0戌57 時分時分	清明 穀雨 初0廿7 十時五時 子3辰16 時分時分	立夏 小滿 十17廿6 一時七時 酉37卯38 時分時分	芒種 夏至 十21廿14 三時九時 亥59未44 時分時分	小暑 十8 五時 辰22 時分

納音 霹靂火
太歲 廿八宿 斗
潘蓋 運 世
大耗 妯 鼎 觀
十未歲 值年 招杜羅
本命星 巨門
守護菩薩 虛空藏
年星 九紫
八白 四綠 六白
七赤 九紫 二黑
三碧 五黃 一白

09

農曆日	國曆 日柱 宿	國曆 日柱 宿	國曆 日柱 宿	國曆 日柱 宿	國曆 日柱 宿	國曆 日柱 宿
初一	1 26	2 25	3 27	4 25	5 24	6 23
初二	1 27	2 26	3 28	4 26	5 25	6 24
初三	1 28	2 27	3 29	4 27	5 26	6 25
初四	1 29	2 28	3 30	4 28	5 27	6 26
初五	1 30	3 1	3 31	4 29	5 28	6 27
初六	1 31	3 2	4 1	4 30	5 29	6 28
初七	2 1	3 3	4 2	5 1	5 30	6 29
初八	2 2	3 4	4 3	5 2	5 31	6 30
初九	2 3	3 5	4 4	5 3	6 1	7 1
初十	2 4	3 6	4 5	5 4	6 2	7 2
十一	2 5	3 7	4 6	5 5	6 3	7 3
十二	2 6	3 8	4 7	5 6	6 4	7 4
十三	2 7	3 9	4 8	5 7	6 5	7 5
十四	2 8	3 10	4 9	5 8	6 6	7 6
十五	2 9	3 11	4 10	5 9	6 7	7 7
十六	2 10	3 12	4 11	5 10	6 8	7 8
十七	2 11	3 13	4 12	5 11	6 9	7 9
十八	2 12	3 14	4 13	5 12	6 10	7 10
十九	2 13	3 15	4 14	5 13	6 11	7 11
二十	2 14	3 16	4 15	5 14	6 12	7 12
廿一	2 15	3 17	4 16	5 15	6 13	7 13
廿二	2 16	3 18	4 17	5 16	6 14	7 14
廿三	2 17	3 19	4 18	5 17	6 15	7 15
廿四	2 18	3 20	4 19	5 18	6 16	7 16
廿五	2 19	3 21	4 20	5 19	6 17	7 17
廿六	2 20	3 22	4 21	5 20	6 18	7 18
廿七	2 21	3 23	4 22	5 21	6 19	7 19
廿八	2 22	3 24	4 23	5 22	6 20	7 20
廿九	2 23	3 25	4 24	5 23	6 21	7 21
三十	2 24	3 26			6 22	

李居明, 宿曜萬年曆, 民間出版, Hong Kong, 2008

STEP ONE:

And now we have the Year Pillar as shown in this birth chart.

Hour	Day	Month	Year
X	X	X	己
X	X	X	丑

The next step is to obtain the month pillar and day pillar. Since this person was born on January 1st, turn to the page where the specific date is located. Once January 1st has been identified, the month can be found on the upper row of the calendar represented by the Yang Fire Rat (丙子). The month is circled on the upper row in the image while the day is circled on the specific day, which is January 1st. January 1st is represented by the Yin Metal Pig (辛亥).

柱	宿	十月小 乙亥 五黃			十一月大 丙子 四綠			十二月大 丁丑 三碧			農曆月 月柱 九星
		國曆	日柱	宿	國曆	日柱	宿	國曆	日柱	宿	農曆日
申	氐	11 17	丙寅	心	12 16	乙未	斗	1 15	乙丑	虛	初一
酉	房	11 18	丁卯	尾	12 17	丙申	女	1 16	丙寅	危	初二
戌	心	11 19	戊辰	箕	12 18	丁酉	虛	1 17	丁卯	室	初三
亥	尾	11 20	己巳	斗	12 19	戊戌	危	1 18	戊辰	壁	初四
子	箕	11 21	庚午	女	12 20	己亥	室	1 19	己巳	奎	初五
丑	斗	11 22	辛未	虛	12 21	庚子	壁	1 20	庚午	婁	初六
寅	女	11 23	壬申	危	12 22	辛丑	奎	1 21	辛未	胃	初七
卯	虛	11 24	癸酉	室	12 23	壬寅	婁	1 22	壬申	昴	初八
辰	危	11 25	甲戌	壁	12 24	癸卯	胃	1 23	癸酉	畢	初九
巳	室	11 26	乙亥	奎	12 25	甲辰	昴	1 24	甲戌	觜	初十
午	壁	11 27	丙子	婁	12 26	乙巳	畢	1 25	乙亥	參	十一
未	奎	11 28	丁丑	胃	12 27	丙午	觜	1 26	丙子	井	十二
申	婁	11 29	戊寅	昴	12 28	丁未	參	1 27	丁丑	鬼	十三
酉	胃	11 30	己卯	畢	12 29	戊申	井	1 28	戊寅	柳	十四
戌	昴	12 1	庚辰	觜	12 30	己酉	鬼	1 29	己卯	星	十五
亥	畢	12 2	辛巳	參	12 31	庚戌	柳	1 30	庚辰	張	十六
子	觜	12 3	壬午	井	1 1	辛亥	星	1 31	辛巳	翼	十七
丑	參	12 4	癸未	鬼	1 2	壬子	張	2 1	壬午	軫	十八
寅	井	12 5	甲申	柳	1 3	癸丑	翼	2 2	癸未	角	十九
卯	鬼	12 6	乙酉	星	1 4	甲寅	軫	2 3	甲申	亢	二十

節氣：
- 十月小（乙亥）：小雪 初六 午25時分 ／ 大雪 廿一 辰3時分
- 十一月大（丙子）：冬至 初七 丑38時分 ／ 小寒 廿一 酉58時分
- 十二月大（丁丑）：大寒 初六 午16時分 ／ 立春 廿一 卯40時分

李居明, 宿曜萬年曆, 民間出版, Hong Kong, 2008

STEP TWO:

With the additional information, the Year, Month and Day is now complete in the chart. The only information that we require now is the hour pillar.

Hour	Day	Month	Year
X	辛	丙	己
X	亥	子	丑

There is a table that makes determining the hour pillar straightforward for practitioners, as presented below. Most Thousand Years Calendar provides the hour pillar information by referring to the self element.

Birth Hour Branch / Self/Hour	Rat 子 11pm-1am	Ox 丑 1am-3am	Tiger 寅 3am-5am	Rabbit 卯 5am-7am	Dragon 辰 7am-9am	Snake 巳 9am-11am	Horse 午 11am-1pm	Goat 未 1pm-3pm	Monkey 申 3pm-5pm	Rooster 酉 5pm-7pm	Dog 戌 7pm-9pm	Pig 亥 9pm-11pm
甲	甲子	乙丑	丙寅	丁卯	戊辰	己巳	庚午	辛未	壬申	癸酉	甲戌	乙亥
己	甲子	乙丑	丙寅	丁卯	戊辰	己巳	庚午	辛未	壬申	癸酉	甲戌	乙亥
乙	丙子	丁丑	戊寅	己卯	庚辰	辛巳	壬午	癸未	甲申	乙酉	丙戌	丁亥
庚	丙子	丁丑	戊寅	己卯	庚辰	辛巳	壬午	癸未	甲申	乙酉	丙戌	丁亥
丙	戊子	己丑	庚寅	辛卯	壬辰	癸巳	甲午	乙未	丙申	丁酉	戊戌	己亥
辛	戊子	己丑	庚寅	辛卯	壬辰	癸巳	甲午	乙未	丙申	丁酉	戊戌	己亥
丁	庚子	辛丑	壬寅	癸卯	甲辰	乙巳	丙午	丁未	戊申	己酉	庚戌	辛亥
壬	庚子	辛丑	壬寅	癸卯	甲辰	乙巳	丙午	丁未	戊申	己酉	庚戌	辛亥
戊	壬子	癸丑	甲寅	乙卯	丙辰	丁巳	戊午	己未	庚申	辛酉	壬戌	癸亥
癸	壬子	癸丑	甲寅	乙卯	丙辰	丁巳	戊午	己未	庚申	辛酉	壬戌	癸亥

STEP THREE:

This table is very simple and easy to use. Sticking with the example we have here, the example uses the Yin Metal as the self element. Assuming that the example is born between 1am-3pm, you would then look at the Ox (丑) hour. Match the two symbols and you would obtain the Yin Earth Ox (己丑) as the birth hour.

To complete the Four Pillars chart, we insert the Yin Earth Ox (己丑) into the hour pillar.

Hour	Day	Month	Year
己	辛	丙	己
丑	亥	子	丑

PLOTTING THE LUCK CYCLES

Now that the Four Pillars chart is complete, the luck cycle must be plotted. In order to do so, first we have to determine whether this is a birth chart of a male or female. Second, the year of birth must be taken into account regarding Yin vs Yang. Let's say this is a birth chart of a male. Since the Yin Earth Ox (己丑) is a Yin year, the symbols in the luck cycle would be plotted backwards in accordance to the month. Luck cycles always use the month pillar as a starting point. By counting backwards for the male chart, the first luck cycle would be the Yin Wood Pig (乙亥), followed by the Yang Wood Dog (甲戌) and so forth.

After the pattern of the luck cycle is verified, the next procedure is to determine when the luck cycle begins. Since the luck cycle goes backwards for male, all you need to do is count the number of days back to the last climate divider represented by a marker in the lunar calendar. The previous marker of the lunar calendar for the birth date of January 1, 2010 is on December 7, 2009. There are 25 days from December 7, 2009 to January 1, 2010.

9 19	丁卯	角	10 18	丙申	氐	11 17	丙寅	心	12 16	乙未	斗	1 15	乙丑	虚	初一
9 20	戊辰	亢	10 19	丁酉	房	11 18	丁卯	尾	12 17	丙申	女	1 16	丙寅	危	初二
9 21	己巳	氐	10 20	戊戌	心	11 19	戊辰	箕	12 18	丁酉	虚	1 17	丁卯	室	初三
9 22	庚午	房	10 21	己亥	尾	11 20	己巳	斗	12 19	戊戌	危	1 18	戊辰	壁	初四
9 23	辛未	心	10 22	庚子	箕	11 21	庚午	女	12 20	己亥	室	1 19	己巳	奎	初五
9 24	壬申	尾	10 23	辛丑	斗	11 22	辛未	虚	12 21	庚子	壁	1 20	庚午	婁	初六
9 25	癸酉	箕	10 24	壬寅	女	11 23	壬申	危	12 22	辛丑	奎	1 21	辛未	胃	初七
9 26	甲戌	斗	10 25	癸卯	虚	11 24	癸酉	室	12 23	壬寅	婁	1 22	壬申	昴	初八
9 27	乙亥	女	10 26	甲辰	危	11 25	甲戌	壁	12 24	癸卯	胃	1 23	癸酉	畢	初九
9 28	丙子	虚	10 27	乙巳	室	11 26	乙亥	奎	12 25	甲辰	昴	1 24	甲戌	觜	初十
9 29	丁丑	危	10 28	丙午	壁	11 27	丙子	婁	12 26	乙巳	畢	1 25	乙亥	參	十一
9 30	戊寅	室	10 29	丁未	奎	11 28	丁丑	胃	12 27	丙午	觜	1 26	丙子	井	十二
10 1	己卯	壁	10 30	戊申	婁	11 29	戊寅	昴	12 28	丁未	參	1 27	丁丑	鬼	十三
10 2	庚辰	奎	10 31	己酉	胃	11 30	己卯	畢	12 29	戊申	井	1 28	戊寅	柳	十四
10 3	辛巳	婁	11 1	庚戌	昴	12 1	庚辰	觜	12 30	己酉	鬼	1 29	己卯	星	十五
10 4	壬午	胃	11 2	辛亥	畢	12 2	辛巳	參	12 31	庚戌	柳	1 30	庚辰	張	十六
10 5	癸未	昴	11 3	壬子	觜	12 3	壬午	井	(1 1	辛亥)		1 31	辛巳	翼	十七
10 6	甲申	畢	11 4	癸丑	參	12 4	癸未	鬼	1 2	壬子	張	2 1	壬午	軫	十八
10 7	乙酉	觜	11 5	甲寅	井	12 5	甲申	柳	1 3	癸丑	翼	2 2	癸未	角	十九
10 8	丙戌	參	11 6	乙卯	鬼	12 6	乙酉	星	1 4	甲寅	軫	2 3	甲申	亢	二十
10 9	丁亥	井	11 7	丙辰	柳	(12 7	丙戌)		1 5	乙卯	角	2 4	乙酉	氐	廿一
10 10	戊子	鬼	11 8	丁巳	星	12 8	丁亥	翼	1 6	丙辰	亢	2 5	丙戌	房	廿二
10 11	己丑	柳	11 9	戊午	張	12 9	戊子	軫	1 7	丁巳	氐	2 6	丁亥	心	廿三
10 12	庚寅	星	11 10	己未	翼	12 10	己丑	角	1 8	戊午	房	2 7	戊子	尾	廿四
10 13	辛卯	張	11 11	庚申	軫	12 11	庚寅	亢	1 9	己未	心	2 8	己丑	箕	廿五
10 14	壬辰	翼	11 12	辛酉	角	12 12	辛卯	氐	1 10	庚申	尾	2 9	庚寅	斗	廿六
10 15	癸巳	軫	11 13	壬戌	亢	12 13	壬辰	房	1 11	辛酉	箕	2 10	辛卯	女	廿七
10 16	甲午	角	11 14	癸亥	氐	12 14	癸巳	心	1 12	壬戌	斗	2 11	壬辰	虚	廿八
10 17	乙未	亢	11 15	甲子	房	12 15	甲午	尾	1 13	癸亥	女	2 12	癸巳	危	廿九
			11 16						1 14						三十

李居明, 宿曜萬年曆, 民間出版, Hong Kong, 2008

STEP FOUR:

Divide the number of days by 3 and you will get a luck cycle of roughly 8. Most practitioners would round this to 8 while others who demand accuracy would use 8.33 as the start of the luck cycle. For demonstration purposes, we will use 8 in this example.

Below is the luck cycle plotted for a male's birth system.

68	58	48	38	28	18	8
己	庚	辛	壬	癸	甲	乙
巳	午	未	申	酉	戌	亥

For a female being born on January 1, 2010, the luck cycle would go forward because the Ox (丑) is a Yin year. There are four days until the climate divider on January 5, 2010. If you divide four by three, you would get a luck cycle beginning at 1.33, but for demonstration purposes, we will round up to a whole number and begin with 1.

11 30	己卯	畢	12 29	戊申	井	1 28	戊寅	柳
12 1	庚辰	觜	12 30	己酉	鬼	1 29	己卯	星
12 2	辛巳	參	12 31	庚戌	柳	1 30	庚辰	弘
12 3	壬午	井	1 1	辛亥	星	31	辛巳	翼
12 4	癸未	鬼	1 2	壬子	張	2 1	壬午	軫
12 5	甲申	柳	1 3	癸丑	翼	2 2	癸未	角
12 6	乙酉	星	1 4	甲寅	軫	2 3	甲申	亢
12 7	丙戌	張	1 5	乙卯	角	2 4	乙酉	氐
12 8	丁亥	翼	1 6	丙辰	亢	2 5	丙戌	房
12 9	戊子	軫	1 7	丁巳	氐	2 6	丁亥	心
12 10	己丑	角	1 8	戊午	房	2 7	戊子	尾
12 11	庚寅	亢	1 9	己未	心	2 8	己丑	箕

李居明, 宿曜萬年曆, 民間出版, Hong Kong, 2008

STEP FIVE:

Since we are going forward with the luck cycle, the first luck cycle would be Yin Fire Ox (丁丑); this is based from the birth month of Yang Fire Rat (丙子) in this specific birth chart.

Below is the luck cycle plotted for a female's birth system:

61	51	41	31	21	11	1
癸	壬	辛	庚	己	戊	丁
未	午	巳	辰	卯	寅	丑

If you are uncertain and require more practice, the best way to do so is to use some of the examples provided in this book. The luck cycles plotted in this book are also rounded to the nearest whole for demonstration purposes. Remember, for precision and accuracy when consulting, it is best to use the exact number. The key to Four Pillars is to understanding cosmic flow, if cosmic flow cannot be analyzed properly, the analysis of the luck cycles and how it affects a birth system would be incorrect.

TEN GODS

Each of the ten gods has a possibility of occurring within a birth chart, luck cycle, annually, monthly or daily. The ten gods are not "gods" – they are simply a standard established for identifying symbols within a Four Pillars chart. The ten gods are composed of the following: Direct Resources (正印), Indirect Resources (偏印), Friend (比肩), Rob Wealth (劫財), Direct Wealth (正財), Indirect Wealth (偏財), Officer (正官), Seven Killings (七煞), Eating God (食神) and Hurting Officer (傷官). Since all of the gods have been discussed within this book, the table below can be used as a reference to determine the ten gods in relation to the self.

Self Element	Friend 比肩	Rob Wealth 劫財	Direct Resource 正印	Indirect Resource 偏印	Hurting Officer 傷官	Eating God 食神	Direct Officer 正官	Seven Killings 七煞	Direct Wealth 正財	Indirect Wealth 偏財
甲	甲	乙	癸	壬	丁	丙	辛	庚	己	戊
乙	乙	甲	壬	癸	丙	丁	庚	辛	戊	己
丙	丙	丁	乙	甲	己	戊	癸	壬	辛	庚
丁	丁	丙	甲	乙	戊	己	壬	癸	庚	辛
戊	戊	己	丁	丙	辛	庚	乙	甲	癸	壬
己	己	戊	丙	丁	庚	辛	甲	乙	壬	癸
庚	庚	辛	己	戊	癸	壬	丁	丙	乙	甲
辛	辛	庚	戊	己	壬	癸	丙	丁	甲	乙
壬	壬	癸	辛	庚	乙	甲	己	戊	丁	丙
癸	癸	壬	庚	辛	甲	乙	戊	己	丙	丁

Sneak Preview to *"Four Pillars of Destiny: Potential, Career and Wealth."*

As I continue to search for research data on the Internet, I decided to browse for the best writers of the past decade. I felt that the most superficial yet effective method was to go to Amazon.com, then click on the top best sellers. One person that caught my attention was Malcolm Gladwell. He is best known for his books *The Tipping Point, Blink, Outliers* and *What the Dog Saw: And Other Adventures.* I pondered: how is it that some authors can repeatedly publish best-selling books, while million of others in the industry can only deliver at best a one hit one wonder? Malcolm Gladwell, born on September 3, 1963, possesses a scholar star underneath his self element with a Hurting Officer found in his stem. This is definitely a recipe for success. Of course, there is no doubt that we must look at the most important aspect of a birth system, cosmic flow.

In his book, Outliers, Gladwell presented me with an additional perspective on my analysis using the Four Pillars system on sports athletes. He also presented examples using Bill Gates, Paul Allen, Steve Ballmer, Bill Joy, Steve Jobs, and many others who have been successful in their careers and why they were able to achieve fame and fortune. What Malcolm lacked in his book was the knowledge of the Four Pillars system which will unearth the missing link to their success. Opportunities, education, timing and the location of birth are only some of the few criteria for success.

Famous sports athletes such as Wayne Gretzky, Christiano Ronaldo, Roger Federer, and Michael Phelps will also be explored in greater depth in my next book. Their natural talents, accompanied by a great cosmic system and cosmic flow, allowed them to achieve greatness within the athletic field. The success that they have obtained is not by a mere stroke of luck.

With my next book, I will explore why it is easier for some to achieve success while others continue to fail repeatedly. People from all corners of the globe will be evaluated, from the Bettencourts to Carlos Slim. Why was Bill Gates able to amass such a great fortune? How did Warren Buffett become an icon in the financial world? Was it by chance that Facebook became such a great hit? Why did Gordon Ramsey rise to prominence in the food and beverages business? And why is Roger Federer one of the greatest tennis players of all time? Cosmic flow and its impact to one's birth system may provide many answers to these questions. Research data will come not only from those who have succeeded in the business and academic world, the data will also come from those who have failed miserably. I have met numerous businessmen who have accumulated well over $100 million USD but to have it swept away within a matter of years. Their birth data and personal recollections of what has transpired will be documented in the book.

References

1. Chung, Lily, *The Path to Good Fortune: The Meng.* St. Paul, MN: Llewellyn, 1997.
2. Chung, Lily, *Easy Ways to Harmony.* [San Francisco, City], CA: Gold Medal Book, 1999.
3. Chung, Lily, *The Truths of Ups and Downs, Cosmic Inequality.* New York, Eloquent Books, 2009.
4. 徐樂吾, *滴天髓微義*, Shanghai Bookstore, Hong Kong, 1984.
5. 徐樂吾, *窮通寶鑑*, Shanghai Bookstore, Hong Kong, 1985.
6. 徐樂吾, *子平四言集腋*, Shanghai Bookstore, Hong Kong, 1985.
7. 徐樂吾, *命理一得*, Shanghai Bookstore, Hong Kong, 1984.
8. 尤達人, *達人命理通鑑*, 台灣集文書局, Taiwan, 1981.
9. 尤達人, *知命四十年*, 台灣集文書局, Taiwan, 1981.
10. 王姿尹, *八字實錄, 女命專論*, 台灣武陵出版社, Taiwan, 2001.
11. 白鶴鳴, *八字八日通*, 香港聚賢館, Hong Kong, 1999.
12. 白鶴鳴, *命理天書滴天髓詳解*, 香港聚賢館, Hong Kong, 1999.
13. 羅量, *點算八字格局*, 香港聚賢館, Hong Kong, 2005.
14. 李鐵筆, *子平真詮評注*, 台灣益群書店, Taiwan, 2006.
15. 李鐵筆, *八字婚姻學*, 台灣益群書店, Taiwan, 2005.
16. 李居明, *蓓曜萬年曆*, 民間出版, Hong Kong, 2008.

CPSIA information can be obtained at www.ICGtesting.com
Printed in the USA
LVOW031948111111

254602LV00003B/20/P